Using Netscape with your Mac

The Netscape Window

Type a URL (Web address) here, and press Enter to go to that page.

The toolbar provides quick access to common commands.

This icon shows you when Netscape is working; the meteorites move across the sky.

Pictures and logos are often links; click on them to see other documents.

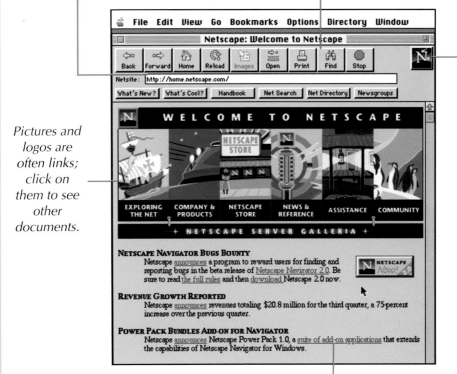

Underlined and colored words are links; click to see another document.

Que® 201 W. 103rd Street • Indianapolis, IN 46290 • (317) 581-3500
Copyright© 1995 Que Corporation

All About URLs

A URL (Uniform Resource Locator) is a Web "address." Here's what one looks like:

`http://home.mcom.com/newsref/news/index.html`

1 This is the type of URL, the "protocol" used to use the resource.

2 This is the host name of the computer containing the file referenced by the URL.

3 This is the directory path to the file.

4 This is the name of the file. (It's not always required.)

You can use a URL by clicking on a link (the URL is inside the link), or by typing the URL into the Location text box and pressing Enter.

To go to the Rolling Stones Web site, type this:
http://www.stones.com/

To go to the University of Texas Macintosh freeware and shareware archivesite, type this:
http://wwwhost.ots.utexas.edu/mac/main.html

To go to the famous Wiretap Gopher site, type this:
gopher://wiretap.spies.com/

To read the alt.binaries.pictures.clip-art newsgroup, type this:
news:alt.binaries.clip-art

URL Types

Here are the different types of URLs:

URL Type	Purpose
http://	HyperText Transfer Protocol—points to a Web document.
https://	Points to a Web document on a secure server.
file:///	References a file on your hard disk.
ftp://	File Transfer Protocol—points to an FTP site where you can transfer files.
gopher://	Enables you to go to a Gopher site.
telnet://	Launches whatever Telnet program you've configured and starts a Telnet session.
tn3270://	Launches your tn3270 program (similar to Telnet).
wais://	Wide Area Information Server—opens a WAIS database. (You can use this only if your system administrator has set up a WAIS proxy.)
mailto:	Starts the Netscape Mail program so you can send an e-mail message.
news:	Opens the Netscape News program and displays a newsgroup.
snews:	Opens the Netscape News program and displays a newsgroup at a secure news server.
about:	Provides information about the program (and some weird stuff). Try the following: about:plugins, about:security, about:mozilla, and about:jwz.

The Newsgroup Window

Double-click on a newsgroup to retrieve messages.

Newsgroup messages may contain links; click on the link to display the referenced newsgroup or Web page.

Click on a message to view the contents.

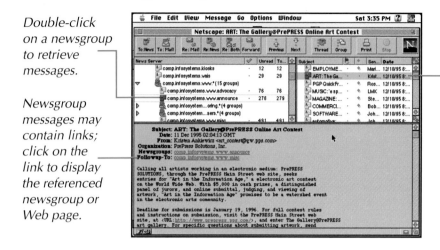

 Post New
Opens the Message Composition window so you can send a message to the newsgroup

 Post Reply
Lets you send reply to the selected message to the newsgroup

 Post and Reply
Lets you reply to the selected message, and send the reply to the author of the original message via e-mail

 New Mail
Click here to write an e-mail message to anyone (not just to a newsgroup)

 Reply
Click here to reply to the author of the selected message via e-mail

 Forward
This lets you forward a message to someone else

 Previous Message
Displays the previous unread message

 Next Message
Displays the next unread message

 Mark Thread Read
Marks all the messages in the thread (conversation) as read, so you won't see them next time you view this newsgroup

 Mark All Read
Marks all displayed messages

 Print
Prints the selected messages

 Stop
Tells Netscape to stops transferring the message

The Toolbar buttons

Back
Click on this button to see the previous Web document.

Forward
Click on this button to see the next Web document—the one you left by clicking the back button.

Home
Click on this button to return to the home page.

Reload
Click on this button to reload the currently displayed document from the Web again.

Images
If you are viewing Web pages with inline images turned off, you can quickly retrieve the missing images from the current document by clicking on this button.

Open
Click on this button to display the Open Location dialog box, into which you can type the URL of a document you want to view.

Print
Click here to print the currently displayed document.

Find
Click here to open a Find dialog box to search the current document for a particular word or phrase.

Stop
Click on this button to stop the current procedure—to stop transferring the Web document or file.

Status Indicator
As long as the meteors are shooting across the sky, Netscape is busy doing something: retrieving a document, trying to connect to a Web server, or transferring a file. You also can click here to return to the Netscape home page.

Security Indicators
There are three different indicators, which show you the type of document you are viewing:

The broken key indicates that this is not a secure document. Either it's on a Web server capable of security, but has not been set up to use the security features; or it's on a Web server that uses a security system that Netscape cannot work with.

The key with the stripes indicates that the document is using "medium-grade" security.

The key with two teeth indicates that the document is using "high-grade" security.

Using

Netscape 2 With Your Mac

Using

Netscape 2 With Your Mac

Joseph Heck

with

Peter Kent

Using Netscape 2 With Your Mac

Library of Congress Catalog No.: 95-72585

ISBN: 0-7897-0729-2

98 97 96   6 5 4 3 2 1

Interpretation of the printing code: the rightmost double-digit number is the year of the book's printing; the rightmost single-digit number, the number of the book's printing. For example, a printing code of 96-1 shows that the first printing of the book occurred in 1996.

Screen reproductions in this book were created using Collage Plus from Inner Media, Inc., Hollis, NH.

Composed in *ITC Century*, *ITC Highlander*, and *MCPdigital* by Que Corporation.

Credits

President
Roland Elgey

Publisher
Stacy Hiquet

Publishing Manager
Jim Minatel

Editorial Services Director
Elizabeth Keaffaber

Managing Editor
Sandy Doell

Director of Marketing
Lynn E. Zingraf

Senior Series Editor
Chris Nelson

**Acquisitions and
Product Manager**
Cheryl D. Willoughby

Acquisitions Editor
Doshia Stewart

Product Director
Oran J. Sands

Production Editor
Elizabeth A. Bruns

**Assistant Product Marketing
Manager**
Kim Margolius

Technical Editor
Jonathan M. Wagner

Technical Specialist
Nadeem Muhammed

Acquisitions Coordinator
Ruth Slates

Operations Coordinator
Patty Brooks

Editorial Assistant
Andrea Duvall

Book Designer
Ruth Harvey

Cover Designer
Dan Armstrong

Production Team
Brian Buschkill
Heather Butler
Damon Jordan
Michelle Lee
Karen Walsh
Jody York
Karen York

Indexer
Ginny Munroe

I'd like to dedicate this work to my grandfather, Joseph Frederick Heck (Fritz) for being the man that imbued me with the passion to delve into new fields and make complex things seem simple.

— J. Heck

About the Author

Joseph Heck lives with his wonderful wife and two cats in Columbia, MO. He maintains the central WWW server as well as providing technical support for the University of Missouri. In his free time, he enjoys metalarts and a variety of far too many hobbies. You can reach him on the Internet at **http://www.missouri.edu/~ccjoe/**.

Peter Kent lives in Lakewood, Colorado. He's been training computer users, documenting software, and designing user interfaces for the last fourteen years. Working as an independent consultant for the last nine years, Peter has worked for companies such as MasterCard, Amgen, Data General, and Dvorak Development and Publishing. Much of his consulting work has been in the telecommunications business.

Peter is the author of *Using Microsoft Network* (Que), *Using Microsoft Internet Explorer* (Que), and the best-selling *The Complete Idiot's Guide to the Internet* (Que). He's also written another seven Internet-related books—including *The Complete Idiot's Guide to the Internet for Windows 95* and *The Complete Idiot's Guide to the World Wide Web*—and a variety of other works, such as *The Technical Writers Freelancing Guide* and books on Windows NT and Windows 3.1. His articles have appeared in many periodicals, including *Internet World, Dr. Dobb's Journal, Windows Magazine, The Dallas Times Herald,* and *Computerworld*. Peter can be reached via CompuServe at 71601,1266 and the Internet at **pkent@lab-press.com**.

Acknowledgments

I'd like to acknowledge the W3C (World Wide Web Consortium), Netscape Communications, Inc, and the initial drive of Dr. Douglas C.Engelbart, without whose vision this would have never happened.

— J. Heck

We'd Like to Hear from You!

As part of our continuing effort to produce books of the highest possible quality, Que would like to hear your comments. To stay competitive, we *really* want you, as a computer book reader and user, to let us know what you like or dislike most about this book or other Que products.

You can mail comments, ideas, or suggestions for improving future editions to the address below, or send us a fax at (317) 581-4663. For the online inclined, Macmillan Computer Publishing has a forum on CompuServe (type **GO QUEBOOKS** at any prompt) through which our staff and authors are available for questions and comments. The address of our Internet site is **http://www.mcp.com** (World Wide Web).

In addition to exploring our forum, please feel free to contact me personally to discuss your opinions of this book: I'm at **osands@que.mcp.com** on the Internet.

Thanks in advance—your comments will help us to continue publishing the best books available on computer topics in today's market.

Oran J. Sands
Product Development Specialist
Que Corporation
201 W. 103rd Street
Indianapolis, Indiana 46290
USA

Contents at a Glance

Table of Contents

8 Saving Stuff From the Web   95

Part III: Traveling the Internet

Part IV: Netscape's Advanced Features

Introduction

Everyone and his or her dog seems to be using Netscape these days. A little over a year or so ago, almost nobody had heard of it. Now it's *the* most popular Web browser. Of course, a little over two years ago nobody had heard of the Internet, and now you can hardly pick up a paper or turn on the TV without hearing something about it. That's the way the Internet works—at warp speed. Changes that might take a couple of years in most types of software—in the world of word processing, spreadsheets and graphics—happen in a few months on the Internet. While most program updates are released every year and a half or longer, the leading Internet programs are released every few months. Here we are, little more than a year into Netscape's life; we've seen several 1.x versions, and we're already looking at version 2.0—a version with dramatic improvements and additions.

In the middle of 1994 the word on the Web was that *the* best browser was Mosaic. But rumors were flying that the core developers of Mosaic had left to form their own company. When Netscape arrived, it was only a matter of months before Mosaic was out, and Netscape was "The Browser."

Right now Netscape is still on top (though it's being given a real run for its money by Internet Explorer, Microsoft's WWW browser). Netscape's publisher, Netscape Communications has gone public in a blast of publicity and hype; the founders have become instant multi-millionaires. (In one case a half-billionaire, on paper anyway; there's some question as to whether Netscape stock is *really* worth $100 a share.) *Forbes ASAP* magazine has even suggested that Marc Andreessen, one of the founders of Netscape Communications, might be the next Bill Gates, a rather astounding compliment, even if it is based on plenty of conjecture.

All this fuss thanks to a computer program, Netscape Navigator, or simply Netscape for short. Perhaps the best (certainly one of the two best) Web browsers available for the Macintosh.

Definitely the most popular—more people use this browser than all others combined.

But none of this really matters if you are using Netscape. What counts is simple: how do you use the program effectively and efficiently. That's what this book is all about. I'm going to explain how you can make the most of Netscape, how you can surf the Web at high speed, and mess around in other areas of the Internet, search FTP sites, dig around in Gopher sites, read newsgroup messages, search WAIS databases, and plenty more.

What makes this book different?

This book explains how to work with Netscape, from the basics (installing it and moving around in Webspace) to more advanced stuff (FTP sessions, using newsgroups, working with Java applets, frames, and plug-ins).

You can use Netscape without my help. You'll quickly figure out how to click on links to move around, even how to enter URLs to jump directly to a Web site. But will you understand what the cache is all about (and the dangers that the cache can pose to your career!); will you understand how and why to use drag-and-drop bookmark entries, how to manage newsgroup messages, why another Netscape window just opened even though you did nothing to make it do so? Will you be able to figure out why your friend swears there's an inline video at a particular page, yet Netscape just shows a static image? Will you understand how to create your own Web pages (or even *why* you should bother)?

By the time you've finished this book, you'll know more about working on the World Wide Web than 99% of all Web users. You'll be able to use Netscape quickly and efficiently, and find what you need when you need it.

You don't have to be a power user to work with this book. I'm assuming that you have the basics down—how to use a mouse, how to open menus and work in dialog boxes—but I won't give you abbreviated instructions that only a computer geek could understand. I'll tell you clearly what you need to do to get the job done. This is a book for people who want to understand how to be a Netscape user right now, with a minimum of fuss, but a maximum of benefit.

How do I use this book?

You can dip into this book at the point you need help—you don't have to read from page one to the end if you don't want to. I've put plenty of cross references in, so if you reach a point where you need some background information that I've covered earlier, you'll know where to go.

There are a number of ways for you to find information, too. There's a detailed Table of Contents—in most cases you'll be able to skim through this and find exactly where to go. There's an index at the back, of course, to help you jump directly to a page. The problem with indexes, though, is that they refer to words, rather than procedures. That's why we've also included an Action Index, just before the normal index. Quickly read through the Action Index sometime—you'll find that it's essentially a list of procedures, things you want to do with Netscape, with the number of the pages you'll need to go to for the instructions.

It's a good idea to spend a few minutes just leafing through the book, finding out what's there. That way, when you run into a problem, you'll have an idea of where to go to find the directions you need.

How this book is put together

I've divided this book into several parts, according to the different functions and procedures. Part I provides a quick explanation of the Internet and the Web, and explains how to find and install Netscape. Part II describes working on the World Wide Web. Part III explains how to use Netscape to work with non-Web Internet systems (newsgroups, FTP, e-mail, and so on). Part IV explains Netscape's advanced features—security, Java applets, scripting with JavaScript, and frames. Part IV also explains how to use the Web Weaver to create your own home page, and even publish on the Web.

Part I: Before We Surf

In chapter 1, I've explained what the Internet and Web actually are, to make sure we start off with a clear understanding. I'm not going into a great deal of detail, though; by now, a couple of years into the Internet boom, you've probably heard the basics before. In chapter 2, I describe where you can find Netscape, the different versions that are available, and how you can install it.

Part II: Caught in the Web

Part II of this book is dedicated to the Web proper. Chapter 3 describes how to start Netscape, and what you'll find when you do. I explain how to begin moving around on the Web—the basic point-and-click moves. Then, in chapter 4, I explain the more advanced navigation techniques, such as entering URLs. I also explain the purpose and use of the cache.

Chapter 5 describes what you'll find as you move "further into the Web," some of the less common Web-page components, such as forms, tables, frames, scripts, and more. Chapter 6 describes the two systems you can use to make finding your way around much easier: the history list and bookmarks.

In chapter 7, I've explained how to search for information on the Web—how to use the special directories and "search engines" that help you find the information you need. Chapter 8 tells you how to save what you find; how you can save documents, pictures, and URLs for future use.

In chapter 9, we'll get to the really fancy stuff, the multimedia. This chapter explains how to install the special viewers you'll need to hear music and watch video. Then, in chapter 10, I'll describe specific viewers that you might want to install, and where to find them.

Part III: Traveling the Internet

There's plenty more on the Internet *outside* the Web, and in this part of the book, I explain how you can use Netscape to work with other parts of the Internet.

In chapter 11, you'll find out about the Internet's software libraries, the FTP sites, and how you can copy files from these libraries back to your computers; you can grab programs, sounds, clip art, documents, and more. Chapter 12 discusses Netscape's e-mail system; how you can send and receive e-mail directly from your Web browser.

Chapter 13 describes what happens when you click on a news link (a link to an Internet newsgroup), or how you can turn Netscape into a newsreader and directly to a newsgroup—it's all about UseNet News. Chapter 14 explains a few more non-Web systems that you can access through Netscape: Gopher and Telnet.

Part IV: Netscape's Advanced Features

This part of the book describes Netscape's more advanced features, things you might not run into often quite yet, but which point in the direction that the Web is moving. In chapter 15, I'll explain how to use Netscape's security features to make sure your online transactions are safe. Chapter 16 describes what will prove to be an exciting new feature, built-in Java support. In chapter 17, we go over the complement to Java, JavaScript, which is a new feature that enables Web authors to make their documents "come alive" with HyperScript-like commands. Chapter 18 is all about the way that Netscape handles frames, another new feature that improves the Web hypertext format.

In this section, I'll also explain a subject that you might not have considered quite yet: Web authoring. In chapters 19 and 20, you'll learn how to create your own home page (it's really quite easy), and even how to set up your own Web site so other people can view your words of wisdom.

In part V, you'll find a Help Index. Go forward a few pages and you find another index, an Action Index. If you're looking for a particular procedure or action, look in here; it will point you to the page that helps you find the information you need.

Information that's easy to understand

This book uses a number of special elements and conventions to help you find information quickly—or to skip things you don't want to read.

Web addresses (URLs) and newsgroups are all in **bold type**, like this: **http://www.netscape.com** and **rec.food.sourdough**, as is text that I'm instructing you to type, and new terminology. Messages that appear in message boxes and status bars are in *italic*, as is link text (that is, the text in a Web document which, when clicked on, takes you to another document or file). Items that can be selected from drop-down list boxes are also in *italic*. Program or HTML text is in `this special font`.

Throughout this book, we use a comma to separate the parts of a menu command. For example, to start a new document, you choose <u>F</u>ile, Open <u>F</u>ile. That means "Open the <u>F</u>ile menu, and choose Open <u>F</u>ile from the list."

And if you see two keys separated by a plus sign, such as Ctrl+X, that means to press and hold the first key, press the second key, and then release both keys.

TIP **Tips either point out information easily overlooked or help you** use your software more efficiently, such as through a shortcut. Tips may help you solve or avoid problems.

CAUTION **Cautions warn you about potentially dangerous results. If you** don't heed them, you could unknowingly do something harmful.

Q&A *What are Q&A notes?*

Q&A notes appear as questions and answers. We try to anticipate user questions that might come up and provide answers to you here.

Plain English, please!

These notes define technical terms or computer jargon.

Sidebars are interesting nuggets of information

Sidebars include information that's relevant to the topic at hand, but not essential. You might want to read them when you're not online. Here you may find more technical details, or interesting background information.

Part I: Before We Surf

1

The Internet and Web—A Quick Intro

● **In this chapter:**

- **What is the Internet?**

- **What Internet services are available?**

- **Using the World Wide Web**

- **Web browsers (clients) and servers**

- **What's HTTP, what are URLs?**

- **Web browser tools you'll use**

Four years ago, the Information Superhighway was a dream without function. The Mosaic was created, and the "Information Superhighway" started to become synonymous with the World Wide Web. Today, the biggest thing out on the Internet, and growing still, is the Web . . . . ●▶

Lots of features, lots of future. The World Wide Web is a "service" on the Internet, like many others. It's been common in Internet books over the past couple of years to describe in great detail what the Internet is—but I think the need for that is diminishing. I suspect that most of you will already be quite familiar with the Internet, and wouldn't want to read another detailed "this is the Internet" book. On the other hand, there's still some confusion about the Internet and all the different systems involved with it. And many people still don't understand the Web and its relationship to the Internet.

To take care of that, we'll start with a chapter that explains a little about the Internet, and a bit more importantly, background information about the World Wide Web.

What is the Internet

The Internet is a network of networks. A **computer network** is a group of computers that are connected so they can communicate with each other. The computers send messages to each other, and share information in the form of computer files. The Internet connects tens of thousands of these networks, with more being added constantly. On those networks are millions of computers.

No doubt you've noticed all the Information Superhighway hype over the past couple of years. Thanks to heavy media coverage, the Internet is growing rapidly. Though few people had even heard of it three years ago, now almost everyone's heard of the Internet—even if they don't really know what it is.

The networks that make up the Internet belong to government bodies, universities, businesses, local-community library systems, and even some schools. More than ninety percent of the registered networks are within the United States and ninety-seven percent are within North America.

Who owns the Internet?...

When I'm asked "Who owns the Internet?" I use the analogy of a phone system. A phone system has lots of different "switches," owned by different organizations, all connected together. When someone in Denver tries to phone someone in New York, he doesn't need to know how the call gets through—which states and cities the call passes through. The telephone network handles it all for him. These private companies have decided the mechanics—the electronics—of the process, and it doesn't matter one whit to the average caller how it's done. The Internet works in much the same way. Just as there's no single telephone company, there's no single Internet company.

Nobody "owns" the Internet. Who owns the world's telephone system? Nobody. Each component is owned by someone, but the system as a whole is not owned by anyone. The Internet is a network that hangs together through mutual interest. The world's telephone companies get together and decide the best way the "telephone system" should function. They decide which country gets what country code, how to bill for international calls, who pays for transoceanic cables, and the technical details of how one country's lines connect to another.

The Internet is very similar. It began in the early '70s, with various government computer networks, and it has grown as different organizations realized the advantages of being connected. Its origins can be traced back to ARPAnet, a Department of Defense computer system that was used to link a variety of research centers together. But the Internet has grown tremendously since its birth. All sorts of organizations connected their networks, each with its own particular configuration of hardware and software.

In the past, the Internet was a non-commercial system; businesses using the Internet was even frowned upon. In spite of that, the largest growth of the Internet has been in the pastr two years as the system has become commercialized. This has brought millions of dollars into the Internet, allowing development of new software, new connections, online businesses, and so forth.

So what's available?

Why would you want to use the Internet? Let's get a little more specific, and look at the services available to you on the Internet.

Service	Description
E-mail and Mailing Lists	Send e-mail messages to anyone in the world (well, assuming that person has an Internet e-mail account). You can also subscribe to e-mail-based discussion groups.
Newsgroups	Thousands of discussion groups, on almost any subject you can think of.
World Wide Web	Millions of interconnected documents scattered around the world with an incredible amount of information. Using the World Wide Web, we can browse through these **Hypertext** documents which include text, sounds, pictures, video, and even 3-D images. And the primary concern of this book, of course, is Netscape—a Web **browser**.
Gopher	A menu system that lets you wander through computers on the Internet, searching for documents. Up until early 1994, it really seemed like the Gopher system would play a critical role in the future of the Internet. Now you hardly hear about Gopher; everyone's more interested in the World Wide Web.
FTP	File Transfer Protocol; one of the core "systems" of the Internet—a system that lets you transfer files to and from computers all over the world. It's like a giant software library—billions of files—that contains programs, sound clips, music, pictures, video, and documents.
Telnet	A system that lets you log in to someone else's computer. Some people actually invite the public into their computers; you might get to play chess, view a government job listing, or search a NASA database.
WAIS	Wide Area Information Servers. You don't hear a lot about these right now; again, the Web is all that seems to interest people. Still, WAIS is there and in the background, providing some additional features to Web servers, allowing you to search through massive amounts of information easily.
Internet Relay Chat	A giant, world-wide "chat" service. You type messages that other people can read and respond to immediately. It's a real-time form of messaging.

Plain English, please!

Hypertext is a concept in which a line of text can point to some other information, either in another document or the same one you're browsing. As you are reading the document you'll see some form of hypertext link; generally underlined text in a different color. Clicking on the link takes you to different information—usually relating to the original words.

Browser is the name given to a program which works on your computer to receive information from the Internet and display it to you in a helpful, friendly manner. **99**

This is not an all-inclusive list. There are other services you can use, and other services that you use without knowing it. But this list covers the basics, the most common and popular services.

If you already know a little about the Internet, you may be surprised to hear that we'll be covering several of the services (listed above) in this book.

No, this isn't a book about the Internet—it's a book about Netscape, which runs on the World Wide Web. But Netscape can also use FTP and Gopher to access their services and, with the aid of another program, launch Telnet sessions. In part III of this book, "Traveling the Internet," we're going to jump from the World Wide Web proper into some of the other Internet services you can use from Netscape.

All about the World Wide Web

This book is about Netscape, not the Internet in its entirety. It's probably a good idea to understand a few basics about the Web before we jump straight in. What is the Web? How does it all fit together?

As you've already heard, the Web is a hypertext system of documents linked together electronically. The Web lets you "navigate" between documents by clicking on the links in documents—and lets you go directly to a document by providing your browser (your Web program, Netscape) with the document's address.

In order to understand the workings of the World Wide Web, let's start with its basic building blocks.

HTML—Web bricks

The primary building material on the Web is the **HTML** document. HTML means **HyperText Markup Language.** HTML documents are computer files containing ASCII text—just plain ole text.

The text contains special codes or **tags**; the codes are created using the normal ASCII-text characters, but they are codes nonetheless. They are not there for you to read, they are there for recognition by Web browsers, in this case Netscape.

After Netscape has read the codes (this happens very quickly, by the way) the browser then displays the text on your computer screen. It strips out the codes and formats the text according to the code's instructions. What do you see? A document, much like a word processing document, is displayed within the content area of the browser.

You really don't need to know what these HTML codes are, unless you want to publish your own Web documents. You'll learn more about the codes in chapter 19, but for now take a quick look at figure 1.1. It is a document displayed in Netscape, after the browser has formatted the HTML document.

Fig. 1.1
Here's what the Netscape Store document looks like in Netscape.

Where is all this?—the Web server

So where, physically, are these documents stored? They are on computer systems throughout the world. How do you get to them? A Web **server** makes them available. This is a program that receives requests from your browser, and transmits the Web documents back to you. What term should we use for the actual information stored on the computer? Each individual HTML file is known as a **document** or **page**. You'll also often hear the term **site**, to mean a collection of documents about a particular subject, stored on a particular computer. It is also sometimes used to refer to a computer that contains a number of documents or pages.

Smaller bricks—other media

The Web is based on text, but there's plenty more out there, too. Just about any form of Internet tool or computer file can be linked to the Web. You'll find pictures, sounds, video, FTP sites, Gopher sites, WAIS database searches, 3D images, and more.

You'll usually find that you start by reading a document, then jump from that document to something else. Many documents have **inline graphics** pictures that are linked into the documents and appear when you display the document (you can see a picture in figure 1.1, for instance). How can these pictures be linked to an ASCII document? A special HTML tag tells the browser where the picture is (generally in the same directory as the HTML document), and the browser grabs the picture and inserts it in the correct position.

Along with the inline graphics, you'll also see what are called **Hypergraphics**, or more commonly known as **imagemaps**. These images are not just simple links to other documents, but contain multiple areas (known as "hot spots") within them that are linked to other documents.

TIP   You may have noticed that so far there's hyper-this and hyper-that. It all started with Hypertext—the concept that some words can be "special"—pointing to more information or another reference. The concept was taken the next step further—so that pictures could be links to other data—that's the Hypergraphics. The whole lot of it is also known as "hypermedia." Fortunately, the "hyper" fad doesn't seem to have caught on as securely as the "cyber" fad, and now they're just mostly known as "links on the Web."

Your HTML "Player"—Browsers

If you want to listen to a music CD, you need a CD player. If you want to listen to an LP, you need a record player. If you want to see a word processing document, you need a word processor. And if you want to see an HTML file, you need a Web browser or Web client, such as Netscape.

> ❝ *Plain English, please!*
>
> Browsers are sometimes also known as Web **clients**. A Web **server** is a system that contains Web documents, and lets people in to view those documents. A **client** is the program that is serviced by the server—it's the program that displays the Web documents. The term browser, however, is more commonly used. ❞

Browsers can be very simple, letting you view nothing but the text in Web documents. They let you move between documents, but little else. Or they can be very sophisticated, letting you save information, play sounds and video, and create bookmarks so you can find your way back. Netscape is one of the best browsers available, providing lots of neat features.

How does the browser get the data?

When you want to view a Web document, Netscape has to transfer the document from a site—just about anywhere in the world—back to your computer. How's that done?

The Internet has all sorts of **Transfer Protocols**, systems used for transferring different forms of data across the Internet. These include (among others) SMTP, the Simple Mail Transfer Protocol (used for sending e-mail); NNTP, Network News Transfer Protocol (used for transmitting newsgroup messages all over the place); and HTTP, HyperText Transfer Protocol. HTTP is the system used by the Web to transfer data to and fro.

By the way, like many writers and Web users, I refer to the Web as if you were traveling around on it. I (and others) say "go to the such and such site," "navigate to something or other," and so on. Strictly speaking, of course, you are not going anywhere. (Your chair should remain firmly attached to the floor.) Rather, documents are being sent from the Web server to your computer. But in many ways the "travel" analogy works well. You are getting documents, pictures, and sounds from all over the world. While you physically remain in one spot, intellectually you are on a journey.

URLs—the Web address

Everything on the Internet needs some kind of address—otherwise, how would you find anything? The Web's no different. Each resource on the Web has an address or URL—**Uniform Resource Locator**. Here's one, for instance:

http://www.iuma.com/IUMA-2.0/pages/registration/registration.html

The URL starts with **http://**. This indicates the site is a normal HTTP (HyperText Transfer Protocol) site; you are going to an HTML document. Sometimes the URL starts with something different. If it starts with **ftp://**, for instance, it means you are on your way to an FTP site. As you'll see in chapters 11 "Software Libraries—Using FTP" and 14 "Not by Web Alone— Gopher, Finger, Telnet, and More", Web browsers can access other Internet systems, not just HTTP.

Next comes the address of the host computer (the address of the computer that has the Web server you are contacting), in this case **www.iuma.com**. Following that is the address of the file directory containing the resource— **/IUMA-2.0/pages/registration/**. In the UNIX world, directories or folders are indicated with forward slashes (/). Most Internet Web sites are running on UNIX computers (though that may change, servers are being developed for all the microcomputer platforms), and the forward slash has become the standard for URLs, regardless of the type of computer the document is found on.

Finally, you have the resource itself—**registration.html**. In this case you can tell that it's an HTML document. The .html extension makes that clear. (Don't be surprised if the document ends in .HTM, this is because older Windows machines were limited to three character suffixes.)

Sometimes the URL won't have a filename at the end. That's not necessarily a mistake. For instance, if you are going to the Ziff-Davis Publishing Web document, you'll use the **http://www.ziff.com/** URL. This specifies the host, but no directory or document. That's okay because their Web server is set up to show you the document they want you to see.

What can you do with it?

What are you going to do with a URL? Well, you can get almost anywhere on the Web by simply following links in documents. But you may spend several weeks trying to get where you want to go! The URL is an address. Web browsers have a way you can go directly to a particular URL. I'll show you how to get Netscape to go where you want it to go in chapter 4, "Advanced Navigation."

 TIP   **You may hear or read something like "point your Web browser to . . ."** This simply means use your browser's URL command to go directly to the document.

You'll find URLs all over the place. In *Newsweek's* regular Cyberscope column, in various directories of resources on the net, in newsgroup messages, and throughout this book.

Tools to simplify life

We've pretty much covered the basics of the Web itself, but before we move on, let's consider some of the ways that Netscape can make traveling the Web easier for you.

First, it's nice to be able to save the document you are viewing. Netscape lets you do so in a number of ways; you can save a text file directly to disk, copy text to the Clipboard, even drag text from the browser to another program.

Then how about downloading files? There are lots of files on the Web that are "pointed to" by links in text documents. Netscape will let you transfer those files back to your computer. In fact, you'll even be able to carry out FTP sessions, to grab files not just from Web sites but from File Transfer Protocol sites, libraries of programs, sounds, documents, and plenty more.

The home page (or is it start page?)

Here's an argument I'm not going to win—"What is a home page?" It's a greatly misused term, that's what it is! You'll often hear the term used to refer to a particular Web site's main page. You might hear someone say, "Hey, dude, check out the Rolling Stones' home page," (it's not a home page, dude, but, nonetheless, it's at **http://www.stones.com/**). It would be more correct to call it the Rolling Stones Web site or page or document.

Home page is actually a browser term, not a Web site term. It's the page that appears when you first open your Web browser. A company could set up a document for all of its employees. When they start their browsers they see this home page, with all the links they'd normally need. A service provider could set up a home page so that when a subscriber started a browser, it displayed that page. And you can even create your own home page, with links to all the sites you commonly use (see chapter 19, "Creating Your Own Web Page").

The home page is a starting point. Most browsers have a button (or command) that will take you directly back to the home page, regardless of what you're browsing on the Web. (If every document on the Web is a home page, what sense does having a home page button make? Which home page should it take you to?)

Anyway, I've pretty much lost this argument. Many HTML authors are creating what they are terming "home pages," so the term now has, in effect, two meanings.

Where've I been?—The history list

Some kind of **history list** is useful. This is simply a list of the documents you've viewed in the current session. A history list lets you quickly select a document and return to that document.

There are different forms of history lists. Some show all the documents you've viewed in the current session, others show documents from previous sessions, sometimes back weeks or months. Netscape currently has a very basic history list, which only keeps track of the current session, but doesn't show all the documents from the session, as you'll learn in chapter 6, "The History List and Bookmarks."

Hey, this is a cool site!—Bookmarks

A bookmark system lets you save the URLs and the titles of documents to which you think you'll want to return. It's easy to get lost on the Web. Spend an hour online, close your browser, then try to repeat your path through the Web. Just remember poor old Hansel and Gretel trying to find their way through the woods. And you are traveling across the world!

Bookmarks, though, let you create a list of this useful stuff, then use the list to go directly back to one of the sites.

What was that again?

We've covered the basics but, as you'll soon find out, there's plenty more. Before we go on, here's a quick summary of a few Web and Netscape terms:

Term	Definition
Bookmarks	A URL that has been saved in some kind of system from which you can quickly select it, so you can jump back to a useful or interesting site.
Browser	A program that can read HTML documents, and lets you navigate through the Web. Sometimes known as a Web client.
Home page	It's the first page that appears when the browser starts. (Okay, a lot of people seem to want to use it to indicate the main page on a Web Server as well.)
History list	A list of all the places you've been on the Web in the current session. Lets you jump directly back to a particular document.
HTML	HyperText Markup Language, the "coding" system used to create a Web text document.
HTTP	HyperText Transfer Protocol, the system used to transfer Web data between the Web site and your browser.
Hyperlink	A connection from something you're browsing to more information—most commonly from a piece of text or a picture to another Web page.
URL	Uniform Resource Locator, a Web "address," used to tell a browser where to find a document or other resources on the Internet.
Web Server	A Web server is a computer running a program that provides information to a Web browser. Web documents are managed by the server.
Web Site	A group of related Web documents on one computer—with this definition, a computer may contain several Web sites. Some people use it to mean a computer containing Web documents.

2

Finding and Installing Netscape

● **In this chapter:**

● What sort of connection do I need?

● Finding, downloading, and installing Netscape

● How do I install the program?

It's not hard, but you need to get and install Netscape before you can use it . . . . ▶

Where can you get Netscape? A variety of places. Perhaps you've been given a copy by your company. Many companies are buying site licenses that allow everyone, it seems, to use Netscape, from the CEO to the cafeteria staff.

Perhaps you bought some software, and got Netscape with it; I've seen the browser bundled with other Internet programs. Or maybe nobody's given you a copy, so you want to go get one. I'll explain where you can find it. First, though, note that we're only interested in the 2.x versions. You can probably find earlier versions lying around, but this book is about version 2.0. And we're only interested in the Macintosh version. There are versions for a variety of operating systems, and all are very similar. But the focus of this book is on the Macintosh program: Netscape 2.0.

66 *Plain English, please!*

Why am I calling this program Netscape? Why not Navigator? The Netscape Navigator browser is generally known as Netscape, even though Netscape is the company name (Netscape Communications). It might make more sense to call it Navigator (after all, we abbreviate Microsoft Word for Windows to Word for Windows, not Microsoft; and Lotus 1-2-3 to 1-2-3, not Lotus). But originally the company name was Mosaic Communications, and the browser was called Netscape Mosaic, named after the first graphical browser (the founders of Mosaic Communications worked on the Mosaic browser). The browser's name was, therefore, shortened to simply Netscape, and that's how it became known. Tell people you are working with Navigator and they won't know what you are talking about. Tell them you are using Netscape, and they will.

The browser is called "Netscape," the same as the name of the company that made it. 99

What sort of connection do I need?

In order to use Netscape to "surf the Web" you'll need a TCP/IP connection to the Internet. What's this? It's a "protocol" that computers on the Internet use to communicate with each other. If you're really curious, TCP/IP stands for **T**ransmission **C**ontrol **P**rotocol/**I**nternet **P**rotocol.

There are two basic kinds of TCP/IP connections; LAN and dial-in connections. A LAN connection is one from a Local Area Network to the Internet. Your company may have already connected its network to the Internet. As long as you have access to the Internet from your computer, using the LAN's TCP/IP connection, you can use Netscape.

A dial-in connection is one that is made over the telephone lines. You use your modem to dial into another computer that will then allow your software to set up a TCP/IP connection. You may have heard this referred to as a SLIP, or PPP connection—these are simply different types of TCP/IP connections designed for use over the phone lines.

This book does *not* explain how to set up TCP/IP connections. If you want to use Netscape at work, talk to your LAN system administrator. If you want to set up a TCP/IP connection at home, you need to contact a service provider (a local provider, or one of the major online services such as CompuServe or America Online). Most providers or services will help you set one up. From here on, I'm assuming that you already have your TCP/IP connection, and are ready to install and run Netscape.

Finding, downloading, and installing Netscape

You can download a copy of Netscape directly from the Internet, from a variety of Web and FTP (File Transfer Protocol) sites. If you already have Web access, start by going to the Netscape Web page at **http://home.netscape.com/**. You'll find information there about how to download Netscape. You can download a version that you may use to evaluate the software, without charge. Or you can go to the Netscape store and buy a fully-supported version immediately.

If you can't get through to the Netscape site (you probably will be able to, but there's a chance it will be too busy or down), try this site: **http://mistral.enst.fr/netscape/**.

If you have FTP access, try **ftp://ftp.netscape.com**. This site is often very busy, though. If you can't get through, try one of these "mirror" sites:

ftp://ftp.netscape.com

ftp://ftp2.netscape.com

ftp://ftp.eos.hokudai.ac.jp/pub/WWW/Netscape

ftp://ftp.leo.chubu.ac.jp/pub/WWW/netscape

ftp://ftp.cs.umn.edu/packages/ftp.netscape.com/2.0b3/mac/

ftp://server.berkeley.edu/pub/netscape/

 *Plain English, please!*

> **Mirror sites**—A mirror site is one that contains the same files as the site it is mirroring. Thus, Netscape's mirror sites should contain the same software as the main Netscape sites, so you can download software from a mirror site when you can't get into the main site. **"**

Netscape is free—*Not!*

There's a rumor going around that Netscape is free software. In most cases it's not. You can download Netscape and use if for free in two cases: if you are (to quote from the license agreement) "a student, faculty member or staff member of an educational institution (K-12, junior college, college or library) or an employee of a charitable non-profit organization; or your use of the software is for the purpose of evaluating whether to purchase an ongoing license to the software. The evaluation period for use by or on behalf of a commercial entity is limited to 90 days; evaluation use by others is not subject to this restriction."

So, if you are not covered by the educational, charitable, or non-profit umbrella, after you've decided you like and want to continue using Netscape, you should register it. You can choose <u>H</u>elp, Registration <u>I</u>nformation within Netscape for more details. The registration price is currently $39.

Installing the program

If you bought Netscape, or otherwise received it on a diskette, just follow the instructions that come with the program. If you are downloading the program, just double-click on the Icon that appears on your desktop and it should install Netscape for you. You'll first see a "splash screen" something like figure 2.1.

Fig. 2.1
The "splash screen" just gives you information about who you got the program from and what you're installing. In effect, they're advertisements.

Follow the instructions on your screen. This is a very quick and easy installation process.

Fig. 2.2
The Read Me button shows the licensing information for Netscape, but to get it installed, all you need to do is hit the Install button.

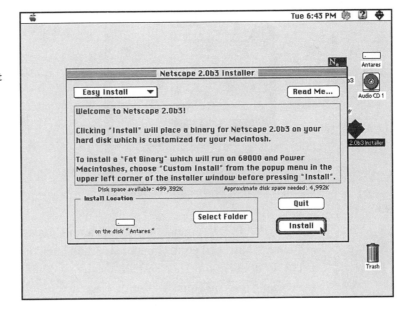

TIP **It can take a long time for the Netscape installation program to** appear—so long that you may think it's not going to start. But if you hear your hard disk churning, just wait a little while and it will start eventually.

There are a lot of options that you can play with in Netscape. We'll just hit upon some as we go through the book and the features. You can also do a lot of customization of Netscape to simply make it look different—we'll go customizing Netscape as we go through the book.

Starting Netscape

Depending on how you have configured your TCP/IP connection, there are several ways to start Netscape. Use these methods to start:

Fig. 2.3
MacSLIP is only one of the ways to get a connection to the Internet—you could also be using InterSLIP, MacPPP, or be directly connected!

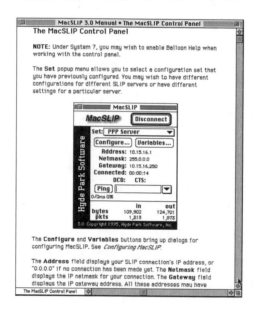

- Start your TCP/IP connection. For example, if you are using MacSLIP, open the MacSLIP control panel and then click on Connect to start your TCP/IP connection. Then start Netscape by double-clicking on the Netscape icon on your desktop.

- Before you start your TCP/IP connection, double-click on the Netscape icon on your desktop and Netscape will open. You can have MacSLIP set up to automatically open its Connect dialog box so you can connect to your service provider.

- Open a .HTM or .HTML file by dragging it onto the Netscape icon on your desktop.

After you've started Netscape, you should see an initial picture show up on the window as in figure 2.4 below. After the picture shows, Netscape will automatically open your home page—the page that it always starts with.

Fig. 2.4
The splash screen will also give you some quick information regarding how it's setting things up—telling you about initializing the network and what version of Netscape you're using.

The home page

Having opened Netscape, you should see a window, what we'll call the **Browser** window and in it is the Netscape **home** page. This is the page that Netscape will automatically open when you first start the program. What does the Netscape home page look like? At the time of writing, it looked like the page shown in figure 3.3. This page is stored on the Netscape Communications host computer, and they add and remove announcements as necessary. In chapter 3, "The Opening Moves," we'll go over how to change your home page if you want to.

Fig. 2.5
This is what the Netscape home page looked like in December 1995. The Web is dynamic, and that's almost constantly reflected in the documents as people and companies update pages, creating and removing information as they like. By the time this book is published, this page will have probably changed.

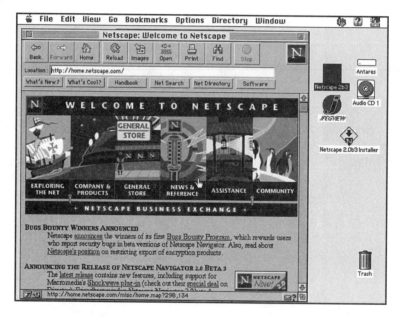

You'll see a detailed listing of all the parts of the browser, as well as the listing of the menus on the insert that comes with this book.

Part II: Caught in the Web

3

The Opening Moves

● **In this chapter:**

- **What the Web document contains**

- **Your first clicks**

- **Don't Wait—Start working right away**

- **Lost yet? Finding your way back**

- **Special text, special backgrounds**

- **You can change Netscape's appearance**

- **Changing your home page**

Now we are ready to begin navigating around the Web. . .

What does a Web document contain?

Before we get started, notice what you are seeing in the Netscape browser—the Web document. You'll remember that a Web document is really a simple ASCII text document. This document contains two basic components:

- Text that the author of the document wants your browser to display so you can read it.

- Text that provides instructions to the browser, telling it how to display the document.

You'll learn more about these special instructions in chapter 19, "Creating Your Own Web Page," when we talk about creating your own home page. For now, take a quick look at the following:

```
<HTML>
<head><title>Information SuperLibrary</title></head>
<BODY bgcolor="#FFFFFF">
<P ALIGN=CENTER><A HREF = "/35179372512002/cgi-bin/imagemap/
general/graphics/new/super.map"  >
<IMG ALT="" BORDER=0 SRC="super.gif"ISMAP></A><P>
<CENTER>
<IMG ALT="Top 5% of the Web!" SRC="top5.gif">
</CENTER>
<CENTER>View our <A HREF = "/35179372512002/general/map/
index.html"  >text only</A> version.<P>
<H2>Browse One of Our Subjects...</H2>
<FORM method = "POST" action = "/35179372512002/cgi-bin/find-
books.cgi"  >
<input type=submit value="Go to">
```

This is from the current main page at the Macmillan Publishing Web site (**http://www.mcp.com**). All the text between the angle brackets (between **<** and **>**) are instructions. The rest of the text is text that you'll see on your screen.

So, when a Web server sends a document to Netscape, Netscape reads this text, and displays the page as it's instructed. In other words, it looks at all the special commands inside the document, strips the codes out of the document, then displays the text on your screen in the manner instructed by those commands. But what about the pictures? How do they get there? In the previous example, you can see a line like this:

```
<IMG ALT="" BORDER=0 SRC="super.gif"ISMAP></A>
```

This is a special instruction that says "get the image file called SUPER.GIF, and place it right here.

A couple of more things you should be aware of. Each Web document has its own address, a URL (Uniform Resource Locator). You can see this in the Location bar, immediately below the toolbar. It may look complicated, but it's really not; I explained what it all means in chapter 1, "The Internet and Web—A Quick Intro."

Finally, a Web document contains two basic forms of information. First there's stuff that just sits there, that you can read or view, the text and pictures. Then there is the **Hypermedia**, pictures and text that also contain pointers to more information.

When you click on one of these Hypermedia links, something happens. Generally speaking, clicking on one of these links sends a message to a Web server asking for another document. This document could be another HTML page, it could be an image, or it could be some kind of unusual file format— a sound or video file, for instance. Netscape is also adding features now that will allow the browser to do some things based on what you click on. We'll cover these features more in chapter 17, "Netscape Scripting with JavaScript."

How, then, do you know where these links are? In figure 3.1 you can see several links. Links on text are shown with underlining and, at first, a different color from the normal text. Links on pictures are not so easily identified. Some will have a blue border around them. This happens in cases in which the Web author has turned the entire picture into a link using the same technique that he might use to convert a word or sentence into a link.

But other image links don't use this method, and so don't have the blue border around them. Point at a picture with the mouse and see if the mouse pointer changes to a small hand. If it does, you are pointing to a link. If it doesn't change, though, move the pointer around a little; some parts of a picture may contain a link, while others don't.

 TIP **Another good way to figure out what you're pointing to is to keep** an eye at the bottom of the browser window, where it will show you the URL of the link you're currently pointing to. If you're not pointing to a link, it will be blank.

Fig. 3.1
Text links at Yahoo
(**http://
www.yahoo.com/**)
are underlined and
colored. That's going
to be the easiest way
to identify links. You
can also just use the
images for clues—the
swirls above the text
look like buttons—and
they are.

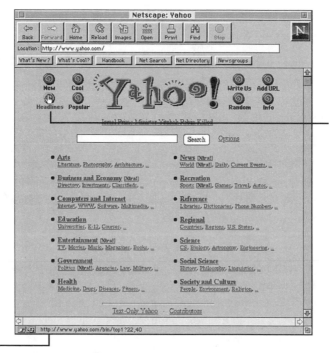

*The hand pointer
indicates that you
are pointing at a
link, not just an
image to be
viewed.*

*The status message
shows the URL of the
document referenced
by the link you are
pointing at.*

Also, notice the status message at the bottom of the window. While you are
pointing at a link, information about that link will be shown in the status
message. Point at a simple link and you'll see the URL of the document or
file that the link "points at," the document or file that will be transferred
when you click on the link. Point at an **imagemap**, a picture with multiple
hotspots (areas containing links), and you'll see the URL of the image itself,
plus some numbers indicating the area of the image to which you are
pointing.

 Plain English, please!

An **Imagemap** is another form of **Hypermedia**. Essentially, an imagemap
is a picture that points to one or more different information sources
depending on where you click in it. The term comes from the program
"imagemap," which uses a map of where the various points link to.

Your first clicks

Let's begin with a few clicks. First, click on the "What's Cool" button in the Directory Button bar. (If this bar isn't displayed—it's below the Location bar—choose Options, Show Directory Buttons.)

This opens a list of interesting locations on the Web. You can now begin clicking on links, to go to any site that takes your fancy. Simply move around, clicking on link after link, to see what happens. Note that when you click on a link, the link changes color for a moment (it changes red). This is so you can tell for sure that you got a good click on the link, and Netscape knows what you want to do.

 TIP **For now I want to stick with simple Web documents. You may** click on a link that displays a picture by itself, or perhaps causes a sound to play; that's fine (I'll explain all this in chapter 10). But if you click on a link and see a dialog box asking you to save a file or asking how to handle some kind of strange file format, cancel out of the dialog box and try some other link. We'll cover these subjects later in chapter 9, "Audio and Video" and chapter 10, "More on Viewers."

Watch the status messages

When you click on a link, you may want to watch the status messages, in the status bar at the bottom of the window. You'll see a variety of messages, such as these:

Reading file—Netscape is grabbing the document out of the document cache, rather than from the World Wide Web itself. See chapter 4, "Advanced Navigation," for information about the cache.

Connect: Looking up host: **www.mcp.com**—This tells you that Netscape is looking up the host address part of the URL (the Web address), to try to find the host computer that has the Web server specified by the link you clicked on.

Unable to locate host: **www.ieee.com**—If the link you click on has a bad host address, you'll see a message saying that Netscape can't find the host. You'll also see a dialog box saying that "the server does not have a DNS entry." This means that when Netscape contacted DNS (Domain Name Service, the Internet system that keeps track of all the host addresses), it was told that the host address did not exist.

 TIP **Netscape is not always correct about the host not having a DNS** entry. If you're not connected to the Internet when you're using Netscape, it can't ask the DNS service to look up a name. Instead of responding that you're not connected to the Internet, it just says it can't find an entry for that particular host name.

Connect: Contacting host: **www.mcp.com**—Netscape has sent a message to the server, and is waiting for an acknowledgment that the server has got the message.

Interrupt the current transfer—Hold on, something's gone wrong. Wait a moment and maybe Netscape will be able to get things moving again.

Connect: Host Contacted: Waiting for reply—Netscape has sent a message to the Web server, and is waiting for it to respond.

Transferring data—The server has begun sending the document to Netscape.

45% of 80k—A message, similar to this, indicates how much of the document has been transferred, and the size of the document. If the document contains inline images, you may see several of these messages, for the text itself and each image. In some cases you'll also see information about how fast the data is being transferred, and an estimate of how much longer it will take. Watch the progress bar to the right of the status messages, too, to see a graphical representation of the amount that's been transferred.

Document: Done—That's it, Netscape's got the entire document, images included.

  TIP **If you begin a transfer, and decide that you want to stop (perhaps** it's taking too long, or you realize you clicked on the wrong link), click on the Stop button or press the ⌘ + . (period) key.

Don't wait—start working right away

In the olden days on the Web—okay, a bit more than a year ago—when you clicked on a link, the document would start transferring, and you'd have to stare at a blank screen for a while, twiddling your thumbs. After all the information had been transferred, your browser would then display it on the screen.

That's all changed. As soon as Netscape has received some text, it displays it on your screen. You can start scrolling around in the document, reading the text, while Netscape continues getting the rest of the text, and then gets the pictures. For instance, take a look at figure 3.2. This shows a document with a missing picture; Netscape has transferred the text, put the images it already grabbed (the large one on top), and is now transferring the rest of the pictures (smaller icons throughout the rest of the document).

But there's more. There are two types of special images, designed to be used as inline pictures, that transfer to Netscape very quickly; **interlaced GIF** and **progressive JPEG**. You can recognize interlaced GIFs by the fact that you see all of the image very quickly, but it's very fuzzy. Then, as more of the image is transferred, it gets sharper. The progressive JPEG image simply loads very quickly and smoothly. Of course, not everyone is using these special formats. If a Web author is using simple .GIF, .JPEG (or .JPG), or .XBM images, they'll transfer a little more slowly. (These are the three image types that can be used for inline images; .XBM is a UNIX format that you don't run into so much these days.)

So, what are you going to do while Netscape is transferring all the text and pictures? You can read the document and view the images that have already arrived. And if you find a link you want to use, don't wait. Simply click on the link—Netscape will stop transferring the current document, and start working on the document referenced by the link you clicked on.

Fig. 3.2
Netscape is still transferring the pictures, though it's got all the text (this is from the Apple Computer Web site, at **http://www.apple.com**).

Moving around the document

You can move a document around, so that you can view it all. There's no set length for a Web document; some are visible in entirety in the window, others may be hundreds of lines long, most of which will be off-screen.

You can use the window's scroll bars to move up and down, of course, and side to side. You can also use these keys:

- Up and Down Arrows—move up and down a line or two at a time.

- Page Up and Page Down—move up and down about a screenful at a time.

- Spacebar—move down about a screenful at a time.

- Home—move to the top of the document.

- End—move to the bottom of the document.

TIP   **These keystrokes only work if the "focus" is in the content area; if** you try to use the keys and they don't work, click inside the Netscape window and then try again. Also, note that if the focus is on the Location bar or Directory Button bar, using these keystrokes may cause Netscape to select another document.

Your links will change color

You may notice as you move around that links change color. At first, all the links are blue, then some of them become purple. The purple links are links to documents you've already seen. Not just links you've clicked on, but links to documents that you've already visited. For example, you are in document A and click on a link that takes you to document B. Later, while in document C, you see a purple link, one you've never clicked on before (because you've never been in document C). You point at the link, then look at the status messages, and see that the link points at document B. Netscape figures this out when it transfers the document, and changes the color accordingly.

How long will these links remain colored purple (or whatever other color you choose as the "followed-link" color)? By default they'll stay that way for 30 days. However, you can tell Netscape to use a different time period, or tell it to use the followed-link color forever. Choose Options, General Preferences and click on the Appearance tab. You should see the window as shown in figure 3.3. Then you can choose any of these options in the box labeled Link Styles or you can click on the Expire Now button to immediately expire (remove the followed color) the links.

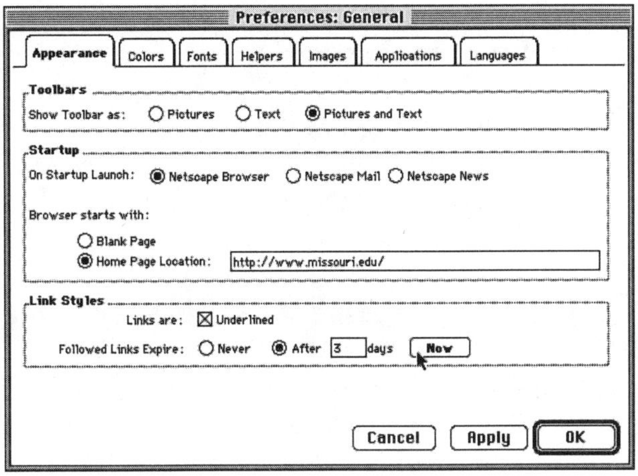

Fig. 3.3
Netscape offers many preferences such as color fonts and appearance.

Lost yet? Finding your way back

Eventually you'll reach a place in which you are stuck. There's no way forward—no more links you can click on. Or maybe you simply don't want to go forward, you want to return to where you've just been. So let's look at a few ways to return.

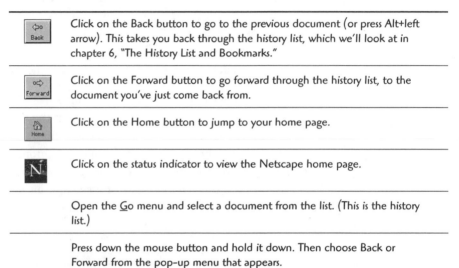	Click on the Back button to go to the previous document (or press Alt+left arrow). This takes you back through the history list, which we'll look at in chapter 6, "The History List and Bookmarks."
	Click on the Forward button to go forward through the history list, to the document you've just come back from.
	Click on the Home button to jump to your home page.
	Click on the status indicator to view the Netscape home page.
	Open the Go menu and select a document from the list. (This is the history list.)
	Press down the mouse button and hold it down. Then choose Back or Forward from the pop-up menu that appears.

That's all the navigating we're going to be doing in this chapter. I'll explain a few more techniques in the following chapters, though. Before we move on, let's look at a few things you may notice as you travel around the Web.

Special text, special backgrounds

Now and again you'll run across Web pages in which all the colors seem wrong. The text color is not the color you are used to, the links—are they links?—are different colors, the background is completely different, and so on.

Netscape has a series of default colors, but Web authors can override these colors if they wish. They can make a particular word or paragraph a different color, or they can use a different color background—or even a special pattern. Look at figure 3.4, for instance. You can see that the document background is white, not the normal gray. This author has defined his own background color.

Fig. 3.4
The **http://
www1.cis.ufl.edu/
perl/** document shows
an example of how an
author may choose to
pick a special back-
ground, in this case
white to contrast more
with the black text.

You can override his overriding if you want! You can tell Netscape that you
don't want to allow an author to pick backgrounds and text colors. You'll do
this in the Colors area of the Preferences dialog box. For an example of how
that overriding looks, see figure 3.5. You'll notice that the background has
gone. The text has now changed back to the normal colors.

Fig. 3.5
We've overridden the
author's overriding!
Now we have default
colors, and have
removed the back-
ground.

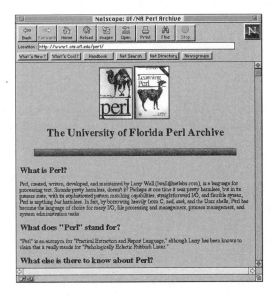

You can change Netscape's appearance

Before we go on, I just want to mention that there are *lots* of ways to modify Netscape's appearance; you can remove the location bar, toolbar, and directory buttons, change the size of the toolbar buttons, change the background color and link colors, and so on.

Changing your video mode

Also, remember that Netscape's appearance is to some extent dependent on how you've set up your video monitor. If you are using a 16-color video mode, many images you see on the Web will appear rather murky. A 256-color mode is better. (There are some, but not many, images using more than 256 colors.) Also, you may find that the Netscape window is rather cluttered. Because we have to shoot my screen snapshots down so much to get them to the correct size to be laid out in a book, I use a resolution of 640 by 480 pixels. These numbers refer to the number of pixels (the smallest part of the video image that can be displayed on your screen) across the screen and down the screen. But 640 by 480 isn't really very convenient, because everything's very large using this resolution. If I used 832 by 624, or even 1,024 by 768, Netscape would be able to display more of each document inside the content area of the window.

The problem with this, however, is that a high resolution "squeezes" things. The text and pictures in the document will become smaller (how do you think it gets more into the content area?). So there's a trade-off. The larger your screen, the higher resolution you can use comfortably, the smaller your screen the more difficult high resolutions will be to work with. Also, the higher the screen resolution you use, the more work your video has to do. At very high resolutions you may find that things work more slowly. And you may also find that you can no longer use a 256-color mode.

So experiment a little. Try all the different resolutions you can, while still keeping 256 colors. You can change these options by opening the Monitors control panel as shown in figure 3.6.

Select the Options button. When the dialog box opens, click on the settings you want to try. You should see some options similar to the ones that are displayed for me as shown in figure 3.7.

Fig. 3.6
The Monitors control panel will only show you the options you have available with your video driver. Macintosh AV machines will tend to be able to display more colors at high resolutions.

Fig. 3.7
Remember: The higher the resolution, the smaller the stuff is going to look on the screen. Small text at high resolutions can be very difficult to read!

Changing your home page

So you have some basic ideas of how to work on the Web, and you've probably taken some time to go looking about (if you haven't, you might want to). One of the things you might want to do is change your home page. This might have already been done for you—some places set up their home pages to the front page of a company, online provider, or university. You might even just want to change it to one you create (which we'll get into in chapter 19, "Creating Your Web Page").

Changing your home page is pretty easy. Choose Options, General Preferences and click on the Appearance tab. You'll see a screen like the one shown in figure 3.8. You can type in the URL of the page you want to be your home page, by clicking in the text box labeled "Home Page Location." The default home page for Netscape is **http://home.netscape.com/**. When you're done, click on the OK button and it's changed. Now whenever you click on the home button, you'll go to the home *you* specified.

Fig. 3.8
If you're new to the
Internet and the Web,
you might want to just
stick with Netscape's
home page. Then
again, there's a lot of
other really cool places
you could start at too.

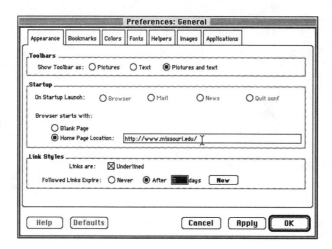

Advanced Navigation

● **In this chapter:**

- Speed things up—removing pictures

- Travel directly to Web pages with URLs

- Running two (or more) Web sessions

- Opening files on your hard disk

- And now...the cache

- Searching within documents

You've got the basics to using Netscape to navigate around the Web. Now let's show you how to really move! . . . . ⊘

Getting around on the Web isn't hard, but it can be tedious. In this chapter, I'll show you how to speed things up by going directly to pages, showing you how to make the documents appear faster, and how to run multiple browser windows at once. These are the advanced moves; the stuff you need to know to work efficiently on the Web.

Speed things up—removing pictures

The Web is a very colorful place. Web authors really get into their work, in many cases including wonderful art in their works, photographs of themselves or their dogs, fancy "buttons" and "toolbars." But all this is a double-edged sword. Sure, it makes the Web an interesting place to visit, but for many of us, it also makes it a very *slow* journey. Many people, perhaps most, are now working on dial-in lines, using modems to transfer the information from the Web back to their computers. And the really fancy stuff that's found on the Web can move very slowly, even with a fast modem.

TIP If you're using a modem, you really want to have something that's at least 14.4Kbps—(that's a speed). 14,400 baud. It's relatively easy and cheap to find 28.8Kbps modems (frequently referred to as "twenty-eight eights"), and soon we'll start seeing things like ISDN, which is even faster. For the best response, you want the fastest connection you can get.

After working on the Web for a while, when all these pictures are no longer a novelty, you might want to speed things up. By *removing* the pictures, you can move through pages in which you have little interest very quickly, and view the pictures only in the pages in which you want to view the pictures. You'll find you move around on the Web much faster.

Simply choose <u>O</u>ptions, <u>A</u>uto Load Images, removing the check mark from this menu option, as shown in figure 4.1 below. The next time you go to a Web page you won't see the pictures.

Fig. 4.1

If you want to keep Auto Load Images off for the next time you start Netscape, you might also want to click Save Options from the bottom of the Options menu.

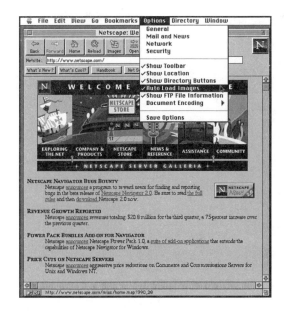

Well, that's not quite true. If you have previously viewed this page with its pictures, Netscape would have kept a copy of the images in the cache—which we'll go into later in this chapter. If Netscape already has a copy of the pictures in the cache, it will display them for you, regardless of your setting with Auto Load Images. If you go to a Web page with pictures that aren't in the cache, Netscape can't retrieve the pictures.

However, you'll discover that not only do you sometimes *want* to view a missing picture, but sometimes you'll *need* to. So many Web pages these days contain images that are essential, that you'll soon reach sites that you can't move through without viewing a picture first. This page has been retrieved with Auto Load Images turned off, and you can see in figure 4.2, the little icons that Netscape uses to replace missing images. There are no text links on this page, so if you want to navigate "through" this page, you'll have to view those pictures.

Notice, though, the pop-up menu on the Web page. You can display this menu by pointing at the icon and holding down the mouse button. Notice that the menu has a Load this Image option. If you select this menu option, Netscape will retrieve the missing image for you. (There's also a View this Image option, with the name of the image file in parentheses. This displays the image by itself in the Netscape window. You won't be able to use any links contained by the image if you use this option. See chapter 8, "Saving Stuff From the Web," for more information.)

Fig. 4.2
I retrieved this Web page (**http://www.aloha-hawaii.com/**) with Auto Load Images turned off. This is generally not considered great HTML, as some people can only use text versions of browsers, and they'd have to guess on how to get through here.

But this Web page has several missing images, so you might want to use another method; click on the Images button in the toolbar. This will tell Netscape to retrieve *all* the missing images in the current Web page.

Travel directly to Web pages with URLs

Now and then you'll find a URL Web "address" in a newspaper or magazine. Or perhaps you'll run across one in a newsgroup message, or a friend e-mails you something she's just found.

Now you need to know how to go directly from here to there. You don't want to follow links to this document, you want to go directly to it. There are several ways to do this:

- Click inside the text box in the Location bar (remember, the Location bar will be labeled **Netsite** if the current document is on a Netscape server), then type the URL. Then press Enter. For instance, type **http://www.mcp.com/** and then press Enter to go to the Macmillan Publishing Web site.

> **TIP** **You can omit the http:// bit, and often the trailing / as well. When** you press Enter, Netscape will add it for you. In this example you'd type **www.mcp.com** and press Enter.
>
> You can also use the text box to jump within one server—just by adding or taking away from the URL that's already listed there.

- Copy a URL into the Clipboard from another application, and then paste it into Netscape's Location bar and press Enter. (You can press ⌘+V or choose Edit, Paste.)

- Click the Open button, or choose File, Open Location; the Open Location box appears. Type (or paste) the URL and choose OK. (This dialog box is simply an alternative to the Location bar, in case you choose to remove the Location bar from the screen by choosing Options, Show Location.)

> **TIP** **Sometimes you'll find that a URL doesn't work, perhaps simply** due to a typo. Try this. Remove the rightmost portion and try again. For instance, if you try **http://www.missouri.edu/ccjoe** and it doesn't work, try **http:// www.missouri.edu/**. (The first URL wouldn't work because there's a typo; it should be **~ccjoe**, not **ccjoe**. You can actually get to my Web page by using **http://www.missouri.edu/~ccjoe**.)

Now, what was that URL?

Let's say you entered a URL a few days ago. Now you want to return to the same document, but you don't remember the URL. You can use the history list, or the bookmarks (if you placed the document there). We'll learn more about those in chapter 6, "The History List and Bookmarks."

How can I share URLs?

You might want to share URLs that you've found. You can copy them from Netscape and paste them into letters, memos, e-mail, and so on. Here's how.

If you want to copy the URL of the page you are currently viewing, click in the Location text box. The entire text will be highlighted. Then press ⌘+C or choose Edit, Copy. This copies the text of the URL into the Clipboard. Then you can change to another application, be it a word processor or e-mail, and paste the URL.

If you want to copy a URL from a link—in other words, you haven't gone to the Web document, so the URL isn't in the Location text box—point at the link, click on it and hold down the mouse button. When the pop-up menu opens, choose Copy this Link Location; the URL referenced by the link is copied to the Clipboard. You can also use Netscape's e-mail system to send links to other people—but we'll look at that in chapter 12 ("E-mail with Netscape").

Q&A   ***What's that horizontal squiggle character I keep seeing in URLs?***

A character that is seeing a lot more use in URLs than normal text is the tilde "~". This is a hold-over from UNIX land, and you'll normally see it on UNIX Web servers to denote a user's home directory. For example, my Web server user's pages is listed using the tilde: **http://www.missouri.edu/~ccjoe/.**

Running two (or more) Web sessions

Netscape enables you to run more than one Web session at the same time. You can have one Navigator window open displaying the latest Dilbert cartoon, and another downloading a file from the RealAudio Web site, for instance.

There are a couple of ways to start new sessions. You can point at the link and hold down the mouse button; a pop-up menu will open. Choose New Window with this Link. A new Netscape window will open and the referenced document is opened in there. You end up with two windows open, each displaying a different document.

The other method is to choose Window, New Web Browser. Another Netscape window will open, displaying your home page. You then can begin navigating through the window in a different "direction"—you have two sessions running at once.

TIP   **It might be more convenient if the Window, New Web Browser** command opened a window and displayed the *current* document, not the home page. However, you can quickly open the current document in the new window by choosing Go, 0 (or pressing ⌘+0) to select the previous entry in the history list.

Opening files on your hard disk

Eventually, in your exploration of the Web, you will end up with .HTM or .HTML files on your hard disk. You'll have them in your cache (which we'll discuss next), you may save documents using the File, Save As command (see chapter 8, "Saving Stuff From the Web"), or perhaps you'll even create your own (see chapters 19, "Creating Your Own Web Page" and 20, "Advanced Web Authoring"). Netscape provides a way to open these files:

Choose File, Open File. The Open box opens. Use the dialog box to find the .HTM or .HTML file you want to open. Click on this file, then click on the Open button. Netscape will display that document.

 You can also open files by dragging them from the desktop onto the Netscape icon—even if it's running. This will open the document you dragged onto the icon in the current Navigator window that Netscape is running.

 You can open other items, too. You can open .GIF, .JPG, and .JPEG files (these are graphics files). You can also select Text (*.txt) to open text files.

And now...the cache

It's time to learn about the cache and the Reload command. I've mentioned it a number of times already, because it seems to touch on so many areas. So let's learn about it in detail.

When you go back to a Web document that you've previously viewed, you might notice that it's displayed much more quickly. That's because Netscape isn't taking it from the Internet; it's getting it from the **cache**, an area on your hard disk in which it saves pages. Needless to say, this is really handy. Not only does it speed up working on the Web, but Netscape doesn't throw away the cached pages when you have finished your session, you can view a page later without having to reconnect to the Internet.

By default, Netscape is set up to 1 MB of disk space as the cache. The hard-disk cache is set by default to be in a folder called "Cache f." The location is set as:

Your Hard Drive

   System Folder

      Preferences

         Netscape f

            Cache f

This cache can get very big—as big as you allow it. Choose Options, Network to see the Preferences dialog box, and then click on the Cache tab. You'll see the information shown in figure 4.3. Note that the Disk Cache Directory line shows which directory is being used as the cache. You can enter a different directory if you want. For instance, if you have a different hard drive, you can move your cache file to that one by selecting the Browse button and choosing where you want to locate the cache on your other hard drive.

TIP   **On Macintosh systems, folders are listed by names separated by** colons. That's why you can't use the **:** character in a filename.

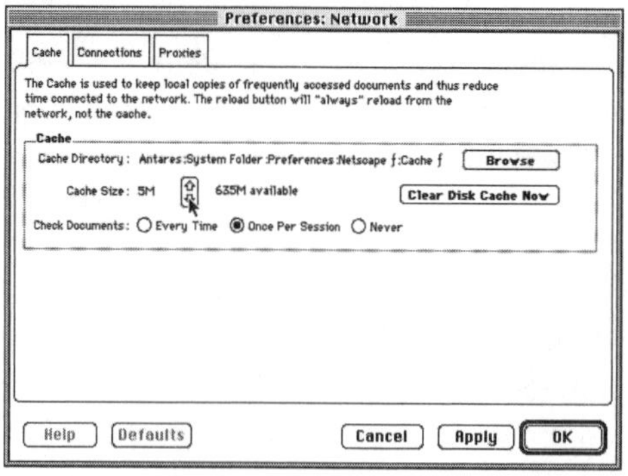

Fig. 4.3
The Preferences: Network dialog box lets you determine the size of your cache and where you want it located.

You can also configure the cache size, by pressing the up and down arrows next to the listed size. It will jump in increments of 1Mb. How large should these numbers be? Well, the larger the numbers, the better—though, as with everything involved with computers, there's a trade-off. If your hard-disk cache is big enough you'll be able to store documents from weeks ago, months ago even. Of course, you'll also be taking up more space on your hard drive for this.

Note, however, that you are not reserving an area of your hard disk for the cache. For instance, if you have a 30 MB disk cache, Netscape doesn't create a 30,000-KB file so other programs can't use that disk space. Rather, it simply means that Netscape can use that much disk space for the cache, *if available*.

So what's the catch? Why not make your cache as large as possible? Because if you do so you'll be using up resources that other applications may need. Fill up your hard-disk cache, and there'll be that much less disk space to save files from other programs. Reserve a large area of memory, and other programs won't be able to use the memory. Also, Netscape Communications say that a very large disk cache may cause Netscape to close slowly.

Notice also that this dialog box has a Clear Dis<u>k</u> Cache Now button. Click on this button to remove all the data from the cache. In this case, it literally deletes all the files from your hard disk cache. Before you do that, read on, because the cache can provide a storehouse from which you can extract information, even after you've logged off the Internet.

CAUTION

Be careful with that cache—it's a record of everything you've done! Let's say, for instance, that you like to sit in your cubicle at work, and use Netscape to cruise around the naughty bits of the Web. Well, this disk cache keeps a record of all those files you saw, and if you're the paranoid type, you might want to delete those files. Otherwise, someone can possibly sit down and look through all the files you've been seeing.

Netscape verifies the cache for you

In some cases Netscape tries to verify the page for you, to see if the document on the Web has changed since the last time a copy of it was placed in the cache. That is, it sends a message to the Web server from which the document originally came, asking if the document has changed. If the Web server responds that the document *has* changed, then Netscape asks the server to send a new copy; if it hasn't changed, Netscape simply retrieves it from the cache.

When does Netscape send this verification-request message? That depends on what you've selected in the Preferences dialog box.

There are three Verify Documents option buttons: Once Per Session, Every Time, and Never. If you choose the Once Per Session option (that's what Netscape is normally set to) button, Netscape will ask for verification the first time you go to a document. If you go to the document later in the same session, it won't bother verifying the document; it will assume that it hasn't changed during the session. For instance, let's say you visited the Rolling Stones Web page (**http://www.stones.com/**) yesterday. Today, you open your browser and go back to the Rolling Stones page; does Netscape ask the Web server if the page has changed? Yes, if Once Per Session is turned on. And if it finds that it's changed, it will retrieve a new copy and place that in the cache.

If you leave the Stones page and return to the Stones page later, Netscape retrieves the document from the cache—it won't bother reverifying the document.

Then there's the Every Time option button. This tells Netscape to always verify the document, to see if there have been any changes, regardless of how many times you have viewed the document during the session. Finally, there's the Never option button, which tells Netscape not to bother verifying documents; as long as the document is in the cache, Netscape will use that document. It will never check to see if a document has changed, so it will never automatically update the document. Documents will only change in two circumstances; if the document "falls out" of the cache (because the cache filled up and Netscape removed old documents to make room for new ones), or if you use the Reload command (as we'll see in a moment).

Which of the cache options should you use? I prefer Once Per Session, because I travel to sites that change a lot, but not every five minutes. If I chose never, I'd have to constantly be hitting the Reload button to make sure the information hasn't changed. Some people may prefer to use the Never option, because it does make traveling the Web faster if you've already been to some of the sites.

When is a page verified?

Now you've got the verification set up, you should be aware that the verification message is also dependent on *how* you access a page. Assuming you've turned on verification, Netscape will verify a document if you reach that document by clicking on a link, choosing a bookmark, entering a URL into the Location text box, or clicking on the Reload button. However, when you use the Back command or select an item from the history list (see chapter 6, "The History List and Bookmarks").

Netscape does not bother to verify the document. It simply grabs it from the cache (under the assumption that you are requesting a previously viewed page, anyway).

What's Reload?

Reload is a "cure" for the cache. What happens if you return to a Web document that's stored in the cache? Netscape gets it from the cache, right? However, that means you are not getting the latest document. Now that won't always matter, but in a few cases, it does.

For instance, let's say you want to return to a site that has constantly updated news (such as **http://www.cnn.com**). If you already viewed this page once this session, that document will probably still be there. You'll likely be seeing the old document, though the corresponding document stored out on the Web might have changed in the last minutes.

The cure for old stale Web pages is to Reload them. Click the Reload button, or choose View, Reload. Netscape overwrites the current document in the cache, replacing it with the latest version.

There is one more related command. View, Reload Cell is used to update the contents of a table. We'll look at tables in more detail in chapter 5, "Moving Further into the Web."

Searching within documents

Some Web pages are pretty big. In fact some are *very* big—dozens of pages long—with links from the top of the document to "sections" lower down.

Netscape helps you search long documents. Click on the Find button, or choose Edit, Find, and the Find dialog box opens (see fig. 4.4). Type the word or words you are looking for, choose Match Case (if necessary). Press the Find button, and Netscape will move the document so that the first line containing the word or words you are searching for is at the top of the window.

Fig. 4.4
Using the Find dialog box can often be faster than clicking on one of those links that jumps down through the document. Sometimes those links won't use a cached document and will cause Netscape to try to reload the entire thing again.

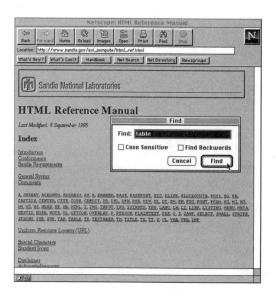

If the first occurrence of the word isn't what you want, you can press ⌘+G or select Edit and Find Again. Or you may want to close the dialog box, then read what Netscape found for you. Then choose Edit, Find Again (or press ⌘+G) to quickly continue the search.

Moving Further into the Web

● **In this chapter:**

- **Tables**

- **Forms**

- **Secure sites**

- **Password-protected sites**

- **Frames**

- **Java applets**

- **Push and pull commands**

- **Microsoft, Netscape, and the rest of us**

The Web is full of a lot more than just simple text and images.
Here's a list of just some of what is available out there . . . ▶

So the basics are there—they make up the majority of the Web that we know today, but it's not a static thing. New things are all over the place, and newer stuff is being invented every day.

Forms

A form is a special interactive Web document. It contains the sorts of components that we've become familiar with while working in today's graphical user interfaces: text boxes, option buttons, command buttons, check boxes, list boxes, drop-down menus, and so on.

You can see an example in figure 5.1. This shows part of the form used for searching the Web; in fact, I found this particular form at Yahoo (**http://www.yahoo.com/search.html/**). Looking for some information on Wales? Netscape? or better yet—CNN?

This form contains drop-down menus (click on the box with a slight shadow and a list of choices will appear), a text box into which you type your query, and a couple of control buttons—used to determine how and what you want to search.

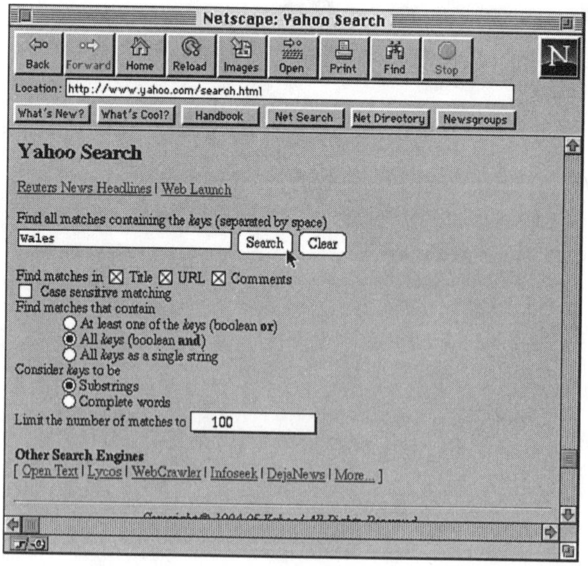

Fig. 5.1

Forms allow you to send information back to the Web server—so you can look for more information or reply to a survey, for instance.

Tables

A table is…well, you know, a table. It's a set of columns and rows in which text—and sometimes pictures—has been organized. You can see an example in figure 5.2.

(While Netscape can display tables, a number of older browsers cannot.) Often a table is simply used to format information in a document in a different way.

Fig. 5.2
Although some of the HTML codes that Netscape uses for its tables aren't in any standard, the basic HTML for tables has now been adopted into HTML 3.0—which means you'll be seeing a lot more of it.

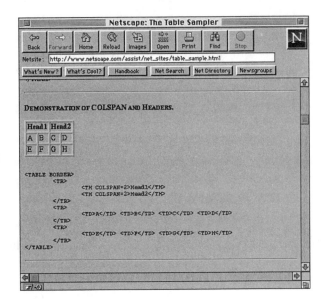

Secure sites

When you enter information into a form and send that information back to the Web server, what happens to the information between here and there? It could be intercepted by someone and read (actually it's not very likely that it'll be intercepted, but that's another story, which I'll get to when we cover security in detail in chapter 15, "Security on the Internet). If you've just transmitted your credit card number, or other information you don't want some snooper to see, you could be in trouble.

Netscape provides a special way to send information securely. If the form you are viewing comes from a special https:// server (a Netscape secure server), then when the information is sent back from the form to the server it's encrypted. When the server receives the information, it then decrypts the information. In between your computer and the server, the information is useless; anyone intercepting the information will end up with a load of garbled rubbish. There are other proposed security features, but Netscape's is the most used and best known.

Password-protected sites

There's another form of security we should discuss, the password. This has nothing to do with encryption. It's simply a feature that allows Web authors to deny access to users unless they enter the correct password. For instance, you may have noticed by now that there are a number of, ahem, sexually oriented Web sites. Some of these contain "teasers," just a little bit of smut available to anyone who cares to view. But to get to the real stuff you have to register, and once registered you are given a password. You can then enter the "private parts" of the site using this password. Well, okay, it's not just sex sites that use this system, there are other by-subscription-only sites, too. Companies can use this system to create Web sites for their customers, and reserve a special area for access by registered customers only, for instance. Anyone who wants to set up a "pay-per-view" site can use a password system to do so.

How do you use a password? Well, when you click on a link that a Web author has set up to provide access to a restricted area, you'll see the dialog box in figure 5.3.

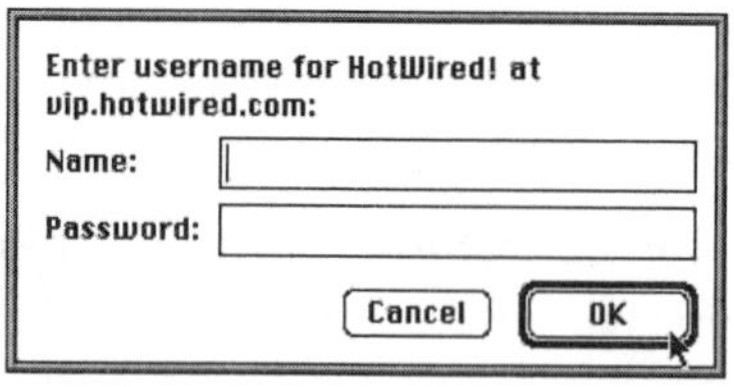

Fig. 5.3
Enter your user ID and password to get into a password-restricted site. Many sites will allow you to register when you get there and start browsing immediately.

```
Enter username for HotWired! at
vip.hotwired.com:

Name:     [                    ]

Password: [                    ]

          ( Cancel )  ( OK )
```

Frames

Netscape now allows multiple panes within a Web document; in Netscape-speak these are known as frames. For instance, you can see an example in figure 5.4. There are two frames in this window (**http://webspace.sgi.com/Mission/index.html**); the left frame contains a bunch of graphics that link to other pages, and the right frame contains the mission statement for Webspace. Click on one of the callouts in the eye diagram, and the associated text in the right frame changes.

Fig. 5.4

As you can see, frames make an easy way to break up the HTML document to get more into the same area—kind of like opening a new window, except you don't have to.

Right now you won't find many Web documents containing frames, so I'm relegating this subject to the "Netscape's Advanced Features" section of the book, where I'll explain more (see chapter 20, "Advanced Web Authoring").

Targeted windows

Netscape now allows Web authors to control where pages show up —they've called this feature targeted windows. Using a targeted window allows a Web author to choose where a link will show up—possibly creating a new window, putting it into a frame already currently displayed, or overwriting the window that is currently active. In other words, when you click on a link, the next Web page doesn't always show in the same window. You could have two windows open; the first one, in which you clicked on the link, and the second one, displaying the document referenced by the link.

Java applets

Probably the hottest thing on the Internet since the Web itself is Java. Java is a programming language (yes, all this hype over a language), but to be fair it's quite a special language. Java is a simpler form of the well renowned programming language C.

The other special aspect of Java is that it's being made so that it can run on any machine—Macintosh, IBM, UNIX workstation—anything. You will be able to download these programs and run them through the WWW, allowing your machine to work like everyone else's. Not surprisingly, a lot of people are excited about the possibilities because it could mean simplifying some programs by only having to write them once.

Currently, however, it's really lagging behind for the Macintosh, and as of the writing of this book it hasn't appeared yet. A number of people have announced that it will be available in the spring and summer of 1996, so keep your eyes open.

JavaScript

JavaScript is another new feature for Netscape—and this one does work with Macintosh systems!

JavaScript is not really anything like Java, except that it works in the WWW and has a similar name. It's a macro language for the WWW that allows various pieces of the Web page to talk to each other. For example, using JavaScript a Web page author can have a summary field change when you type a number into an entry field. A Web author can also create a JavaScript that links certain components together; say when you press on a radio button in a form, a Java applet will run showing you an animation of your selection.

Authors can use JavaScript to make their forms a bit smarter. When you try to submit a form, a JavaScript script can check the information you've entered into the form to make sure that it makes sense. It could check to see that your credit card number is in the correct format, or that you've entered all the information required. JavaScript can also be used to display or play special introductory information—perhaps music—when you first open a document, or play some kind of goodbye statement when you leave the document.

At the time of writing, JavaScript was still under development, so there really aren't many sites doing much with it. I would imagine you could expect to see more of this popping up in the Web!

Multimedia

You'll find all sorts of different file formats on the World Wide Web. There are different varieties of still pictures, video and animation, sounds, electronic documents, 3-D images, and so forth on the Web. Any file format that can be played or displayed on your computer can be linked to a Web page. What happens when you click on a link that takes you to one of these file formats? If Netscape can handle the file itself, it does so; it will display the document or picture in the window in the normal way. But if the file is a format that Netscape can't handle, it has two options; it may send the file directly to a program that can handle it, or it may ask you what to do. We'll take a look at this subject in chapter 9, "Audio and Video," and chapter 10, "More on Viewers."

Pushing and pulling

Pretty soon you may notice that Web pages start to do things by themselves. Rather than information arriving at your screen because you've directly requested it—by clicking on a link or entering a URL—Web pages will soon be using **server push** and **client pull**.

The first of these, **server push**, occurs when the Web server continues sending information, even though you haven't requested it. For instance, you might click on a link to display a Web page. Then, a few minutes later, the Web page changes; you haven't requested more information, but the server has sent updated information. And the server continues periodic updates until you close the page.

Client pull is similar, except that the request for updates comes from Netscape. For instance, you open a page. At the same time that the server sends the page, it sends a special program. (You don't see this, it all happens in the background.) This program tells Netscape when to request updates. After the defined interval Netscape sends a request to the server asking for the information. Again, this will continue until you leave the page.

These systems appear very similar to each other—you usually won't know which method is being used. They are very useful for any information that changes rapidly: stock quotes, weather, news headlines, an auction of some kind. Right now, they're mostly used for simple animation.

Microsoft, Netscape, and the rest of us

There's this little competition going on—between Microsoft and Netscape Communications. You see, when Netscape was founded not so many months ago, the company set out to create the very best Web browser that it could. But in order to make the browser really neat, they decided they'd also have to create new HTML codes. You'll remember that in chapter 1, I explained how the source HTML document contains special codes (tags) that a browser reads in order to figure out how to format the document. Well, the original idea behind the Web was that everyone would play by the same set of rules, that a governing body would publish a set of HTML codes that everybody could incorporate into their browsers if they wished.

That governing body is trying, but commerce is jumping ahead of them in leaps and bounds. Netscape Communications started it by creating their own special HTML codes, designed to work with Netscape. That didn't stop other browser publishers from adding support for Netscape features, of course, but it did give Netscape a lead, and very soon Netscape was the most popular Web browser in the world. To be fair, they also proposed these tags become open standards, and some of them have been adopted more widely. Even still, little signs were appearing in Web documents saying things like "Optimized for Netscape," or "This document looks better in Netscape," or whatever.

Well, Microsoft wanted a bit of the Web pie, and along with Windows 95 they released Internet Explorer, which they intended would give Netscape a real run for its money. Why am I telling you about Windows 95? Well, the end result is that Microsoft began doing the same thing, creating their own HTML tags. They encouraged people to design their Web pages using these neat features—and to put up little signs in their Web pages saying "Optimized for Internet Explorer."

The result of all this is not that surprising. Now both companies are working to develop all these new codes and it's jumping ahead of the folks trying to keep track of it all pretty fast.

Here are a few of the features that Microsoft has developed with Internet Explorer, but Netscape can't handle (yet...):

non-scrolling backgrounds	This feature creates a background that doesn't scroll as you move down the document. Rather, the text simply scrolls over the top of the static background. If you find a document with this feature you may not know it; Netscape simply treats it as a static background.
colored table cells	Background colors can be added to table cells; Netscape simply ignores the colors.
background sounds	A sound plays automatically when you display the document—it may play once, or may play over and over again as long as you are viewing the page. Netscape simply doesn't play the sound.
marquees	This is a piece of text that moves across a document, like text on one of those electronic signs you see in airports and sports arenas; the text moves across the page, right to left. Netscape displays marquees as static text.
inline videos	This is a small movie that sits inside the Web document and runs automatically. If Netscape sees one of these it may display the video as a static picture, or it may display a rectangle on the screen, showing where the video should be.

Netscape may well add marquees, background sounds, inline videos, and other Internet Explorer features. If you want to see if the version of Netscape you are using can now work with these features, go to **http://www.microsoft.com/windows/ie/ie20html.htm** or **http://www.microsoft.com/windows/ie/iexplorer.htm**, where you can find some of the Microsoft examples.

The History List and Bookmarks

● **In this chapter:**

- **Using the history list—the path of where you've been**

- **Keeping your favorite pages organized...the bookmark system**

- **How do you share your bookmarks with your friends? Create a book-mark file!**

- **Using your bookmarks with Netscape—Dragging and dropping bookmarks**

With all this information now at your fingertips, you need to have a way to keep track of what sections you like...and how you got there . . . . ⬧

Hypertext has been around for a long time; it was invented years before the Web appeared on the scene. In fact, it was invented in the 1960s by Dr. Douglas Engelbart. While they invented it quite a number of years ago, nobody really used it on a wide scale until the Macintosh came around. One of the first programs to come out for the Macintosh was HyperCard, which was one of the first widely used instances of hypertext and hypermedia. In fact, it's still used today, although the Web has certainly overshadowed it now. One of the keys to getting hypertext widely used was having different documents (what are now Web pages) be addressable from any machine, anywhere. After that was developed, and the Web exploded, some old problems came to bare.

And it's long been known that one of the most serious problems with hypertext and hypermedia is that people tend to get lost—that is, they don't have a good sense of where they are in relationship to where they've been. It's hard to get lost in a book; you read from the front to the back, or maybe you might dip into the book in the middle. The book has a direction, from page 1 through page 300 or 400 or whatever. But hypertext has no direction. Or rather, it has too many directions.

There are literally billions of different paths that can be taken through the World Wide Web. To make it worse, the paths are constantly changing. New ones appear every minute, and some that were there yesterday are gone today. Play around on the Web for a while and you'll soon find that you can get lost, that you're not exactly sure where or how you found that interesting document about aliens and UFOs at Groom Lake (try **http://www.cris.com/~psyspy/area51/index.shtml**), or where that cool information about the latest developments in QuickDraw 3D for the Macintosh was located (**http://product.apple.com/qd3d/**).

Netscape can help you out. It has a couple of essential features that will assist you in your travels around the Web: the **history list** and the **bookmarks**. We'll start with the history list.

Using the history list

A history list is, quite simply, a list of documents you've viewed during the current Web session. (At the time of writing, Netscape only lists documents from the current session, not previous sessions; this may change, though, as many browsers now maintain very large history lists that can go back days or even weeks.) The history list is created automatically. Each time you view a document, that document is added to the history list.

There are a couple of ways that you can use the history list. The quickest and easiest is to use the Back and Forward buttons. (Or choose <u>G</u>o, <u>B</u>ack, or <u>G</u>o, <u>F</u>orward; or use ⌘+Left Arrow or ⌘+Right Arrow.)

These will move you back and forward through the list. Back to the previous document, back to the one before that, forward to the one you've just come from, and so on.

The other way to use the history list is to open the <u>G</u>o menu and select a page from the bottom. You'll find a list of documents that you've viewed recently, probably something similar to what's shown in figure 6.1. You can jump to any one of these documents by simply pulling down the document you want to see and releasing the mouse button.

Fig. 6.1
You can also use the keyboard shortcuts listed next to the items in your history list. Press ⌘+0, or ⌘+1 ...up to ⌘+8—they point to your current document and then the documents back from there.

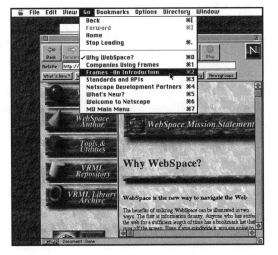

Not *all* the documents!

I stated that the history list is a list of documents viewed during the current session. But it's not a list of *all* of the documents you've viewed, unfortunately. Here's how it works. Let's say you are in document A, and click on a link to go to document B, then go to C, then to D, then to E. Now you use the history list to return to document B. In document B you select another link that takes you to, say, document 1. Now take a look in the history list. You'll find that documents C, D, and E are no longer there; they've been thrown out of the list.

I realize this is confusing, but here's the problem. The history list can only keep a list of documents down one route—a single line straight back from where you came. If you go back a few steps, and then take a side trail from there, the history list only keeps the documents that point back to your home.

The bookmark system

Though Netscape's history list isn't perfect, the bookmark system is a lot more helpful. Bookmarks are just what they sound like—they are markers on Web pages. Just as you might place bookmarks inside this book to mark a page you want to look at later, Netscape's bookmarks enable you to quickly return to a Web page. (You are not literally adding a bookmark to a Web page, of course; rather, you are creating a list of URLs, Web addresses, and using that list to help you find your way back to the pages.) Bookmarks stay until you remove them; they are not limited to the current session, you'll be able to use them weeks or months later.

There's a wide variety of things you can do with bookmarks. You can add bookmarks, you can order your bookmarks into a hierarchy of menus, you can edit the bookmarks themselves (including adding comments about what you think!), or you could create a bookmark file to share your bookmarks with someone else.

Adding a bookmark

This is the simplest procedure. If you find a Web page that you think you'll want to return to later, simply choose Bookmarks, Add Bookmark. That's it, the bookmark has been added. If you now open the Bookmarks menu you'll see that the document title has been added to the bottom of the menu. You'll be able to return to the document at a later date by simply opening the menu and pulling down to the entry.

There are a few problems with this menu entry, though. You may not want to use the document title. Some are too vague or verbose, and it's nice to be able to modify them. Also, the list in the menu is not in alphabetical order, making it hard to find things after a while. And all the bookmarks are lumped together, with no kind of hierarchy. Don't worry, though, we can solve all these problems in the Bookmarks window.

Modifying your bookmarks

Open the Bookmarks window by choosing <u>W</u>indow, <u>B</u>ookmarks. You'll see something like the window in figure 6.2 (assuming you've added a few bookmarks). As you can see, all the bookmarks have been placed into a single "folder." We're going to create a hierarchy of folders, though, so we can organize the bookmarks more efficiently.

Fig. 6.2
You might want to create some sort of organization to your bookmarks—if you're anything like me, you'll have hundreds in no time.

First, click on the entry after which you want to place a folder. (In other words, you can insert folders inside the list of bookmarks if you wish, or place all the folders together at the top of the list.) Then choose <u>I</u>tem, Insert <u>H</u>eader to open the Bookmark Properties dialog box as shown in figure 6.3. Type a name into this box.

Fig. 6.3
Make the folder name
something descriptive.
This is your organiza-
tion and you need to
be happy with it.

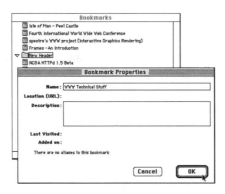

You can also enter a description—a few words explaining what the folder is intended to hold. Click on the OK button and your new folder will appear inside the Bookmarks window.

Now you can move bookmarks into the folder. Click on a bookmark, and then hold the mouse button down. Still holding the button down, drag the bookmark onto the folder and release the button. You can move several bookmarks at once. Hold down the command key while you click on each one that you want to move, then point at one and drag that single bookmark into the folder—the rest will move along with it. You can also select a contiguous block of bookmarks by clicking on the first in the block, holding the shift key down, and clicking on the last in the block.

 You can also move bookmarks using the menu commands. Select them and then choose <u>E</u>dit, <u>C</u>ut. Then click on the folder into which you want to place them and choose <u>E</u>dit, <u>P</u>aste.

Create as many folders as you want. You can even create folders within folders. Click on a folder, then choose <u>I</u>tem, Insert Folder. Note that when you create a hierarchy within your Bookmarks window, you are automatically modifying the <u>B</u>ookmarks menu, too. When you open the menu you'll find that each folder is represented by a cascading menu. The folder name appears in the menu with a small triangle to the right. If you pull down to the entry, you'll see another menu open displaying the contents of the folder.

More bookmark operations

After you've created a bookmark hierarchy, you might want to modify your bookmarks further. Here's what you can do:

Rename a bookmark	Click on the bookmark, choose Item, Properties, then type a new name. You can also modify the URL and add a description (see fig. 6.4).
Copy a bookmark to another folder	Click on the bookmark, choose Edit, Copy, click in the folder you want to copy to, and choose Edit, Paste. Or just drag the bookmark into whatever folder you like.
Delete a bookmark	Click on it and press Delete (or ⌘+D).
Find a bookmark	Choose Edit, Find, type a word (part of the bookmark title, URL, or description), and press Enter. This will look through all of your bookmarks—even the ones in closed folders.
Open or close a folder	Click on the little triangle to the left of the folder.
Insert a menu separator	To place a separator line on the Bookmarks menu between items (remember, the menu reflects the windows format), click on the entry *after* which the line should appear and choose Item, Insert Separator.
Add a bookmark manually	Click where you want to place the bookmark, then choose Item, Insert Bookmark. Type a name and the URL, and a description if you wish.
Sort the bookmarks	Select the bookmarks you want to sort and choose Sort, by Name.

Fig. 6.4
Remember that the
Find command can
locate things by
description—so if you
have a lot of similar
bookmarks, Find can
be very handy!

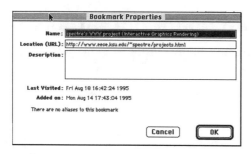

TIP **You can also open a bookmark into the current Navigator window**
by just double-clicking on it. That can make for a fast way to browse
through things if they're all still in your cache.

Using the bookmarks

How do you actually use your bookmarks? You've seen how you can select
a bookmark from the <u>B</u>ookmarks menu. To go to a bookmarked document
from the Bookmarks window, you can use several methods. Double-click on
the entry, drag a bookmark into the Navigator window, click once and press
Enter, or click once and choose <u>I</u>tem, <u>G</u>o to Bookmark.

TIP **When you go to a bookmark from the Bookmarks window, the**
window remains displayed. You won't automatically switch back to the
Navigator window. Click on the Navigator window below to return to it.

Creating bookmark files

You can create and import bookmark files. This provides several benefits. It
allows another hierarchical level of organization. You might have one bookmark file for business-related Web sessions, and one for your personal
interests. Or one for each member of the family, or each co-worker using the
computer.

It also provides a convenient way to share bookmarks. Create a bookmark
file then put it on a floppy disk and take it home to load into your personal
copy of Netscape, or give it to a friend or colleague. And it allows you to
import other lists of links, perhaps from other programs, and use them as
bookmarks.

There are two basic procedures to moving bookmarks in and out.

Create a bookmark file	Choose File, Save As to create an HTML document containing all of your bookmarks. You can then open this in Netscape, or import it into another copy of Netscape on another computer.
Import a bookmark file	To add the contents of a bookmark file to your current bookmarks, choose File, Import. This will place all the new bookmarks at the top of the list.

Dragging and dropping bookmarks

Not only can you drag and drop bookmarks within the Bookmarks window, you can drag and drop between windows, too. If you drag a bookmark from the Bookmarks window onto Netscape, Netscape will load the document referenced by the bookmark.

7

Searching for Information on the Web

● **In this chapter:**

- ● **Netscape's search tools**

- ● **Using the search engines**

- ● **The Internet directories**

- ● **Directories of Directories**

- ● **More specific stuff**

The Web is huge...so where's the road map? . . . . ➤

The Web is enormous, and thousands of new pages are being added every week. How can you possibly know what's out there, how can you find the information you need? For instance, I recently wanted to find information about a particular printer I was considering buying. I was sure that the company that made the printer must have a Web site—most companies in the computer business seem to have sites up and running these days. But what was the URL I needed to get to the site? I also wanted to find the public-television Web site, so I could search for a particular show I was interested in. How was I going to find that site?

Of course I could spend several years, wandering through hyperlinks on the Web, and maybe eventually I'd wander into the pages I needed. Or I could go to a search or directory site, and search a vast index of Web sites, or view lists of sites broken down by category.

Netscape's search tools

Netscape provides you with several search tools. Well, they're not really Netscape's tools, but Netscape puts them within a couple of click's distance, making them quickly available. You can use these buttons and commands to find sites:

Net Search Directory Button (Directory, Internet Search)—Takes you to a document that enables you to search the InfoSeek search engine, and get to several other search sites.

Net Directory Directory Button (Directory, Internet Directory)—Takes you to a page with links to a variety of Internet directories.

What's New Directory Button (Directory, What's New)—Displays the Netscape Communications What's New page. You won't use this to search for a particular site, but it provides links to interesting new sites on the Web.

What's Cool Directory Button (Directory, What's Cool)—Displays the Netscape Communications What's Cool page, with a variety of links to interesting sites. Again, you won't search, but it's interesting just to peruse.

Directory, Internet White Pages—This takes you to a list of links to directories of Internet e-mail addresses, so you can track down other users.

> ## 66 *Plain English, please!*
>
> Directories and search engines—What's the difference between an Internet directory and an Internet search site? A directory provides categorized lists of Web pages. You can select a category, then a sub-category, then another sub-category, and so on, until you find the site you want. A search site lets you use a **search engine**, a program with which you'll search a database of Web pages that someone else maintains. Type in a keyword and click on a Search button or press Enter, and the search engine searches the database for you. Some sites—such as Yahoo—contain both directories and search engines. 99

Using the search engines

Let's begin by looking at the Internet search engines—the programs that allow you to search a database. Click on the Net Search directory button, or choose <u>D</u>irectory, Internet <u>S</u>earch. Scroll down the page that appears, and you'll see something like figure 7.1.

Fig. 7.1
The Internet Search page, which lets you search InfoSeek as well as Deja News, Excite, Lycos, and WebCrawler.

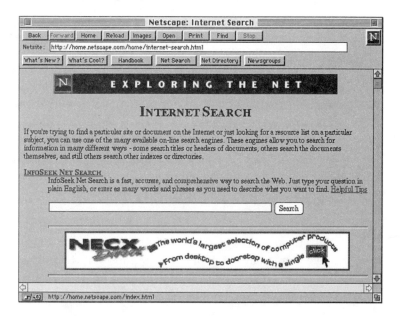

You now need to type a search term into the list box. What are you going to type, though? You could just type a single word, but you may want to get fancy, in which case you should read the instructions. Notice the special query operators link above the text box. Click on that to go to a document that describes exactly what you can type. Read this, because it gives you a lot of suggestions and hints. See table 7.1 for a few things you could enter.

Table 7.1   Tips for Using Search Engines

Words between quotation marks	This tells InfoSeek to find the words in that exact order, next to each other. For instance, `"the here and now"`
Proper names	These should be capitalized correctly: `Colorado, England, Gore`
Words separated by hyphens	This tells InfoSeek to find the words as long as they are close together in the document: `diving-scuba`
Words in brackets	These should appear together, but not necessarily in the order you've entered them: `[diving scuba]`

Each search engine is a little different, allowing different sorts of search terms. You can always search by simply entering a single word, but the more you know about each search engine, the more efficiently you will be able to search. When you first go to a search engine, look around for some kind of link to a help document. You might even want to make a bookmark folder of them.

Now, back to InfoSeek. When you've finished reading the help information, click on the Back button to return to the page with the text box (see fig 7.1). Enter the word or phrase you want to search for, then press Enter, or click on the Run Query button. Netscape sends the information to InfoSeek, and, with a little luck, you may see a result page like figure 7.2. On the other hand, you may see a message telling you that the search engine is busy; try again in a few moments and you may well get through.

What, then, has InfoSeek found. Well, when I searched for Wales it found 100 links to Web sites that contain information about England. (InfoSeek may have more than 100 such links, but I just use the free search. If I signed up for the commercial service, there would be no limit; that is, it would show me everything it can find related to Wales.)

The document I'm viewing doesn't show me all 100 links. It shows me the first 10, but there's a link at the bottom of the page to show me the next 10. It found links to things such as the *Welsh Genealogy, some photos from Wales,*

Wales Tourist Board, Rhwydwaith Gwybodaeth Cymru, Wales Information Network, Anglesey, Wales and plenty more. If any of these links interest me, all I need to do is click on the link, and away I go, possibly over the North Atlantic and into Wales.

Fig. 7.2
InfoSeek found a few links relating to Wales.

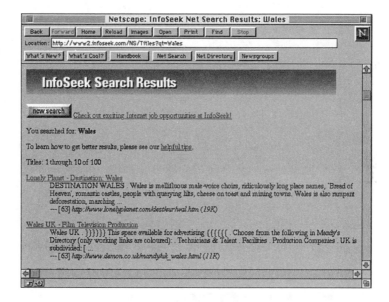

More search engines

InfoSeek is but one of many search engines on the Web. If you click on the Net Search button again, then scroll down the page, you'll find links to Lycos, WebCrawler, Déjà News (which searches newsgroups—you'll learn more about them in chapter 13, "UseNet News"), and Excite (which lets you search Web sites, newsgroups, classified ads, and NetReviews—reviews of Web sites).

One good search engine that isn't currently listed in the Internet Search document is Yahoo, but it is listed as a directory site, and we're going to take a look at those in a moment.

Search multiple engines quickly!

There are many more search engines, and you can quickly search dozens of these things using a couple of special forms. At the bottom of the Internet Search document you'll find a couple of links to lists of search engines:

W3 Search Engines. This is neat. Not only will you find a list of many search engines, but you'll also be able to search directly from the W3 Search Engines form. **http://cuiwww.unige.ch/meta-index.html**

CUSI (Configurable Unified Search Interface). Another great site for searching, this one also allows you to search a variety of engines from one form. It's perhaps a little easier to use than the previous one. **http:// Web.nexor.co.uk/susi/cusi.html**

You might also check out the **Search Engine Room**, which contains links to a number of search engines, though you can't search without going to the engine sites first: **http://www.nosc.mil/planet_earth/Library/sei_room.html**

Q&A *Which is the best search or directory site?*

There is no "best." I really like Excite (**http://www.excite.com/**) and Jump City (**http://www.jumpcity.com/**), but you may find other sites that you prefer. Each is different and work in a different way. And each will give you a different result. Try a few—for that matter, try a bunch—and see which you like.

The Internet directories

Now let's see the Internet directories. Click on the Net Directory button, or choose <u>D</u>irectory, Internet <u>D</u>irectory. Right at the top of this document is the Yahoo directory. As I mentioned a moment ago, Yahoo has a search engine. If you'd like to use this, click on the *Yahoo Directory* link and you'll go directly to the Yahoo site. When you get there, you'll see the document shown in figure 7.3.

Q&A *They're doing all this for free?*

Well, it's free to us. Many of the large servers out there are making up their money by advertising—which you'll no doubt see on Yahoo, Lycos, Excite, and many of the other search engines. Remember, if you want to skip the images (advertising in this case) you can always turn off the Auto-Load Images.

One of the other reasons it's free is because there isn't any sort of easy payment system in place on the WWW. There are lots of ideas, but as of the writing of this book, paying in small increments for services just doesn't exist.

Fig. 7.3

Yahoo provides lists of Web sites, broken down by category—and it does it for free.

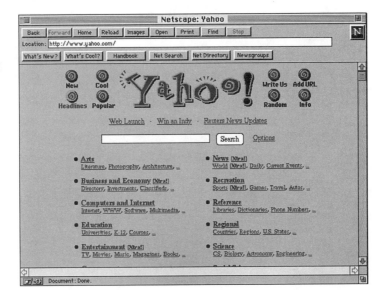

Notice the category links: Art, Education, Health, Social Science, and so on. Each of these links points deeper into the Yahoo system, a level lower down in the hierarchical system of document categories. For instance, click on *Recreation* and you'll see a document from Yahoo with a list of more categories: *Amusement/Theme Parks@*, *Aviation*, *Drugs@*, *Motorcycles*, and so on. What does the @ sign at the end of some of these mean? It means that this entry is a sort of cross reference, that you will be crossing over to another category if you select this link. For instance, click on *Drugs@* and you'll see the page in figure 7.4, which is in the Health:Pharmacology:Drugs category. It contains links related to recreational drugs (from alcohol to XTC), political and legal issues, pharmacology, and many other subjects.

Now, notice that figure 7.4 contains links shown with bold text and numbers in parentheses after them (such as *Alcohol (2)*), and links that are not bolded (such as *DEA List of Controlled Substances—Uses and Effects*). The bold links take you further down the hierarchy. You'll see another document containing more links. The number in parentheses after the link shows how many links you'll find in that document.

The regular-text links are links across the Internet, to Web documents containing the information you're looking for. Select *A short introduction to smart drugs*, for instance, and you'll find yourself viewing a document from Finland.

Fig. 7.4

Finally you'll arrive at a page with links out across the Web

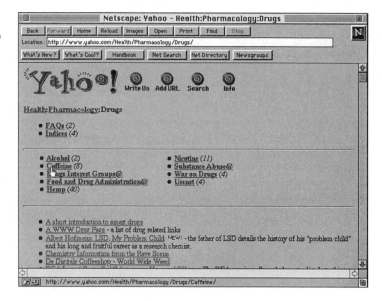

More directories

Go back to the Internet Directory (press the Net Directory button) page, and scroll down a little to find links to more directories:

The Mckinley Internet Directory—This is a directory of Web pages, Telnet, Gopher, FTP, newsgroups, and mailing lists. The entries are also rated by reviewers.

Point—Another directory that rates sites.

World Wide Arts Resources—A directory of Web sites related to artists and the arts.

Excite—Select from a list of a few dozen categories, or search the database. In addition to searching the WWW, it also maintains archives of UseNet newsgroups, and reviews of various products and sites, providing a large information source. Each link has a short description, which is very handy.

World Wide Web Servers—A list of Web servers. It won't help you find a particular subject, but will allow you to select Web servers by country or state.

Virtual Tourist—This site provides a map of the world; click on a region to see a smaller scale map, click on a country to see a map showing where the servers are, or a list. Click on a button to see a list of Web servers, color-coded according to the city (see fig. 7.5).

Fig. 7.5
The Virtual Tourist provides a wonderful way to see where the world's Web servers are.

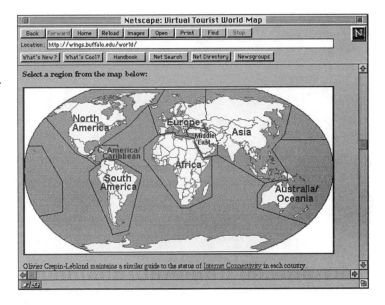

Other Search Sites

There are loads of other Web sites set up specifically to help people search for a subject of interest. I'm going to describe a few of them now. (You may want to go my co-author's page **http://www.mcp.com/authors/pkent/**, which he set up some time ago when he wrote *The Complete Idiot's Guide to the World Wide Web.*) You'll find links to *Chapter 25*, which contains links to all the sites I'm about to mention, and to *Chapter 26*, which contains links to a potpourri of interesting sites.

Let's take a look at a few other directories you may want to visit.

Directories of Directories

We'll start with a general category, a list of Web documents that will help you find more specific directories.

TIP **Remember that URLs sometimes end with .html, and sometimes** with **.htm**. Make sure you use the correct one. And if it doesn't work, try the other.

The World Wide Web Initiative

"Everything there is to know about the World Wide Web is linked directly or indirectly to this document." From the W3 Organization, the people planning the future of the Web.

http://www.w3.org/hypertext/WWW/TheProject

ANANSE—Internet Resource Locators and Search Engines

Links to lots of other directories.

http://ananse.irv.uit.no/law/nav/find.html

List of Robots

This is a directory of programs that dig around on the Web, creating indexes and measuring its size.

http://web.nexor.co.uk/mak/doc/robots/active.html

General search engines and directories

The following lists are directories of Web documents. You can search or browse for just about any subject.

Jump City

I really like this one. You can search Web sites and newsgroups, or view category lists (à la Yahoo). The items that are found have short reviews, so you know what you are getting.

http://www.jumpcity.com/

The World Wide Web Worm (WWWW)

The World Wide Web Worm is a system that digs around on the Web looking for documents. It follows links through the Web, and builds an index of Titles and URLs. You can enter keywords to search for any subject—you'll find detailed instructions on how to search.

http://www.cs.colorado.edu/home/mcbryan/WWWW.html

WebCrawler

This system crawls around on the Web, creating an index. You can search that index.

> http://www.webcrawler.com/

The WebCrawler Top 25

The WebCrawler also publishes a document that lists the 25 most-referenced documents on the Web. That is, the documents that are referenced by other document links more than any others.

> http://www.webcrawler.com/WebCrawler/Top25.html

The JumpStation

Another simple index that you can search.

> http://www.stir.ac.uk/jsbin/js

Wandex

Wandex—the World Wide Web Wanderer Index—lets you search an index of thousands of documents.

> http://www.netgen.com/cgi/wandex

The Spider's Web

Over 1000 links to "cool places."

> http://gagme.wwa.com/~boba/spider1.html

Nikos

This is an index created by Rockwell Network Systems and Cal Poly, San Luis Obispo. Type the keyword you are looking for.

> http://www.rns.com/cgi-bin/nomad

RBSE's URL Database

The RBSE (Respository Based Software Engineering) spider "walks the web" grabbing URLs. You can search the resulting database.

> http://rbse.jsc.nasa.gov/eichmann/urlsearch.html

Best of the Web '95

A list of the "best" Web documents, chosen in an online contest and announced at the International W3 Conference in Geneva. From the NCSA (Best Overall Site) to the Sports Information Service (Best Entertainment Service), Travels With Samantha (Best Document Design) to the Xerox Map Server (Best Use of Interaction).

http://wings.buffalo.edu/contest/

ALIWEB

ALIWEB stands for *Archie-Like Indexing for the Web*. It lets you search for Web sites in the same way you can use Archie to search for FTP files (we'll get to that in chapter 11, "Software Libraries—Using FTP"). There are several different interfaces—a form-based search, a multiple-keyword form-based search, and a simple index search.

http://web.nexor.co.uk/aliweb/doc/search.html

The Mother-of-all BBS

Search this giant database of Web sites, or select a category first; from Agriculture to Writing on the Net, and subjects as diverse as Underwear and the Sheffield Ski Village.

http://www.cs.colorado.edu/homes/mcbryan/public_html/bb/summary.html

NCSA's What's New on the Web

A list of new Web pages. You can view the current month's crop of new stuff, or go back and view previous months. This is a great way to get a feel for just how much new information is being added to the Web.

http://www.ncsa.uiuc.edu/SDG/Software/Mosaic/Docs/whats-new.html

NCSA's Starting Points

This site is handy for newcomers wanting to get an overview of what's on the Web. You'll find links to useful services and other directories.

> **http://www.ncsa.uiuc.edu/SDG/Software/Mosaic/StartingPoints/ NetworkStartingPoints.html**

The WWW Virtual Library

This is at CERN, the home of the Web. Select a category and you'll be shown a list of related Web sites.

> **http://www.w3.org/hypertext/DataSources/bySubject/Overview.html**

Q&A *What does CERN stand for?*

CERN actually stands for "Conseil Européen pour la Recherche Nucléaire", the original name for this Swiss scientific laboratory that specializes mostly in particle physics. I can well imagine your question—How did CERN come up with the Web?

Actually, it's pretty simple. The Web was a development of a tool that CERN developed to allow it's scientists to collaborate across large distances (such as across Europe). After it was picked up and made popular by Mosaic, and then Netscape, it became the Web as we know it today.

If you're interested in CERN itself, you can get some details at **http:// www.cern.ch/CERN/GeneralInfo.html.**

The CUI W3 Catalog

This directory (the Centre Universitaire d'Informatique W3 Catalog in Geneva) lists thousands of Web pages. You type the word you are looking for, and the catalog looks for matches. It's actually an index of the WWW Virtual Library.

> **http://cuiwww.unige.ch/w3catalog**

Virtual Libraries

This site points you to Web reference documents, such as Scott Yanoff's Internet Services List and Big Dummy's Guide to the Internet. You'll find pointers to useful directories as well as individual documents.

> **http://www.w3.org/hypertext/DataSources/bySubject/Virtual_library**

EINet Galaxy

This site is another directory that can be searched by entering a keyword, or by browsing through links to different subjects. There's also a What's New page.

http://galaxy.einet.net/

The Harvest WWW Home Pages Broker

Another searchable index of Web sites. This system also displays information about a Web document that it finds, even showing part of the document's text.

http://www.town.hall.org/brokers/www-home-pages/

GNN NetNews

This one isn't really a directory, but it's worth mentioning because it's a great way to discover lots of interesting things. It's an online magazine about the Internet. A great place to find out about new programs and services, Internet news stories and controversies, and neat stuff on the net.

http://nearnet.gnn.com/news/index.html

Internet Services List

Scott Yanoff's Internet Services List has been around in text files for about 3 years, but it's now available on the Web, in interactive form, of course. When you find something of Interest—whether a Web site, an FTP site, a chat service, or whatever—you can go right there.

http://slacvx.slac.stanford.edu:70/misc/internet-services.html

Commercial and Business Lists

These are lists of Web documents maintained by businesses.

Open Market's Commercial Sites Index

A large alphabetical listing of commercial Web documents. You can also search for a keyword, or look at the What's New section.

http://www.directory.net/

Interesting Business Sites on the Web

A small list of interesting business Web pages. There's no searching, just select a category—Pick of the Month, Financial Services, Virtual Malls, and so on.

http://www.rpi.edu/~okeefe/business.html

Sell-it On the WWW

This is a Directory of Advertisers' Web sites. You'll find links to companies selling CD-recordings, business supplies, computer equipment, books, and general services and stuff.

http://www.xmission.com/~wwwads/index.html

CommerceNet

A Silicon Valley based directory. You can find out about products and services, associations, news, information and events related to the participants in CommerceNet. Companies like American Express, Amdahl, Apple, Fedex, and many more. (Cool graphics in this directory.)

http://www.commerce.net/

MecklerWeb

Select the category you are interested in—Business and Finance, Travel, Seniors, Arts & Entertainment, Computing, Education, and so on—and you'll see information about companies related to that subject. Or view a list of companies with information at this site. Mecklermedia, the owner of MecklerWeb, publish Internet World magazine.

http://www.mecklerweb.com/

More Specific Stuff

The following are directories that are designed to help you find more specific information.

Web Newspaper List

This lists magazines and newspapers on the Web. It also contains links to other lists of publications.

http://www.jou.ufl.edu/commres/webjou.htm

Campus Newsletters on the Net

This list has links to dozens of college newspapers.

http://ednews2.asa.utk.edu/papers.html

Journalism and Communications Schools

Links to Journalism and Communications colleges.

http://www.jou.ufl.edu/commres/jouwww.htm

The Journalism List

In theory this provides information about Internet and Web resources that might be of use to journalists. But it's a great list for *anyone* who wants to find their way around. Not only does it have Web resources, but newsgroups, finger, FTP, gopher, WAIS, and more.

http://www.jou.ufl.edu/commres/jlist.htm

Internet Law Sites

These are good places on the Web to find information about the law. The General Lists of Various Law Sites (**http://ananse.irv.uit.no/law/nav/law_ref.html**) and Law related sites on the Internet (**http://www2.waikato.ac.nz/law/law-related.html**).

Multimedia Information Sources

This is an index to Web sites related to multimedia. You'll find links to documents with information about current events in multimedia, various company sites, software archives, and more.

http://cuiwww.unige.ch/OSG/MultimediaInfo/index.html

Web Exhibits

This list links to dozens of Web exhibits, from art to the Dead Sea Scrolls.

http://155.187.10.12/fun/exhibits.html

US Government Web

This is a Web site that lets you search for U.S. Government Web documents. White House press releases, the National Trade Data Bank, the President's speeches (audio files), and more.

http://sunsite.unc.edu/govdocs.html

Irena, Australia's Beauty

Irena is, apparently, named after "one of the most attractive women in Australia" (perhaps it's an inside joke understandable only to Australians). It lets you search the Web server at the Australian National University for information on the social sciences, humanities, and Asian Studies.

http://coombs.anu.edu.au/bin/irena.cgi/WWWVL-Aboriginal

Saving Stuff From the Web

● **In this chapter:**

- Saving documents as text and HTML files

- How can I grab images out of Web documents?

- How can I save the document background?

- Printing documents

- Saving URLs

- Transferring files across the Web

The information is there, and there's lots of it. But it's changing constantly. Pages change and sometimes disappear. If you want to keep some of that information, you need to save it yourself . . . . **>**

etscape provides a number of ways for you to get information saved on the hard disk. Here are the things you can save:

- Document text

- HTML "source" document

- Text or HTML source for documents you haven't even viewed

- Inline images in graphics files

- Document background

- URLs to the Clipboard, so you can copy them into another program

- Computer files referenced by links

TIP **Remember, much of what you come across on the Web is** copyrighted material. In fact, unless you are sure that what you are viewing is not copyrighted, you should assume it is. You can take this material for private use, but not for publication. For information about what you can and can't do with copyrighted material, refer to a book on copyright law. (Many writers' references contain copyright-law information.)

Saving document text

Let's begin by looking at how to get text out of a Web document. Use any of these methods:

- Choose File, Save As. In the dialog box that appears (shown in fig. 8.1), you'll notice that a pop-up menu displays TEXT as it's default. Click on Save, and Netscape will save all the text in the document (not the underlying HTML "codes," though).

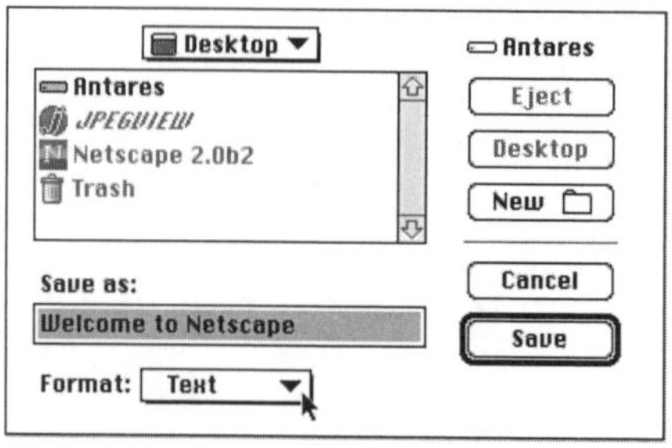

Fig. 8.1
The file name that appears is the same as the title of the Web page. You can change the name for the file if you like.

Desktop ▼		Antares
Antares		Eject
JPEGVIEW		Desktop
Netscape 2.0b2		New 📁
Trash		
Save as:		Cancel
Welcome to Netscape		Save
Format: Text ▼		

- Highlight the text and choose Edit, Copy or press ⌘+C. The text is copied to the Clipboard, so you can now go to another application and paste it.

TIP   **To highlight text, choose Edit, Select All; or point at the beginning** of the text you want to highlight and click the mouse button, hold the button down, and drag the pointer across the text. (Make sure you are not clicking inside a link, of course, or you won't highlight the text, you'll see the pop-up menu.) Make sure the cursor isn't in the "Location" field if it's visible at the top of your screen. If it is, you're only going to select the text in that field.

Save the HTML "source" document

Why would you care about the "source" document? Most people won't want the source document, but if you are interested in creating your own Web pages you will. If you view a source document, you can learn the techniques other Web authors have used to create documents.

The source document is the plain text document that is the basis of the Web page you are viewing. As we saw back in chapter 1, "The Internet and Web— A Quick Intro," each Web document is an ASCII text document with special codes, or tags, which tell Web browsers what to do. When you transfer a document to the browser, the browser "renders" the document; that is, it takes a look at all the codes, then figures out what it has to do to turn the document into something you can read.

To save the source document, choose File, Save As. Enter a Filename, choose a directory, and make sure that *Source* is displayed in the pop-up menu. Then click on Save.

An alternate way of viewing the source and saving it is to choose View, Document Source. This will bring up a text editor with the source file. Generally, it's TeachText or SimpleText, but you can specify it to be different—including just using Netscape. When it appears, use the editor to save the file.

Changing your View Source application

If you wanted to use a specific text editor to view source files, you can very easily change this option. Choose Options, General Preferences... and click on the Applications tab. You should see the window as shown in figure 8.2.

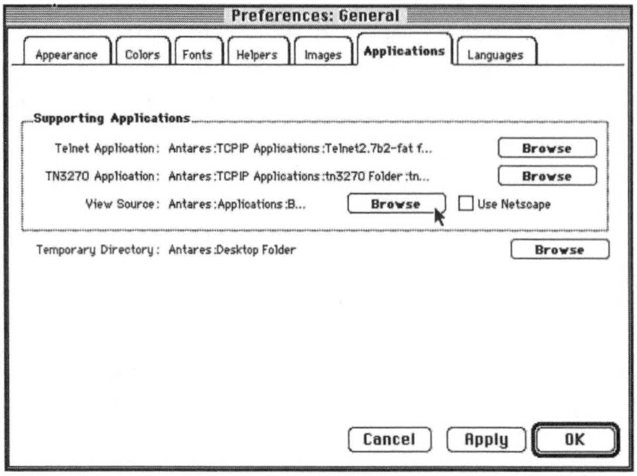

Fig. 8.2
Although Netscape will generally keep you up to date on Applications it's using, you can change them to specific ones for Telnet and TN3270 as well.

You can choose at this point to simply use Netscape to view the source of a Web page, or you can click on the Browse button and use the standard dialog box (shown in fig. 8.3) to choose a different text editor.

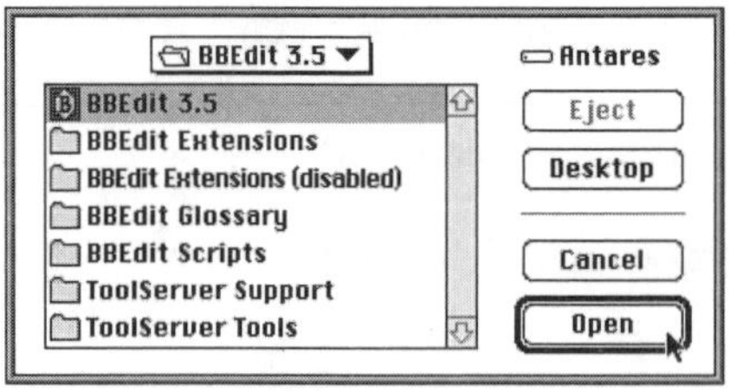

Fig. 8.3
My personal favorite is BBEdit, but you can also use SimpleText or TeachText.

Saving documents you haven't even seen

You don't have to view a document before you save it. As long as you have a link to the document, you can save it without viewing it first. Click on the link and hold down the mouse button until the hidden menu appears, shown in figure 8.4 below. Choose Save This Link As. You'll see the Save As dialog box. After you've entered the document title you want to use (if you want to change it), selected the directory, and clicked <u>S</u>ave, Netscape will transfer the document. It won't display it, though, it will simply save it as instructed.

Fig. 8.4
This will bring up the Save As dialog box, which will let you save either the HTML source for the document or just the plain text in the document.

Saving inline images

You can save pictures that you find inside Web documents. Just as in saving a link you haven't seen, click on the picture and hold down the mouse button until the pop-up menu appears. This time, choose Save This Image As, and you'll see the Save As dialog box. Enter a filename and click on <u>S</u>ave to save it to your hard disk. It will be saved using the original format. If the picture's a .GIF file, Netscape will save it as a .GIF. If it's a .JPG or .XBM, it'll be saved as such.

Note, by the way, that there's a way to display just the image by itself. Click on the image, holding down the mouse button until you see the pop-up menu, and choose View This Image. Netscape will request a copy of the picture from the Web server that has it and display the picture in a document by itself. You won't see the original text or document background, all you'll see is the image you selected.

TIP **You can quickly copy a picture for pasting into another program** using the pop-up menu. Click on the image and hold the mouse button down until you see the pop-up menu. Choose Copy this Image, then go to another application and paste the image.

Save document backgrounds

A new feature that's becoming popular on Web pages these days is the background pattern. A Web author can add a special background to his documents; the background may be a plain color, or perhaps some sort of pattern. Many Web sites use a sort of watermark in the background, with the company name or logo. Others are some kind of marble or rock background. (Some authors aren't doing a good job here. I've noticed that a lot of Web pages are almost illegible these days, thanks to a poorly chosen background color.)

Right now Netscape provides no direct way to save the background image. There is a fairly simply technique by which you can do this, though. You just need to figure out the URL of the background image. Here's how.

1 Choose <u>V</u>iew, Document <u>S</u>ource. You'll see the View Source window.

2 Near the top of the window look for something like this: `<BODY BACKGROUND="/netstore/images/background.gif"`.

3 This is the command that places the background image into the document.

4 Use the mouse to highlight the filename and the path to the file, the text that appears inside quotation marks, immediately after the = sign. In this case, `/netstore/images/background.gif`. (You can highlight text by pressing the mouse button and dragging the pointer across the text, or by placing the cursor at the beginning or end of the text, then pressing Shift and using an arrow key to move across the text.)

5 Press ⌘+C to copy this text to the clipboard.

6 Open a word processor or text editor, and paste the text (⌘+V). Look closely at what you've got. If it's something like our example (`/netstore/images/background.gif`), you don't have the full URL. This is what's known as a relative URL. It shows where the image is in relation to the document. (If the image starts with `http://`, you have the full URL; skip to step 8.)

7 Switch to the Netscape window, click in the Location bar, and press ⌘+C. Go back to the word processor and paste the text. Again, look closely at what you've got. IN our case, we have this:

```
/netstore/images/background.gif
http://merchant.netscape.com/netstore/index.html
```

8 You need to take the beginning of the URL, all the way to the end of the host name, and add it to the beginning of the path to the image file, like this:

```
http://merchant.netscape.com/netstore/images/
background.gif
```

In some cases you may only have a filename (`background.gif`, for instance). This would mean that the image file is in the same directory as the .HTML file. In such a case you would remove the .HTML filename from the full URL, and replace it with the image filename.

9 Copy the new URL and paste it into the Location text box.

10 Press Enter, and Netscape will transfer the image and place it in the Netscape window.

11 Use the pop-up menu to save the image as we described above.

That's it, you've got the background image. Remember, though, you don't *own* this image! You can use it for your own private purposes, but you probably can't publish Web pages using it, without the permission of the artist who created it, or perhaps the author of the Web site from which you took it.

Also, you'll probably see that the image you transferred is just a small square—it doesn't fill a document. A browser knows how to take these small squares and "tile" them all across a document's background.

66 *Plain English, please!*

Tile is a term used to describe how Netscape (or some other program) takes a small image and spreads it out over a larger area. It takes the (usually) square image and places many of them across the screen, like you would tile a floor with square tiles. 99

Printing the document

If you want a paper copy of something you've found in a Web document, you can print the document directly from Netscape. The first thing you'll want to do is define your default page setup (you only have to set this up once, not every time you print). Choose File, Page Setup to see the dialog box in figure 8.5.

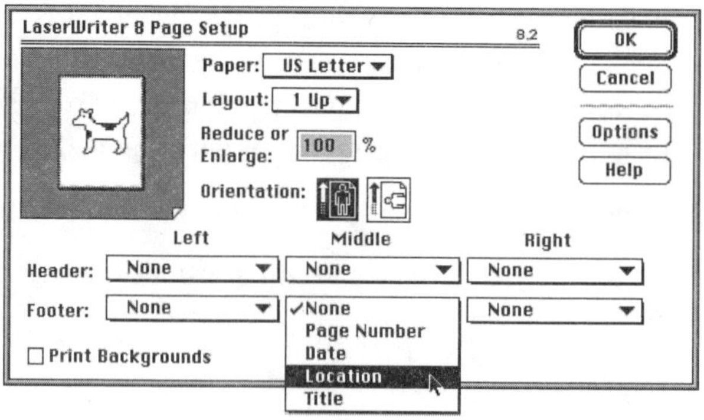

Fig. 8.5
You can set various items to be placed in the margins of printed document—Location URL, Title, Page number, etc.

LaserWriter 8 Page Setup		8.2	OK
Paper: US Letter ▼			Cancel
Layout: 1 Up ▼			Options
Reduce or Enlarge: 100 %			Help
Orientation:			

	Left	Middle	Right
Header:	None ▼	None ▼	None ▼
Footer:	None ▼	✓None	None ▼
☐ Print Backgrounds		Page Number	
		Date	
		Location	
		Title	

TIP **Just so you know, the Page Setup dialog box shown in figure 8.5** may not always look the same. The top stays pretty much constant, but the bottom section will generally change according to what printer you've hooked up to your Mac.

When you are ready to print the document, choose File, Print to see a typical Print dialog box. You can select which pages you want to print (you'll have to guess here a little, because a Web document is a single, perhaps very long, page while it's on the screen), and how many copies you want to print.

Saving URLs to the Clipboard

Once you're a regular Web user, you'll find that you want to save URLs, the Web "addresses." Perhaps you want to share them with a friend or colleague. Maybe you want to include a URL in a memo or article you are writing, or want to save the URL in a database with other research materials. Netscape provides a few ways to save URLs:

- Click in the Location text box and then drag over the line of text that makes up the URL. Once you have the URL highlighted, press ⌘+C; the text is copied to the Clipboard.

- Use the pop-up menu (a text or graphic link), and choose Copy This Link Location. This is a very handy method for copying a URL without even going to the referenced document.

- To copy the URL that identifies a picture in a Web document, use the pop-up menu and choose Copy This Image Location.

Stealing directly from the cache

Long after you've been to a Web document—days or weeks later, depending on how big your hard-disk cache is (see chapter 4, "Advanced Navigation")— you can grab information from that document by digging around in the cache. The cache is not very easy to work in, though.

First, to see where your cache directory is, choose Options, Network, then click on the Cache tab. The Cache Directory text box shows where your cache has been placed. (It's generally in your Preferences folder unless you specified it to be somewhere else.)

Now, use the Finder to open that folder, a picture of my Netscape Preferences and Cache Folder are shown in figure 8.6. You'll find all the inline images—.GIF, .XBM, and .JPG files—from your cached documents, along with the .HTML documents themselves, and a variety of other file formats you may have loaded. You can drag them on to Netscape to see what they are, or open them in another application.

Fig. 8.6
If you want to view the most recent cached files, you might try setting the View option to date by choosing View, By Date.

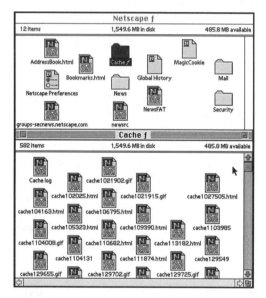

TIP **If you're looking for another image program that's good on a** Macintosh, one I use very frequently is JPEGView. It can invariably be found on the Macintosh software archives - check chapter 11, "Software Libraries—Using FTP," for more information on those archives, or even chapter 7, "Searching for Information on the Web," to go and find it.

Unfortunately, these files have all been renamed, and it's quite difficult to figure out what they are. They've all been given a special *M* number: M007J0PL.HTML, for instance. Double-click on the .HTML files, though, and they'll open in Netscape—though the links to the inline graphics won't work.

 TIP **When Netscape retrieves a file from the cache, it can retrieve the** inline pictures, too. It's only when *you* open an HTML file, by dragging it onto the Netscape program or opening it from the File menu that the problem occurs with the inline images not being found.

Downloading files from the Web

Many links on the Web point not to other Web documents, but to computer files of various kinds. We can group these files into two types:

- Files that you want to transfer to your hard disk. For instance, a link may point to a program that is in an .hqx or .sea file. You want to transfer this program to your computer and then install it or run it.

- Files that you want to play or view; sound files (music and speech), video, graphics of many kinds, word processing documents, Adobe Acrobat documents, PostScript files, and so on.

Of course in order to play or view a file it has to be transferred to your hard disk, and you may choose to save it. So in one sense there's no difference between these two types of files—in each case a file is transferred to your computer. But if you want to play or view a file, that's part of the "hypermedia" or "multimedia" experience of the Web, and so the purpose of the transfer is different.

But it's also different in another way. You may have to configure a special **viewer** so that when Netscape transfers the file it knows how to play or display it. (For the first of these file types, though, Netscape doesn't care what happens to the file; it's simply going to save it to your hard disk and let you figure out what to do with it later.) We're going to look at viewers in chapter 9, "Audio and Video," and chapter 10, "More on Viewers".

For now, we're only interested in the first type of file, one that you want to transfer and save on your hard disk.

File transfers

Why transfer files back to your computer? In chapter 11, "Software Libraries—Using FTP," you'll learn how to use Netscape to run FTP—File Transfer Protocol— sessions. FTP is an Internet-wide system that allows you to copy files to your computer from software archives all over the world. You can get shareware programs, clip art, various documents, sound clips, and more. There are literally millions of files waiting for you at these archives.

But Web authors can also distribute computer files directly from their Web documents. They create special links from their documents to the files that they believe their readers may want to transfer. Clicking on the link begins the transfer to your computer. Here are a few reasons for grabbing files across the Web:

- Many sites are run by companies that want to distribute their shareware, freeware, or demo programs. (We'll look at one of these in a moment.)

- Some authors want to distribute non-Web documents. They may create links to PostScript, Word for Windows, Adobe Acrobat, and Windows Help documents, for instance.

- Some authors have placed clip art archives on the Web. You can transfer the files and then use them in your own Web documents.

As you can see, we have some overlap here between the two types of files mentioned before. The bulleted list points out that a Web author may want to distribute an Adobe Acrobat file (Acrobat is a hypertext document format). But Acrobat files fall into the second category of files, ones that are part of the multimedia experience, that Netscape wants to "play."

Well, they may be files that can be played, depending on two factors:

1 How is the document formatted? The format of the document is determined by it's suffix. If the file has its original extension, and is in its original format, the Web author has set it up so it can be played. For

instance, the Acrobat extension is .PDF, and when the file is transferred Netscape can automatically send this file to an Adobe Acrobat viewer, so you can view the document immediately. But the Web author may have saved the file in a compressed, or archive, format. The extension may be .sit, for instance (a Stuffit compressed file) or .sea (a self-extracting archive file). This means that the Web author expects people to transfer the file, extract the software, and then load the file into another program.

2 Have you set up Netscape to play the file? If you haven't set up Netscape to play a particular file (and we'll discuss that in chapter 9, "Audio and Video"), then the only thing Netscape can do is transfer it to your hard disk. So even if the file extension is .PDF, for instance, if you haven't configured Netscape to "call" an Adobe Acrobat viewer, it can't do so and will want to simply transfer the file and drop it onto your hard disk.

Here's how it works

Let's take a quick look at how all this works. As an example, I'm going to look at the VRML test page (**http://www.vrml.org/vrml/**), which contains a number of VRML files. Clicking on one of the links, Netscape opened the Unknown File Type dialog box, which you can see in figure 8.7.

Fig. 8.7
The Unknown File Type dialog box appears whenever you receive a file that Netscape doesn't recognize.

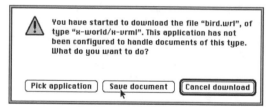

You have started to download the file "bird.wrl", of type "x-world/x-vrml". This application has not been configured to handle documents of this type. What do you want to do?

Pick application   Save document   Cancel download

Why did Netscape display this dialog box? Because it doesn't know what to do with it. It can't do anything with the file itself, because it's not one of the file types that Netscape has been designed to work with. And it doesn't have a "viewer" installed for this file type (it's a .WRL file), so it can't send the file to another program. So it needs your help. You have three choices:

- **Pick Application**—Click here to tell Netscape which program to send the file to (but we'll cover that in chapter 9, "Audio and Video").

- **Save File**—Click here to see the Save As dialog box, in which you can tell Netscape where to put the file once it's transferred it.

- **Cancel Download**—Click here to remove the dialog box and return to the document.

TIP As you'll see in chapter 9, "Audio and Video," you can configure a "viewer" for .wrl files, a program that will open the file and show you the document. We'll cover VRML itself with more detail in chapter 10, "More on Viewers."

CAUTION It's a good idea to check software you transfer with a computer-virus program before using them; many sites on the Internet don't check for viruses, so you don't always know for sure what you are getting. There are a number of commercial and shareware programs available.

Audio and Video

● In this chapter:

- What file formats will I run into?

- What happens when Netscape transfers a file?

- External viewers and inline plug-ins

- External files and embedded ("live") objects

- Installing a "viewer" for .WAV sound files

- Working with plug-ins

- How do I install a viewer through the preferences dialog box?

The World Wide Web is a multimedia system. It's a lot more than text and inline pictures. But to really use all the features the Web has to offer, you need to have some programs to help you out . . . . ▷

What happens when you click on a link in a Web document? Well, it might take you to another Web document. That's pretty much what this book has been about so far. It might also transfer a file, an archive, program, or self-extracting archive file that you want to transfer to your hard disk. We covered that in chapter 8, "Saving Stuff From the Web."

But it might be something different. Here's how Netscape works with a variety of file formats:

File Format	Description
.GIF, .JPG, .JPEG, .JPE, .XBM	These are graphics files. They share one thing in common: they are the formats that are used for inline graphics images. But a Web author may also place one of these files at a Web site with a link pointing to it. The file will be transferred, but it won't be "inline." That is, it won't be part of a Web document—as a graphic separate from a document it's often known as an external image. They will appear in the Netscape window.
.HTM, .HTML	You know all about these—the basic Web document format.
.TXT, .TEXT	A text file. These are displayed in the Netscape window.
Netscape needs a "helper application" for the following file types:	
.AU, .AIF, .AIFF, .AIFC	Sound files used on UNIX, Macintosh, or Windows systems.
.SND	The standard Macintosh sound file format.
.WAV	The standard Windows "wave file" sound format.
.EPS	A PostScript image.
.PS	A PostScript document.
.MOV, .QT	The QuickTime movie format.

File Format	Description
.MPEG, .MPG, .MPE, M1V	The MPEG (Motion Pictures Expert Group) video formats.
.PDF	The Portable Document Format, an Adobe Acrobat hypertext file. This format is becoming a very popular way to distribute electronic documents.
.RAM, .RA	RealAudio. This is a sound format that plays while it's being transmitted. Click on a link to a RealAudio file and it begins playing within a few seconds, rather than making you wait for the entire file to be transferred before starting.
.TIF	A common graphics format.
.WRL	A VRML (Virtual Reality Modeling Language) 3-D object.
.ZIP	A Windows/DOS archive file. These files contain other, compressed, files within them.
.DOC	If you have Microsoft Word, .DOC files will open in that program. However, the .DOC extension could be any number of different Microsoft Word versions. To be safe, you need to have the latest version.
.RTF	Rich Text Format, word-processing files that work in a variety of Windows word processors. Most word processors should be able to open this.

TIP **You'll find compressed files in a variety of formats. If you find a** .ZIP, .LZH, or .ARC file, it's probably for a DOS or Windows computer. The .EXE is often a self–extracting archive very common in the DOS and Windows world. If the file is a .HQX, .SEA, or .SIT file it's a Macintosh file. The .Z, .TAR, and .GZ files are generally for UNIX computers (although the .GZ format can work on all three of these computer types, you'll rarely find a .GZ file for the PC or Mac).

Have I missed some? Sure, there are as many possible file formats on the Web as there are file formats in existence. But the ones I've mentioned here are the ones you'll most likely find (in fact, even some of the ones I've mentioned are not used very often on the Web—I think I've covered the ground pretty well with this list).

Let's take a look at how Netscape figures out what it's supposed to do when it transfers a file.

What happens when Netscape transfers a file

When you click on a link, the Web server sends information about the file that is about to be transferred. Netscape looks at this information, to see what type of file is being sent. The Web server may send the MIME information (we'll get to that later in this chapter), which tells Netscape exactly what the file is. If the server doesn't send the MIME information, Netscape takes a look at the file extension and uses that to figure out what sort of file it is. Here's the procedure it follows:

1 If the file is a Web document (MIME type text/html which has an extension of .HTM or .HTML), it knows just what to do—display the file in the Netscape window, because it's a Web document.

2 If the file is a text file (MIME type text/plain, extension .TXT), it's not a true Web document, but it can be displayed easily nonetheless (it's a text document), so Netscape displays it in the window. (You'll often find .TXT files when working in Gopher sites.)

3 If the file is an inline-image file (MIME types image/jpeg, image/gif, image/x-xbitmap, extension .JPG, .JPEG, .JPE, .GIF, or .XBM), Netscape displays the file in the Netscape window; all of these are graphics types.

4 If the file is "none of the above," Netscape looks at its list of **viewers** (also known as **helpers**), to see if any have been configured. For instance, you may have configured a viewer for .AU files—you can use SoundMachine to play these. Netscape looks in its viewer or helper list, finds that the .AU format is associated with SoundMachine, so it "sends" the file to SoundMachine.

5 If the file is not in the file-association list, Netscape is stuck; there's nothing more it can do, so it has to ask you.

You now have three choices. You can choose Save to Disk to save the file to your hard disk—absolving Netscape from any further responsibility. You can choose Configure a Viewer, to tell Netscape which application it should use to open this file type (we'll look at this in a moment). Or you can choose Cancel Transfer, to remove the dialog box and return to the Netscape window.

The two types of "viewers"

In a moment we'll look at how to configure a viewer. But first I want to describe the two different types of programs that you can use to display file types that Netscape can't handle:

- **External viewers (or helpers)**—Viewers are more properly called external viewers. They're sometimes known as helpers (the tab in the General Preferences dialog box says Helpers). An external viewer is one that Netscape opens when it needs it. Netscape sends the file it's just received to the viewer, and the viewer displays or plays it. For instance, you might configure the program Sparkle to play .MPEG files.

- **Inline Plug-Ins**—These are "viewers" that are built into Netscape. Instead of opening another program and sending the file to that program, Netscape will use special program code that you've added to display or play the file within the Netscape window.

Inline plug-ins are similar to the idea of OpenDoc or Microsoft's OLE (Object Linking and Embedding). One program can use program code from another to display a file within itself. For instance, using Microsoft's Word, you can display Excel spreadsheet data, or Excel can display Microsoft Word data. Inline plug-ins are not OLE or OpenDoc, but the idea is the same; they allow Netscape to display data that it normally would be unable to handle.

For now, though, you should be aware that if there's a plug-in available for a particular file type, it's probably preferable to installing an external viewer program. Rather than waiting for another program to launch and display a file, it will be displayed within Netscape (though there may be cases in which you prefer to have the file type played or displayed outside Netscape). For instance, if you want to view .PDF files and can get the Adobe Acrobat plug-in, use that rather than installing the Adobe Acrobat reader program.

Two types of objects

There are also two different types of objects. There are external objects, and live objects. An external object is a file that is not embedded into a document. You click on a link, and the Web server sends the file referenced by the link. For instance, the link may "point to" an Adobe Acrobat .PDF file (an Acrobat hypertext file, which we'll learn more about in chapter 10, "More on Viewers").

Click on the link and the Web server sends the .PDF file, which is then sent to the external viewer, or displayed in the inline plug-in.

Live objects, though, are embedded into a document. The Web author uses the `<EMBED SRC="file">` tag, so that when you open the document containing the tag, the embedded object is displayed. Netscape will run the appropriate inline plug-in, which will display the document. For instance, an .MPEG file may be embedded in a Web document. When you click on a link that takes you to the Web document, Netscape automatically opens some kind of .MPEG player plug-in, and the video begins playing in a rectangle within the Netscape window.

We'll come back to inline plug-ins later in this chapter. For now, though, we'll stick with external viewers.

Installing a viewer

On the Macintosh, there's generally only a few programs that you'll need (or want) for any kind of file type. Netscape makes installing very easy to work with—all you have to do is get the file. For example, when you first install Netscape, it may not know how to handle .AU files. Choose Options, General Preferences..., click on the Helpers tab, then look for audio/basic; you'll see that in the Action column it says Ask User. In other words, when you click on a link to an .AU file, Netscape will ask you what it should do with the file. You might notice that in the Application column, it also lists SoundMachine. This means that if Netscape can find SoundMachine on your Macintosh (with the help of the Finder of course), it'll use it to play the .AU file.

TIP **You might very well find that Netscape already knows how to deal** with a large number of these applications. If your copy of Netscape happened to come with SoundMachine, then it won't show Ask User under the Action Column. Instead it'll show a little icon of the program, and it'll probably say "Launch."

About MIME

What's this audio/basic thing? That's the file's MIME (Multipurpose Internet Mail Extensions) type. Originally this system was designed to allow Internet e-mail programs to transfer binary files, and it's still in use today for that purpose. But what's really important is that MIME provides a way for a program to identify a file type. When transferring a file (of any kind, including Web documents) to a browser, the Web server always starts out with the MIME description. Netscape uses this information to identify the file type, and then figures out what to do with it (which viewer to send it to, or which plug-in to use). If the server doesn't send the MIME information (say, while you're looking at an FTP site), Netscape then looks at the file extension, and tries to identify the file that way. (Using the MIME information is the pre-ferred way to handle files, though, as a single file type may be identified using a range of different extensions.)

There are two parts to the MIME description: the type and the subtype. For instance, here's a MIME file description: video/mpeg. The type is video (the file is a video file), while the subtype is mpeg (the file is an MPEG file, just one of several different types of video files). If you look in the Helper Applications list you'll see more video/ subtypes: video/quicktime (an Apple video format), and video/x-msvideo (a Microsoft video format).

Adding the .AU viewer

Okay, it's time to add the .AU viewer. Let's begin by making sure we have the program we need: SoundMachine. I'll assume you don't have it—you can find it at Netscape's Helper Application Web page (**http://home.netscape.com/assist/helper_apps/machelpers.html**). Download it if you need to, and then we'll go look at a sound file or two.

CAUTION   **Almost every program for a Macintosh is going to be encoded in**
the format BinHex (the extension .hqx). This is because Macintosh programs
don't have a simple binary format (although the data files usually do). We're
going to have to have BinHex4.0 or Stuffit Expander to decode these
programs. Netscape has probably come with it, and if it hasn't—there should
be someone you can get it from. If nothing else, you may need to use Fetch
initially to get the Stuffit Expander program (Fetch knows how to decode
BinHex format itself and doesn't need another program to do it) so that
you can get other programs as well.

Once you've made sure you have Sound Machine, let's go to the Rolling
Stones Web site: **http://www.stones.com**. When you get there, use the
RealAudio link to go to the Live Audio Clips page (or simply jump directly
there using the URL **http://www.stones.com/audio/index.html**). Now,
scroll down the page, and you'll find various Rolling Stones songs, in a
variety of formats. You'll see AU, WAV, AIFF, and RealAudio (which are .RA
or .RAM). We'll talk a little about RealAudio in chapter 10, "More on
Viewers."

If you didn't have this configured, you would see the Unknown File Type
dialog box. Click on the Configure a Viewer button, and up pops the Configure External Viewer dialog box. All you need to do is tell Netscape which
program you want to use to open this file.

TIP   **If you do have a viewer or browser and it's not showing up**
properly in the Helper Applications window, you might need to rebuild
your Desktop file so Netscape can find the program.

To do this, you'll need to restart your computer. When it's starting up, hold
down the ⌘+Option keys until it asks you "Are you sure you want to
rebuild your Desktop? This may take a few minutes." Click on "OK," and
that should solve the problem.

Adding viewers manually

There's another way to add viewers. You don't have to wait until you click on
a link to a file type that Netscape doesn't recognize. Instead you can go into
the Preferences dialog box and add viewers beforehand.

Choose <u>O</u>ptions, <u>G</u>eneral. When the Preferences dialog box opens click on
the Helper Applications tab. You'll see the dialog box in figure 9.1. The large

list box in the middle shows you many of the MIME types. As we've already heard, some of these are handled by Netscape itself (look in the Action column for image/gif—the action will show INTERNAL).

Fig. 9.1
The Preferences dialog box shows all the viewers configured, and many file types for which you haven't configured a viewer. You can also use the program names listed there to find out what programs you might want to go find on the Internet.

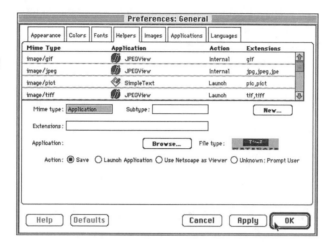

Click on an item in the list, then look below the table. You'll see the File/ MIME Type, the Subtype, and the File Extensions. Below there you'll see four Action option buttons. These allow you to tell Netscape what to do with a particular file type. Click on the file type in the list box, then click on an option button:

Button Type	What it does
View in Browser	This option button is disabled in most cases; it's only enabled if you have selected one of the file types that Netscape can handle directly. You'll only use it if you have previously told Netscape to do something else with one of these file types, which is unlikely anyway.
Save to Disk	Click on this option button if you want to save this file type to disk. As soon as you click on a link that points to this file type, Netscape will open the Save As dialog box.
Unknown: Prompt User	This is the default; if this is selected Netscape will display the Unknown File Type dialog box.
Launch the Application	Select this if you plan to configure a viewer. This tells Netscape to open the application specified in the text box immediately below the option button.

CAUTION   **Don't think you can come into the Helper Applications area, fool**
around with various changes, then click on Cancel to get out without saving
your changes; you can't. As soon as you make a change, it's saved, and
clicking on Cancel will not retrieve the original settings.

Configuring a new viewer is very easy:

1 Click on the file type in the list box.

2 Click on the Launch the Application option button.

3 Click on the Browse button.

4 In the Select an Appropriate Viewer dialog box find the program you
want to use and click on the Open button.

Q&A   *I picked the wrong program! How do I set it correctly?*

Simply click on the file type in the list, then click on the Unknown: Prompt
User option button. Or click on the Browse button and pick another
application to act as the viewer.

Can't find the correct file type?

Now and again you may want to install a viewer for a file type that doesn't
appear in the list. For instance, you may want to use the Adobe Acrobat
player. This uses the application/acrobat MIME type, which, at the current
time anyway, doesn't appear in the list box. Here's how to add it:

1 Click on the Create New Type button to open the dialog box in
figure 9.2.

2 Type the MIME Type (the bit before the /, application), and the MIME
SubType (the bit after the /, pdf).

3 Click on OK to close the dialog box.

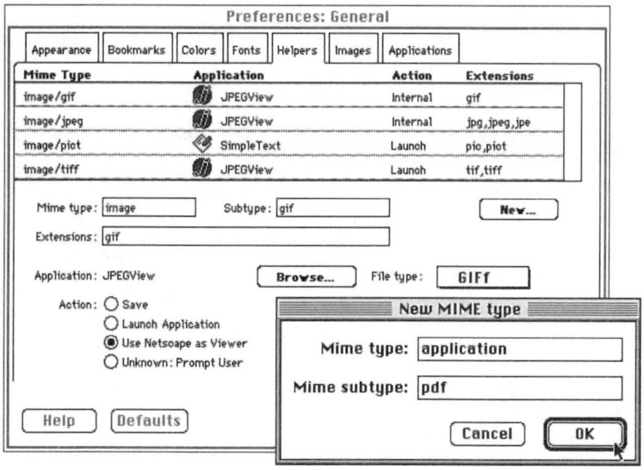

Fig. 9.2
You can add new MIME types as you like, or as they become available on the Internet.

4 Now, with the new MIME type selected, enter the file extension in the File Extensions text box (as shown in fig 9.3). Many file types actually use several different extensions, as you can see by clicking on different file types in the list. In this case, Adobe Acrobat, there's only one common format, .PDF.(if you were adding two extensions, you would separate them with a comma, and no space. For instance: ra,ram).

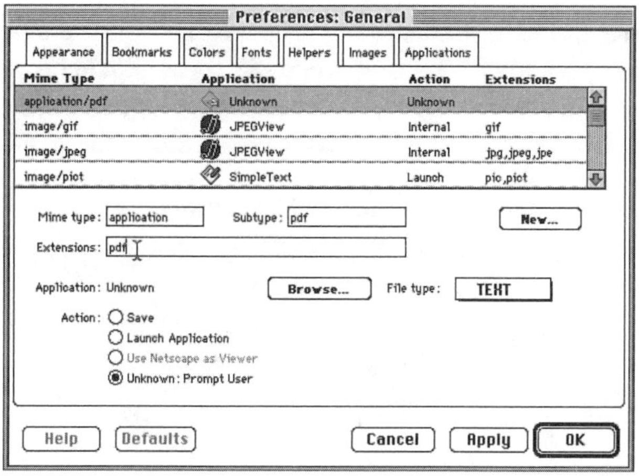

Fig. 9.3
Once you've entered the basic MIME information, you can tell Netscape what program to use with this data.

5 Next, select the appropriate option button. If you plan to use the Adobe Acrobat player (see chapter 10, "More on Viewers"), click on the Launch the Application option button.

6 If you selected the Launch the <u>A</u>pplication option button, click on the
<u>B</u>rowse button to find the application.

Q&A *If I want to configure a viewer for a file type, but I don't know the MIME information, what do I do?*

If you already know of a link to a file of that type, go to the link and click
on it. You may see the Unknown File Type dialog box, which shows you the
MIME type. You can go ahead and configure the viewer right away, as we
saw earlier. However, Netscape may simply transfer the file without knowing
how to handle it, and display garbage text in the Navigator window—all
sorts of strange characters and program code.

Otherwise the programs themselves will generally have this information. Real
Audio makes it very easy—when you install the program, it takes care of
adding all the appropriate information to Netscape for you.

More about plug-ins and live objects

How about installing plug-ins, so you can use live objects? Well, you may
already have plug-ins installed, without realizing it.

Apart from the "Default Plug-in," there's only one plug-in available for the
Macintosh. By the time you read this there should be quite a few more. In
fact, you can find a list of plug-ins at **http://home.mcom.com/comprod/
products/navigator/version_2.0/plugins/index.html**.

How are plug-ins installed? Well, generally it's pretty easy. The plug-in that
I've seen just installs itself. You run the installer and follow the instructions
and everything is taken care of. If you do have to install one by "hand," all
you should have to do is put the plug-in into the Plug-ins folder that appears
in the same directory as Netscape.

Plug-ins will operate in one of three ways:

Plug-in type	What it does
Embedded	An embedded plug-in is one that runs an embedded object. It appears as a rectangular area within the Web document, just as an inline image appears as a rectangular area. The difference is that while the inline image is static, the embedded plug-in will "do stuff" such as play a video, and is interactive—you may be able to use mouse clicks, for instance, to determine what's happening in the plug-in.
Full-screen	The full-screen plug-in takes over the entire Netscape content area. When an external file is transferred to Netscape the full-screen plug-in opens and displays the file contents: it may be an Adobe Acrobat hypertext file or Apple QuickTime video file, for instance. The normal Netscape controls will remain in view, but the plug-in may add controls, too—a video-player plug-in would have start, stop, pause, and rewind buttons, for instance.
Hidden	A hidden plug-in is one that runs without any visible sign. A plug-in that plays sounds, for instance, may be hidden.

Plug-ins have a really incredible amount of possibilities. They'll be able to grab information from other Netscape windows, grab data from the Internet (using URLs), create information that can be used by Netscape or other plug-ins, and so on. It'll be interesting to see just what sort of plug-ins are developed. In the planning stages are plug-ins that will let you index Web documents you view, move through 3-D images, restrict your kids' or students' access to the Internet (by time or specific Internet sites), play RealAudio sounds, and play MPEG audio and video. There are also loads of multimedia plug-ins on their way.

10

More on Viewers

● In this chapter:

- Saving the Multimedia files you play

- Where can I find more viewers?

- RealAudio, real cool

- Why is Adobe Acrobat (.PDF) so important?

- Playing videos

- Making Cyberspace real—Virtual Reality on the Web

Viewers, you'll need to make the most of the multimedia World Wide Web . . . .

I n chapter 9, "Audio and Video," you learned the basics of adding viewers to Netscape. In this chapter I want to cover a bit more information that you'll find useful—how to save the multimedia files that you find on the Web, where you can find more viewers (mostly freeware or shareware), and some details about specific viewers that you'll find useful.

Saving what you've played

Once you've played a file, you can save it for future use if you wish. Most viewers have some kind of command to help you save the file. For instance, you may be using Sparkle to play an .MPEG file. This program has a File, Save As command which lets you save the video to wherever you wish.

But some viewers *don't* provide a way to save files. For instance, SoundMachine will open up with an .AU file, but you can't save with it. How can you save a file that's been played by a program that doesn't let you save it? Grab it from the hard disk.

When Netscape transfers a file, it has to place it on your hard disk. In some cases it places the file in the cache directory (see chapter 4, "Advanced Navigation," for information about the cache). But for most of the files that you'll be using Helper Applications with, Netscape will place them in a "temporary directory." If you haven't specified one, it'll use the Macintosh Desktop. You can specify another location if you want, by choosing Options, General Preferences, and clicking on the Applications tab. The window (shown in fig. 10.1) will show you the location you're currently using, and you can choose a new location by clicking on the Browse button.

CAUTION **When you quit Netscape, it's going to try and clean up those files** it's left in the temporary folder (maybe your Desktop). Just because you see them doesn't mean they'll stay there when you quit Netscape. If you want to keep them, move them into another Folder (or just onto your hard drive) and Netscape won't delete them.

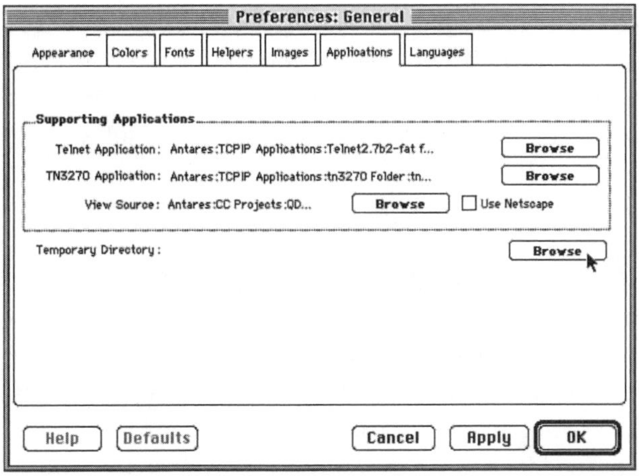

Fig. 10.1
You might want to
leave the Temporary
Directory undefined
because it's easier to
notice those files
showing up on the
Desktop.

```
                      Preferences: General
  ┌─────┬──────┬─────┬───────┬───────┬──────────────┬───────────┐
  │Appearance│Colors│Fonts│Helpers│Images│Applications│Languages│

  ┌─ Supporting Applications ─────────────────────────────────────┐
  │   Telnet Application :  Antares :TCPIP Applications :Telnet2.7b2-fat f...  │ Browse │
  │   TN3270 Application :  Antares :TCPIP Applications :tn3270 Folder :tn... │ Browse │
  │       View Source :  Antares :CC Projects :QD...  │ Browse │  □ Use Netscape │
  └───────────────────────────────────────────────────────────────┘
     Temporary Directory :                            │ Browse │

     ┌──────┐ ┌──────────┐        ┌────────┐ ┌───────┐ ┌──────┐
     │ Help │ │ Defaults │        │ Cancel │ │ Apply │ │  OK  │
     └──────┘ └──────────┘        └────────┘ └───────┘ └──────┘
```

What viewers do I have?

You have plenty of "viewers." As you've already seen, Netscape can deal with
.TXT, .HTML, .HTM, .GIF, .JPG, .JPEG, .JPE, and .XBM files itself. But how
about other types of files? As we saw in chapter 9, "Audio and Video," you
can get the names of the most common viewers from Netscape itself, and
download the most common ones from Netscape's Helper Application Web
page: **http://home.netscape.com/assist/helper_apps/machelpers.html**.

Finding more viewers

You can find more general purpose viewers on the Internet. These are often
freeware or shareware. I've already shown you how to find SoundMachine,
but you may want to take a look at the following sites to see what else you
can pick up:

```
ftp://sumex-aim.stanford.edu/comm/tcp/
http://www.archive.umich.edu/util/comm/
```

TIP **See the rest of this chapter for information about finding viewers**
for RealAudio (.RA, .RAM), Adobe Acrobat (.PDF), Video (.MPEG, .MPG,
.MPE, and .MOV), and VRML 3-D images (.WRL).

If you can't find what you need through these sites, try searching the Web (see chapter 7, "Searching for Information on the Web,") or use one of the Macintosh software archive searches (see chapter 11, "Software Libraries—Using FTP"). I suspect, though, if you can't find what you need in these sites it's just not available.

RealAudio (.RA and .RAM) files

The **RealAudio** links at the Rolling Stones site are to .RA and .RAM files, a new format that greatly improves the way that sound is played over the Web. With the other sound formats we've looked at, you click on a link and then wait. Twiddle your thumbs for a while, or go for coffee, because it can take a long time to transfer a sound file. Once the transfer has finished, Netscape sends it to SoundMachine.

But RealAudio begins playing almost immediately. Netscape begins the transfer, then starts the RealAudio player within a few seconds. (You don't have the RealAudio player yet—I'll explain how to find it in a moment.) The music (or radio broadcast; National Public Radio use RealAudio files for their Internet broadcasts—go to **http://www.npr.org/**) begins playing right away, and continues playing while the file is being transferred. In fact this is the way that a radio works, isn't it? The radio receives signals over the airwaves and plays the signal immediately (it doesn't wait until it's received the entire song and then play it). If you want to try RealAudio, go get the player. You can find it at the RealAudio Web site, **http://www.realaudio.com/**. Read this page; you'll find lots of background information, and links to sites that use RealAudio sounds.

Q&A   So what's the drawback to RealAudio?

The drawback is RealAudio compresses the sound down a lot farther than other formats. It makes it up to 20 times smaller than an .AU file format. The result is you'll hear some static, and music won't sound quite as crisp as you might like. In fact, it sounds like a radio station with some static on the line.

It'll advance as the Internet advances. As we can bring down more information across our telephone lines, they won't compress the data so much—and we'll get better quality while it still plays everything in real time.

On the RealAudio main page, click on the Download link to go to the download page, and click on the "Download the RealAudio Player for Macintosh (version 1.00)" to download the link and transfer the file as shown in figure 10.2.

Once you've downloaded the file, quit Netscape, and you'll probably see the file "RealAudio Installer" on your desktop. If you had Stuffit Expander on your machine, Netscape probably had this file already decoded for you as well.

Fig. 10.2
Many sites that offer news services like this on the Web will also have easy links to the helper applications as well.

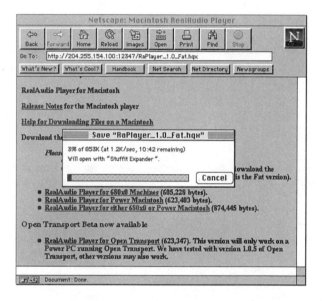

Just double-click on the installer, and the RealAudio program will take it from there. Follow the instructions to install the program. I suggest you select the Easy installation, which lets you choose the directory into which you want to place the program.

The Setup program looks for various Web browsers on your hard disk, and asks if you want to install the RealAudio player for those browsers, too. If you don't have these browsers, you can simply click on the Cancel button. Make sure you select Netscape, though, so RealAudio can configure itself for that program. Finally, the RealAudio player opens and informs you—vocally—that the setup is complete.

That's it, RealAudio is ready to play—if all went well, it even entered the correct information into the Netscape list of viewers (Helper Apps). Let's go back to the Rolling Stones site (**http://www.stones.com/audio/index.html**)

and find a RealAudio file. Or go to NPR (**http://www.npr.org/**), or back to the RealAudio page (or directly to **http://www.realaudio.com/ othersites.html**) where you'll find links to RealAudio sites all over the world.

Playing RealAudio

At one of the sites I've just mentioned, find a RealAudio link and click on it. The RealAudio program opens (it may take a few moments), Netscape starts transferring the file, and the music (or newscast, or whatever) begins! (See fig. 10.3.)

You can click on the Stop button in the RealAudio player (the big black square) to cancel a file transfer. You can use the other controls to determine which parts of the sound file you play.

You can also drag the vertical bar along the horizontal scroll bar—immediately below the toolbar buttons—to move to a different part of the sound.

Fig. 10.3
More and more sites are beginning to use RealAudio. CNN, ABC News, and NPR are all producing broadcasts for the Internet using RealAudio.

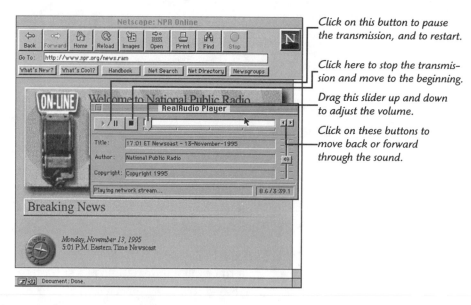

Click on this button to pause the transmission, and to restart.

Click here to stop the transmission and move to the beginning.

Drag this slider up and down to adjust the volume.

Click on these buttons to move back or forward through the sound.

Adobe Acrobat (.PDF) files

We're going to see a lot of .PDF files on the Web very soon, for several reasons. You might think of .PDF as a sort of extension of the Web's "hypertext" or "hypermedia." Adobe Acrobat files are self-contained hypertext documents, with links between pages. Unlike HTML, though, Acrobat files allow the author to determine exactly what the document will look like.

When a browser "renders" an HTML file into the document you see on your screen, the browser decides how to display the different document components—the headers, body text, pull quotes, and so on. But with Acrobat this control is left in the hands of the author; the Acrobat viewer displays the document just as the author intended. Also, Acrobat files are independent of the Web. You can take an Acrobat file and send it to anyone with an Acrobat reader—they don't need a Web browser. In fact, Acrobat began its life far from the Web; it was intended to help companies distribute online documentation to a variety of different computer systems. The same document can be read by viewers on Windows, DOS, Macintosh, SunOS, and Solaris computers, with more viewers to be added soon. It also allows companies to produce online documents that look the same as their paper documents.

 TIP **Apple was one of the first companies to help make the PDF format** viable. It now maintains a complete listing of all its product sheets in PDF format. You can browse through the latest technical details of the Macintosh computer line at **http://www.info.apple.com/productinfo/ datasheets/**.

Two important companies on the Web—Netscape Communications and Spyglass (the people who make Advanced Mosaic, among other browsers)—have decided that Adobe Acrobat will be merged into the Web; both companies plan to make their browsers work with .PDF. Netscape will soon work with Acrobat through the use of an inline plug-in. Also, Adobe is working on a system called *Weblink* (go to **http://www.adobe.com/Acrobat/ Weblink.html** for information) that will allow Acrobat authors to add links from their Acrobat files to Web sites. Users will be able to click on a link in Acrobat, causing their Web browser to retrieve the specified Web document. Once the Acrobat plug-in is available, Acrobat files will appear to work within Netscape "seamlessly;" a link at a Web page will display the Acrobat document within Netscape, and links in the Acrobat document will take you out, back to various Web documents. In the meantime, you'll have to add a .PDF browser if you want to view Acrobat files.

You'll find the Adobe Acrobat reader in a variety of places, but you might want to try the source first, Adobe itself, at **http://www.adobe.com/ Software.html** (the viewer is free; Adobe wants to sell the authoring tool, so they've made the viewer easy to get). Once you've installed the program (just run the file you download and follow the instructions), you can try it out at a variety of sites, perhaps even the one shown in figure 10.4:

Web Sites with Cool PDF Documents

PDF—**http://www.adobe.com/Acrobat/PDFsites.html**

US Patent Office: **http://www.uspto.gov/hearings.html**

Centers for Disease Control Morbidity and Mortality Weekly Report—**http://www.cdc.gov/epo/mmwr/mmwr.html**

Time-Life Virtual Garden—**http://www.timeinc.com/vg/TimeLife/Project/**

TimesFax—**http://nytimesfax.com/**

Axcess Magazine—**http://www.internex.net/axcess**

Fig. 10.4
Seventh Electronic Times, in the Adobe Acrobat Reader. (I found this at **http://sunsite.unc.edu/nppa/epw7/stories/assignment7.html**.)

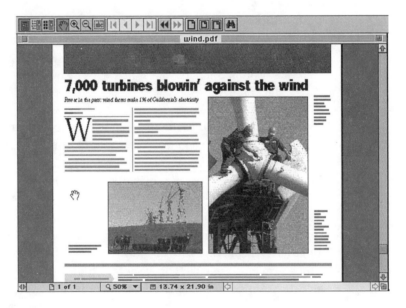

Video Viewers

You'll find a variety of video images on the Web. Perhaps the most popular are the MPEG (.MPEG, .MPG, .MPE) and QuickTime (.MOV) formats, which can be played with the program Sparkle.

I've installed the Sparkle program. (I found it at the **http:// wwwhost.ots.utexas.edu/mac/pub-mac-graphics.html** site, which was linked from the Netscape Macintosh Helper Application Web page (**http:// home.netscape.com/assist/helper_apps/machelpers.html**.) It plays MPEGs and QuickTime movies.

TIP As "neat" as video on the Web may be, it can get old fast. The problem is that transferring video across the Internet is very slow, even if you are using a 28,800 bps modem. If you have an ISDN—Integrated Services Digital Network—connection or a LAN connection, you're okay, but many people are still working with 14,400 or 28,800 bps modems, which take a *long* time to transfer the 5 or 6 MB that many videos on the Web take up. A small video can easily take an hour, or several hours, to transmit when using a 14,400 bps modem! When the transfer begins, wait a few moments for it to settle down, then look at the Saving Location dialog box and see what the estimated transfer time is.

You can see an example of a movie running in Sparkle in figure 10.5. This is from the Enternet Skateboarding Videos, at **http://www.enternet.com/ skate/birdhouse.html**.

Fig. 10.5
Sparkle will also play QuickTime movies, sound included (which isn't usually included with MPEG files).

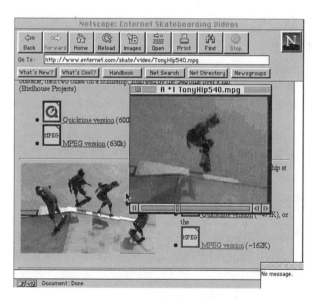

Q&A   ***Where can I find MPEG videos on the Web?***
A good place to start is **http://www.cs.tu-berlin.de/~phade/ mpegwww.html**—you'll find links to dozens of MPEG-related sites. Try **http://www.netvideo.com/technology/videosites.html**, too. Or search for MPEG at a Web search site.

QuickTime is another very popular movie format (.MOV or .QT). You'll need to have QuickTime installed on your Macintosh (which you can get at **http:// quicktime.apple.com/form-qt2mac.html**). Sparkle will play QuickTime movies, or you can use MoviePlayer (which you can download from Apple as well—and comes with the QuickTime distribution).

Once you've downloaded and installed QuickTime, you can go in search of QuickTime movies. The best places to start are **http://quicktime.apple.com/ content.html** and **http://www.iac.net/~flypba/qt.html**, where you'll find lists of QuickTime sites.

MPEG Audio

There's another MPEG format, MPEG audio (MPEG stands for the Motion Picture Experts Group, after the people who came up with the file format). These files have the .MP2 extension. They are a great way to play sound; the files are compressed, so really high quality sounds can be squeezed down into quite a small space. You won't find a lot of these on the Web, though— most sounds are in the .AU, .AIF, .WAV, or .RAM formats.

Just as with the QuickTime and MPEG files, Sparkle will play them wonder-fully—if you can find any.

Virtual Reality on the Web

The newest fad on the Web is 3-D images—in fact, it's 3-D scenes. Click on a link in a Web page, and up pops your 3-D viewer, with a 3-D image inside. Move around in this image, or "walk around" the image (some images are of landscapes and buildings you can "move through," others of objects that you can rotate).

The Macintosh has two kinds of Virtual Reality setups available—one of them is QuickTime VR, the other QuickDraw3D (which is related to VRML).

QuickTime VR

QuickTime VR is an extension to the QuickTime format that's already been so popular on the Internet. You might not see a whole lot of it out there (other than what Apple has produced), simply because it's not available for a wide variety of other kinds of computers.

QuickTime VR creates a scene which you can spin around in and look in all directions (360 degrees actually). It can also create a 3-D object that you can look at and spin around, viewing it from all sides. I picked up the image in figure 10.6 at Apple's QuickTimeVR archive site: **http://quicktime.apple.com/archive/index.html**.

Fig. 10.6
To play the QuickTime VR movies, you need to have the QuickTime VR player. Netscape will see any QTVR movie file you bring down as a normal QuickTime movie—that is, using the extension .MOV.

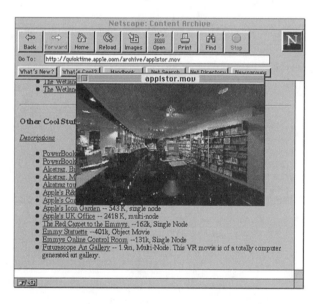

You can get QuickTime VR, as well as the QuickTime VR Player, at Apple's QuickTime VR Web site: **http://qtvr.quicktime.apple.com/**.

TIP **With all of the virtual reality documents and viewers, it's going to** require a fast computer. To really get the best effects, you're going to want to have one of those newer Powermacs. It'll still run on some of the older machines, but this technology is running way ahead of the machines.

Quickdraw3D

Quickdraw 3D is Apple's complementary system to QuickTime VR—it's a three-dimensional realtime rendering package. Of course, Apple has its own format it prefers—3DMF, but the program they wrote to read those files from the Web also reads VRML data. I'll get to VRML in a second, but first a little bit about 3DMF.

3DMF is the file format (and extension actually) for a new MIME type that Apple is supporting for its Powermac line of computers. You can get the basic information about Quickdraw 3D at **http://www.info.apple.com/qd3d/ QD3D.HTML**.

The viewer we're really interested in is Whurlwind, and you can find it to download at **http://www.info.apple.com/qd3d/Test_Drive/Viewers/ Whurlwind.hqx**.

Once you've downloaded Whurlwind, you'll need to set up Netscape to recognize it. Choose the Options, General Preferences and click on the Helper tab. Press the new button, and you should be seeing a window similar to figure 10.7 below.

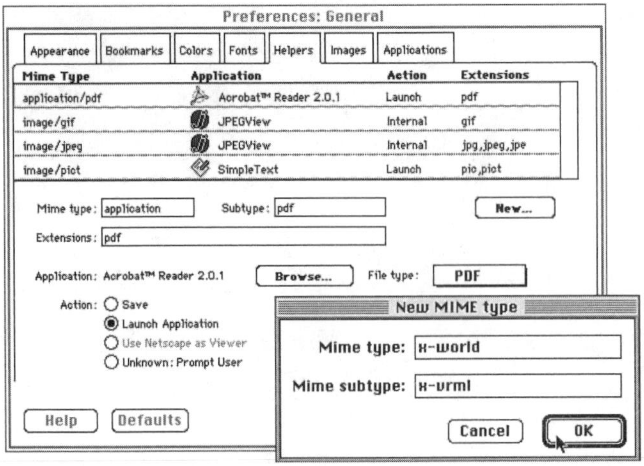

Fig. 10.7
Remember to fill these out in the correct case —case counts on the Internet! "x-world/ x-vrml."

Type **x-world** into the MIME Type text box, **x-vrml** in the Subtype text box and click OK. Type in **wrl** in the extensions text box, and choose the option Launch. Click on the browse button and then find Whurlwind as in figure 10.8 below.

Fig. 10.8
At the time of this writing, Whurlwind was still being developed. Keep checking on the Web site http for any updated viewers.

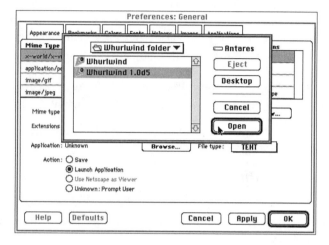

 TIP

Where QuckTimeVR is better to play on the Power Macintosh, the Quickdraw3D requires a Power Macintosh. If you don't have one, you might skip over this section unless you want to see what's coming with the newer technology.

❝ *Plain English, please!*

Viewer? Browser?

Just to confuse the issue, there are a number of programs that are called both **viewers** and **browsers**. You could call Netscape both if you want to (although most people will call it a **browser**), and the program Whurlwind is very similar. Even though it performs the function of a viewer, it's also called a **browser**.

The distinction is really minimal—a **browser** tends to be a program where you can move around in a document where a **viewer** just shows it to you in its own fashion. For example, the VRML documents get a browser (Whurlwind or something else), while Quicktime Movies get a viewer (Sparkle, for example). In the program Whurlwind, you can navigate the information provided—in this case a 3D world. With Sparkle, you just watch as it presents the movie to you. ❞

Apple also provides a 3DMF viewer, but outside of Apple's pages, you probably won't see a whole lot of those files. At least, not yet.

VRML

The format that's all over the Internet, and really making the news, is VRML (Virtual Reality Markup Language). VRML has a very organized following, which you can watch at **http://www.vrml.org**. From here, you can find a number of links to VRML objects you can test.

- **http://nemo.ncsl.nist.gov/~sressler/projects/vrml/vrmlfiles.html** (VRML Samples from the Open Virtual Reality Testbed)

- **http://vrml.arc.org/gallery95/index2.html** (The Arc Gallery—a la VRML)

- **http://www.well.com/user/spidaman/vrml.html** (look under the *Actual VRML sites* heading for links to VRML sites)

- **http://nemo.ncsl.nist.gov/~sressler/hotvr.html** (Hot Virtual Reality Sites)

- **http://www.lightside.com/3dsite/cgi/VRML-index.html** (loads of links, some of which are to actual VRML sites, though most to sites with information *about* VRML)

Now, when you've found a link to a VRML object (it will have the .WRL extension; look in the status bar), click on it and Netscape will transfer the file and load your viewer. You'll then be able to move around in (or about) the 3-D picture. See figure 10.9 for an example.

Fig. 10.9
The finger with the circle above it indicates that the browser Whurlwind is pointing to another URL.

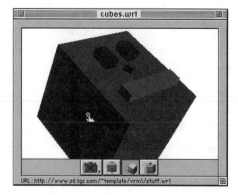

VRML, as you can see from figure 10.9, can also have links to other sites on the Web, including more VRML files. Integrating URLs is just an extension on the hypermedia idea we originally started with, and in the case of VRML allows us to keep a sense of place and scale. You might not want to show everything in an area at once—say an entire house—but you would like to show a room. You could embed links into the virtual room that you create to allow you to connect to other rooms in the house.

 TIP The Web page http://www-dsed.llnl.gov/documents/ WWWtest.html is a good place to try out all sorts of viewers (including VRML viewers). You can also find unusual viewers here; viewers for .PDB "chemical objects," .MA Mathematica files, .V5D dataset objects, and so on.

Note, by the way, that VRML is very new, and there will probably be many changes over the next year. The specifications for VRML 1.0 have just been set down, and like HTML, it is blossoming into several revisions already. Along with the specifications to allow you to link to other VRML worlds, they're adding a way for authors to create animated 3D worlds and eventually to allow people to interact in these worlds, even over a relatively slow link like a modem. In the wake of this book being written, specifications for VRML 2.0 have been proposed and are being debated. A VRML consortium (much like the World Wide Web consortium) is being formed to help develop standards and keep the whole idea open for all of us, and not pinned under one developer.

You'll soon find lots of new and improved viewers, and perhaps new file formats (there are lots of different 3-D file formats, though most of the files you'll find on the Web are currently .WRL files). For information about VRML, go to the **http://www.vrml.com/**, **http://vrml.wired.com**, or **http:// www.lightside.com/3dsite/cgi/VRML-index.html** Web pages. As a final note for exploring the new worlds, I might mention that these worlds will look a little different depending on what kind of VRML browser you're using. The folks that are creating VRML are working on that, but like Netscape and the Web, there are going to be some people ahead of others.

Part III: Traveling the Internet

11

Software Libraries—Using FTP

● **In this chapter:**

- **Using non-World Wide Web resources through Netscape**

- **Using FTP to grab files from the Internet**

- **Finding the files you need at the FTP site**

- **How can I search for computer files on the Internet?**

- **Finding an Archie site**

- **Searching with Archie**

- **Advanced Archie**

The Internet is much more than just the Web, and Netscape can help you use these other services, such as Telnet, Gopher, newsgroups, mail, and much, much more . . . . ▶

So far in this book we've looked at the standard http:// URLs (http stands for *HyperText Transport Protocol*, the basic "language" of the Web). When your Web browser sees a URL that begins with http:// it knows that the destination is a Web document. But some URLs begin with other things, such as these:

- **gopher://**—Takes you to a Gopher-menu system. See chapter 14, "Not by Web Alone—Gopher, Finger, Telnet, and More."

- **ftp://**—Takes you to a File Transfer Protocol site, a site set up so that you can transfer files back to your computer.

- **mailto:**—Used to send e-mail. See chapter 12, "E-mail with Netscape."

- **news:**—A special newsgroup protocol, allowing you to read newsgroups from Web browsers. See chapter 13, "UseNet News."

- **telnet://**—Starts a Telnet session in which you can log on to another computer on the Internet. See chapter 14, "Not by Web Alone—Gopher, Finger, Telnet, and More."

- **tn3270://**—Starts a 3270-mode session, which is very similar to Telnet (you're connecting to a different type of computer, an IBM mainframe). See chapter 14, "Not by Web Alone—Gopher, Finger, Telnet, and More."

- **wais://**—A relatively little-used URL. This one is for Wide Area Information Servers, systems that are used to search databases. Netscape can use the **wais://** URL if you have a special proxy set up; if not, you can still use WAIS through special "gateways." See chapter 14, "Not by Web Alone—Gopher, Finger, Telnet, and More."

- **file:///**—This URL is used to "point" to a file on your hard disk. When you use the File, Open File command, Netscape uses this URL (you'll see it in the Location bar).

- **mailbox:/**—This is a special Netscape URL used by the program's e-mail system (which you'll learn about in chapter 12, "E-mail with Netscape"). It simply tells the mail system which mailbox file to use. (It's not a URL that is used by other Web browsers to point to Web resources.)

In other words, you can access systems that are not true Web systems. You can use Gopher, FTP, and Telnet, you can send e-mail from Web links, and you can read newsgroup messages. There are even special "gateways" through the Web to systems for which your Web browser isn't prepared. For instance, your Web browser cannot communicate directly with Archie, a system used to search FTP sites for computer files (you type a filename, and Archie tells you where to find it). But there are Web documents that do the work for you, using forms. You type the name of the file into a form, and a special program at the Web server communicates with Archie for you.

Finding Internet resources

If you'd like to find the sort of non-Web things that you can get to through the Web, take a look at some of these documents:

Inter-Links

Select a category to see lists of related documents and tools.

> **http://www.nova.edu/Inter-Links/**

Directory of Service Types

If you want to see where you can use WAIS, newsgroups, Gopher, Telnet, FTP, Whois, and other Internet services through your Web browsers, take a look at this Web document.

> **http://www.w3.org/hypertext/DataSources/ByAccess.html**

ArchiePlex

This is a directory of ArchiePlex servers throughout the world—servers that let you search Archie directly from the Web. You'll find sites for browsers both with and without forms support.

> **http://web.nexor.co.uk/archie.html**

Internet Resources—Meta-Index

This is a list of directories containing references to various Internet resources—the Web, Gopher, Telnet, FTP, and more.

> **http://www.ncsa.uiuc.edu/SDG/Software/Mosaic/MetaIndex.html**

FTP—The Internet's file library

We've already seen how to transfer files from the Web back to your computer (see chapter 8, "Saving Stuff From the Web"). The Web contains many files that you might find useful—shareware and demo programs, clip art, press releases, music, video, and plenty more.

But before the Web was born, there was already a system for grabbing files from the Internet, **FTP**, File Transfer Protocol. Using this system you can log into a computer somewhere on the Internet, then transfer files back to your computer.

There are many publicly accessible software archives on the Internet. These are known as **anonymous FTP** sites. This refers to a procedure by which anyone can log in to a public FTP site. When you log in, you use the account name *anonymous*, and then type your e-mail address as the password. (Those unfortunate souls still using the Internet through a command line actually type these entries when they log into an FTP site; Netscape does it automatically for you, though—you won't even see Netscape log in for you.)

 Netscape only works with anonymous FTP. Some FTP sites are set up with *real* account names and passwords—rather than *anonymous* as the account name and an e-mail address as the password. If you have been given access to one of these private FTP sites, you can still retrieve files from it, but it's more difficult.

If you want an FTP program that can do just about anything, try Fetch or Anarchie. You can find these programs at **ftp://sumex-aim.stanford. edu/comm/tcp/** or **ftp://mac.archive.umich.edu/util/comm/**.

For instance, here are a couple of FTP sites that contain a lot of Macintosh shareware utilities: **sumex-aim.stanford.edu/comm/** and **mac.archive.umich.edu/util/**. Or go to **http://hoohoo.ncsa.uiuc.edu/ftp/**, to the Monster FTP Sites list, to find thousands of FTP sites.

What does all this information mean? First, there's the FTP site name (or host name): **sumex-aim.stanford.edu**, for instance. This identifies the computer that contains the files you are after. Then there's the directory name: **/comm/**. This tells you which directory you must change to in order to find the files.

There are two ways to use the Web browser for an FTP session. You'll either click a link to an FTP site that some kind Web author has provided, or enter an FTP URL into the Address box and press Enter. The FTP URL begins with **ftp://**. Let's say, for instance, that you want to go the **ftp.support.apple.com/pub/utils/** ftp site, to see what shareware games are available. You would type **ftp://ftp.support.apple.com/pub/utils/** into the Location text box near the top of the Netscape window, and press Enter. Watch the status bar and you'll see a progress message (*Connect: Contacting Host*). When you connect, you'll see something like figure 11.1. (This site actually has a text message at the top of the directory listing; I scrolled down so we can see more of the files and directories.)

TIP As with the http:// URL, you don't always need to include **ftp://**. If the ftp site name begins with ftp, you can forget the **ftp://** bit. For instance, you can type **ftp.support.apple.com/pub/utils/** instead of **ftp://ftp.support.apple.com/pub/utils/**.

Fig. 11.1
Using Netscape to look at what Apple has to offer for some utility programs.

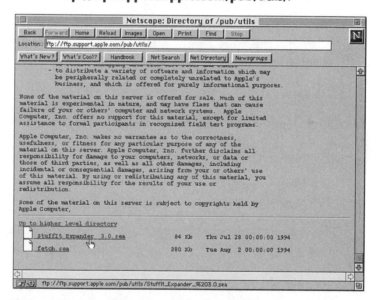

Forward Slash & Back Slash

If you've worked with DOS or Windows machines before, the slashes used in the Internet might confuse you. In the Internet, we generally use the forward slash (/) rather than a backslash (\) to separate each directory in the path. If you're really into Macintosh's directory structures, you'll notice they use the colon (:).

Each file and directory is shown as a link. On the left side of the window you'll see a column of icons—plain white "sheets" to represent files of most kinds, white "sheets" that appear to have writing on them to represent text files, white "sheets" with ones and zeros on to represent program files, and yellow folders to represent directories.

Over on the right side of the window you'll also see a column that describes the item. You'll see descriptions such as these:

Macintosh BinHex Archive—An .HQX file, an ASCII text file that contains some form of binary file—a program file, graphics file, whatever—that has been converted to ASCII so it can be transferred across the Internet's e-mail system. BinHex is commonly used on Macintosh systems. In the UNIX and PC world, the equivalent is UUENCODE (see chapter 10, "More on Viewers").

Macintosh Self Extracting Archive—An .SEA file, an archive file used on Macintosh systems.

Symbolic Link—UNIX allows **symbolic links**, special files that act as links to another directory, shortcuts through the directory system. Selecting a symbolic link is the same thing as selecting a directory.

Directory—A directory containing files and, perhaps, more subdirectories.

Plain Text—A text file; select this to read the file in the Netscape window.

Binary Executable—A program file.

Zip Compressed Data—A .ZIP file containing compressed data (see chapter 10, "More on Viewers").

GNU Zip Compressed Data—A .GZ file, an archive file used on UNIX systems.

UNIX Tape Archive—A .TAR file, another form of UNIX archive file.

No description—If there's no description shown for an item, the item is a file of some other kind. Note that just because Netscape can't figure out what the file type is right now, once you begin transferring the file Netscape will look at the list of viewers to see if you've set up one for this file type. For instance, if this is a .WAV file, the description will be blank; but if you configured Sound Recorder as the viewer, when you click on the link to this file Netscape will transfer it and open Sound Recorder.

You'll find more information about an entry, too. You can see that the file or directory's date and time of creation is shown (the date is very handy, providing an indication of how old the file is). And the size of each file, in bytes or Kbytes, is shown, too.

Click a directory link to see the contents of that directory. Netscape will display another Web document, showing the contents of that directory. There's also a link back to the previous directory—the *Up to a higher level directory* link, at the top of listing. (This is not the same as the browser's Back command, of course. It takes you to the parent directory, the one of which the current directory is a subdirectory.)

 TIP **Don't forget Archie! Archie is a system that lets you search an** index of FTP sites throughout the world for just the file you need. See "How can I find files—Working with Archie," later in this chapter, for more information.

What happens when you click a link to a file? The same thing that would happen if you did so from a true Web document. If Netscape can display or play the file type, it will; if it can't, it will try to send it to the associated application; if there is no associated application, it will ask you what to do with it, allowing you to save it on the hard disk. This all works in the same way as it does when you are at a Web site—Netscape looks at the file type and acts accordingly. For instance, if you've set up StuffIt as the "viewer" for .hqx files, when you click on a link to a .hqx file Netscape will transfer the file and open StuffIt Expander (see chapter 10, "More on Viewers," for more information.)

How can I find my way around?

Finding your way around at an FTP site is often a little difficult. There are no conventions for how such sites should be set up, so you often have to dig through directories that look as if they might contain what you want, until you find what you want.

Remember, though, that Netscape can display text files. When you first get to an FTP site, look for files that say INDEX, README, DIRECTORY, and so on. These often contain information that will help you find what you need. The more organized sites even contain text files with full indexes of their contents, or at least list of the directories and the types of files you'll find.

TIP **Many FTP sites are now accessible directly through Web docu-ments.** For instance, if you're looking for easy to find Macintosh programs, you can look at the site **ftp://mac.archive.umich.edu/**, or you could access it through the WWW directly at **http://www.archive.umich.edu**.

How Can I Find Files?—Working with Archie

With millions of files to choose from, and thousands of FTP sites spread around the Internet, it's difficult to know where to go to find the file you need. That's why Archie was developed.

Designed by a few guys at McGill University in Canada, Archie is a system that indexes FTP sites, listing the files that are available at each site. Archie lists several million files at thousands of FTP sites, and provides a surprisingly quick way to find out where to go to grab a file in which you are interested. Well, sometimes. As you'll find out, Archie is extremely busy, sometimes too busy to help you!

More Client/Server Stuff

As with many other Internet systems, Archie is set up using a "client/server" system. An Archie server is a computer that periodically takes a look at all the Internet FTP sites around the world, and builds a list of all their available files. Each server builds a database of those files. An Archie client program can then come along and search the server's database, using it as an index. Your Web browser is *not* an Archie client. That is, there is no archie:// URL! Rather, you'll have to use an Archie interface on the Web. There are dozens of these. Go to **http://web.nexor.co.uk/archie.html** to find a list. Just in case that's busy, here are several Archie sites you can try:

> **http://www.lerc.nasa.gov/archieplex/**
>
> **http://hoohoo.ncsa.uiuc.edu/archie.html**
>
> **http://src.doc.ic.ac.uk/archieplexform.html**

When you arrive at an Archie site, what sort of search are you going to do? Most of these sites offer both forms and non-forms versions. Netscape is a forms-capable browser, though. That is, it can display the forms components we've seen earlier—text boxes, command buttons, option buttons, and so on. So select the forms search.

> **TIP** **It's generally believed in Internet-land that it doesn't matter** much which Archie server you use because they all do the same thing; some are simply a few days more recent than others. This isn't always true. Sometimes you may get very different results from two different servers. If, for example, one server finds two "hits," another might find seven.

How do I search?

In figure 11.2 you can see an example of an Archie form, this one at the NASA Lewis Research Center located at **http://www.lerc.nasa.gov/archieplex/**. The simplest way to search is to type a filename, or part of a filename, into the Search For? text box and press click on the Submit button. For instance, if you are trying to find the Fetch program I told you about earlier in this chapter, you could type **Fetch** and press Enter.

> **TIP** **To cancel a search, click on the Stop toolbar button or press** ⌘+. (period).

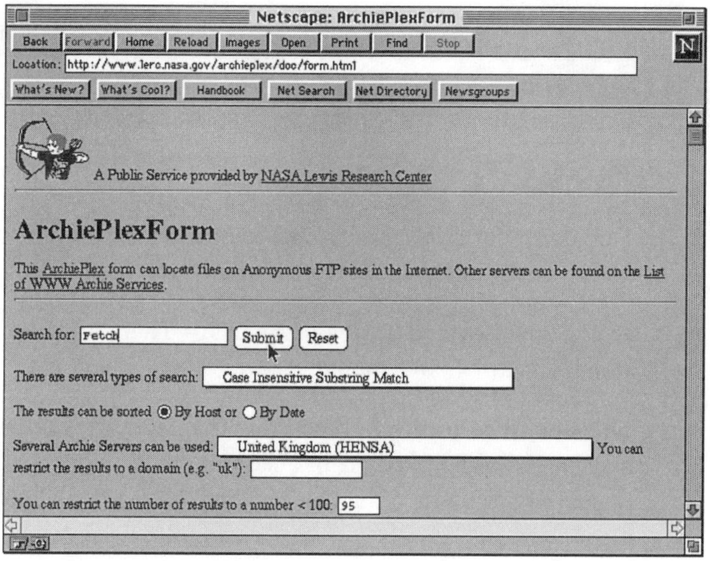

Fig. 11.2
The dozens of Archie Web sites provide a way for you to search for specific files on the Internet.

Archie searches are often very slow. In fact, they often simply don't work, because the Archie server you are working with is busy (I'll show you how to choose another server in a moment). If you are lucky, though, you'll eventually see something like figure 11.3. This shows what the Archie server found; links to the files with the characters "Fetch". You can see that there are links to the host (the computer that contains the file you are looking for), the directory on the host that contains the file you want, or directly to the file you want. For instance, if you clicked on one of the *Fetch.2.1.1.sea.hqx* links, Netscape would begin transferring the file.

Fig. 11.3
You'll find that while Archie searches do find what you're looking for, they'll find a lot of other stuff as well. If you can limit your searches, it's best to do so.

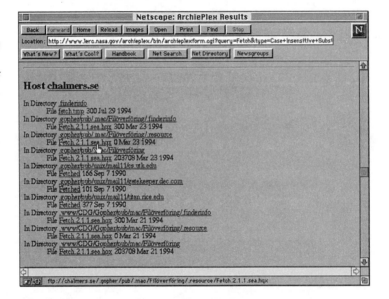

Archie's Options

The Archie form has other components, which provide more options for your search (refer to fig. 11.2). Here's what you'll find.

There Are Several Types of Search—There are four types of searches, which I'll explain in a moment.

The Results Can Be Sorted By—The list of files that is returned to you may be sorted by file date, or according to the host containing the file. The file-date search is a good idea, as it will help you pick the latest version of the file.

Several Archie Servers Can Be Used—There are Archie servers all over the world, and you can select the one you want to use from a list. If you find that the Archie server you tried is busy, or it can't find what you want, try another one. You might want to try servers in countries that are currently "asleep," and, therefore, less busy than during the day.

Restrict the Results To A Domain—You can tell the Archie server that you only want to see files in a particular domain (a particular host-computer type): UK (FTP sites in the United Kingdom), COM (commercial FTP sites), EDU (educational FTP sites) and so on.

You Can Restrict the Number Of Results to a Number—You can tell the Archie server how many results you want to see, though this setting is not always accurate.

The Impact On Other Users Can Be—You can tell Archie to be Nice (Extremely Nice, Nicest, and so on) to other people, or Not Nice At All.

Q&A *Why are the options I'm seeing different?*

Each Archie form is a little different. If you go to a different form from the one I've used as an example, you'll find that many of the labels are different. Still, they're usually close to what I've shown here—you'll be able to figure them out quite easily.

What are the Search Types?

Before you begin searching for a file name, you should figure out the type of search that you want to use. You have the following choices:

Exact or **Exact Match**   You must type the exact name of the file for which you are looking.

Regex or **Regular Expression Match**   You will type a UNIX regular expression. That means that Archie will regard some of the characters in the word you type as wild cards. (If you don't understand regular expressions, you're better off avoiding this type of search.)

Sub or **Case Insensitive Substring Match**   This tells Archie to search within file names for whatever you type. That is, it will look for all names that match what you type, as well as all names that include the characters you typed. If you are searching for *fetch*, for example, Archie will find *fetch.c* and *fetch.sea.hqx*. Also, when you use a sub search, you don't need to worry about the case of the characters; Archie will find *fetch* and *FETCH*.

Subcase or **Case Sensitive Substring Match**   This is like the sub search, except you need to enter the case of the word correctly: if you enter *fetch*, Archie will find *fetch* but not *Fetch*.

TIP   **The Substring Matches won't always find filenames that contain** what you typed. That is, if you type **fetch**, it may not find *fetch.sea.hqx*, or it may only find one or two when there are many files named *fetch.sea.hqx* at many FTP sites. Why? Because it will show you the *fetch* matches before it shows you the *fetch.sea.hqx* matches, so if there are a lot of *fetch* matches it may exceed the find limit (see **You Can** Restrict the Number Of Results to a Number in the table under "Archie's Options"). You can increase the number of results and search again, though, to see if there are any *fetch.sea.hqx* files. Or search for *fetch.sea.hqx*.

More often than not, you'll want to use the sub search (Case Insensitive Substring Match), and you'll probably find that sub has been set up as the default. It takes a little longer than the other types, but it's more likely to find what you are looking for.

You should know, however, that file names are not always set in stone. With thousands of different people posting millions of different files on thousands of different computers, sometimes file names get changed a little. If you have trouble finding something, try a variety of different possible combinations.

A different way to do the same thing—only easier

Since the Internet has become so popular, the sites maintain the massive archives of software have also become very popular. It didn't take long until someone made an index of them that you can search on the web. The two largest software archives (each has over a dozen mirror sites around the world) are **sumex-aim.stanford.edu** and **mac.archive.umich.edu**. At the site **http://www.tocnet.com/~baron/umich/** there is an index of Macintosh programs specifically—so when you type in "fetch" (as shown in fig. 11.4), you won't find dozens of listings of things you aren't interested in.

Fig. 11.4

With this search engine, you can also search the descriptions of the programs, which can make finding that tidbit of software much easier.

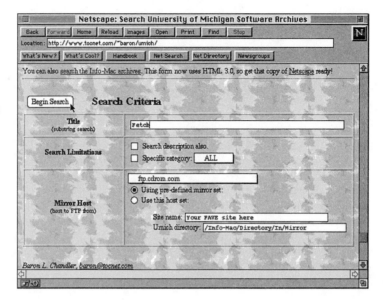

12

E-mail with Netscape

- ## In this chapter:

- Setting up Netscape to work with e-mail

- Sending messages

- How can I send files, Web documents, and URLs?

- The address book

- How can I retrieve e-mail messages?

- Reading and managing messages

Netscape can help you with all of your major Internet chores…including your e-mail . . . .

Many browsers allow you to send e-mail. It's almost an essential browser function these days because so many documents use an HTML code requesting them to send mail; click on a link with this code and the browser's e-mail program opens.

The To field is already filled in for you with the address in the HTML code the author set up. All you need to do is write the message and click on Send.

Until recently, most browsers would let you send e-mail, but you couldn't read e-mail that people sent you. Netscape 1.0 came bundled with a program to allow you to read the e-mail—Eudora. But now, Netscape 2.0 has built in the features so you can read e-mail with Netscape. You could still use Eudora, but Netscape's set it up so you don't have to have two programs. With Netscape 2.0 you can work with attached files, create folders, view your messages in a "threaded" view, and more.

Setting up e-mail

Before you can use the e-mail system, you need to enter information into the Preferences dialog box. Choose <u>O</u>ptions, <u>M</u>ail and News, then click on the Directories tab, to see the dialog box in figure 12.1.

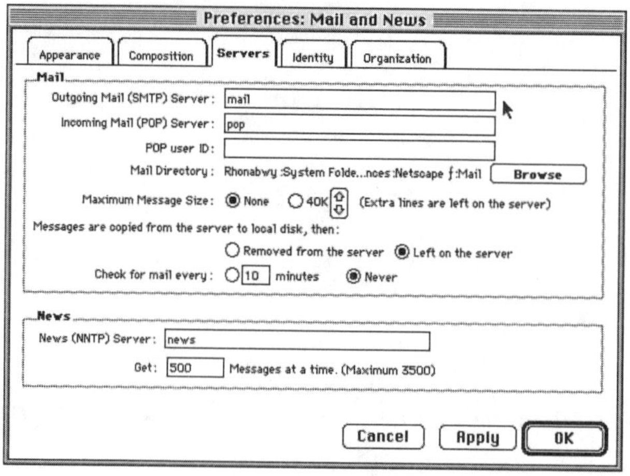

Fig. 12.1
This is the panel where you tell Netscape how to send and receive your mail. If you're having a problem with e-mail, it's probably going to be fixed on this panel.

```
                    Preferences: Mail and News
  ┌─────────┬────────────┬────────┬─────────┬──────────────┐
  │Appearance│ Composition │Servers │ Identity │ Organization │
  ┌─Mail───────────────────────────────────────────────────────
  │    Outgoing Mail (SMTP) Server : │mail                        │    ▶
  │    Incoming Mail (POP) Server : │pop                         │
  │            POP user ID : │                            │
  │         Mail Directory : Rhonabwy :System Folde...nces:Netscape ƒ:Mail  [ Browse ]
  │    Maximum Message Size : ◉ None  ○ 40K ▭  (Extra lines are left on the server)
  │  Messages are copied from the server to local disk, then :
  │                          ○ Removed from the server  ◉ Left on the server
  │         Check for mail every : ○[10] minutes  ◉ Never
  ┌─News───────────────────────────────────────────────────────
  │    News (NNTP) Server : │news                        │
  │              Get : [500]  Messages at a time. (Maximum 3500)
                              [ Cancel ]  [ Apply ]  [ OK ]
```

Right now we're only used to the top area, the Mail area. The News area is related to newsgroups, which we'll look at in chapter 13 "UseNet News." Enter the following information:

Mail (SMTP) Server   You must enter the address of your SMTP (Simple Mail Transfer Protocol) server. This is the system to which Netscape will send e-mail messages (ask your service provider what to enter). If you don't have this field filled out correctly, you won't be able to send mail.

Mail (POP) Server   Enter the address of your POP (Post Office Protocol) server, the system that holds your incoming e-mail until you log on to retrieve it. Again, ask your service provider what to enter here. If you don't have this field filled out correctly, you won't be able to receive mail.

Mail Directory   This is the directory on your hard disk where Netscape will store the mail-related files (the files containing the messages, for instance). There's no need to change this.

Messages are Copied From the Server to the Local Disk and Then   These two option buttons define what Netscape tells the POP server to do with your messages. If you select Removed From the Server, once Netscape has retrieved your e-mail it tells the POP server to delete the messages—if you try to retrieve them later using a different e-mail program they won't be there. If you select Left on the server, Netscape doesn't tell the POP server to delete the messages—you can retrieve them with another e-mail program later. You may want to use this option until you are sure you want to use Netscape to handle all of your e-mail.

Now click on the Identity tab, to see the information in figure 12.2. In this area you are going to tell Netscape how you want to be identified in your messages. Enter these items:

Your Name   Type your name here. This will be included on the From line of your outgoing messages, along with your e-mail address.

Your e-mail   Type your e-mail address. Again, this goes on the From line.

Reply-to Address You can enter a different Reply-to Address, if you wish, so that replies to your e-mail are sent to a different address. Most users will ignore this option—it's useful if you have more than one e-mail address.

Your Organization When posting messages to newsgroups you can include an Organization line that identifies you by your company name, for instance. See chapter 13 "UseNet News" for information about newsgroups.

Signature File A signature file is a text file containing some kind of "blurb" that's inserted into the end of an e-mail message. You've seen other people use these—they often contain the person's name and address, phone numbers, other e-mail addresses, and so on. Sometimes they also contain a favorite quote, or some kind of advertising blurb. If you want to use a signature file, type the text in a word processor or TeachText. Limit it to about 65 characters across, and place a carriage return at the end of each line. Don't use more than four or five lines. Many Internet users get irritated by long signature files. Save the file—make sure you save it as ASCII text, if using a word processor (TeachText saves in ASCII automatically). Then click on the Browse button in the Preferences dialog box to select the filename and place it in the Signature File text box (see fig. 12.2).

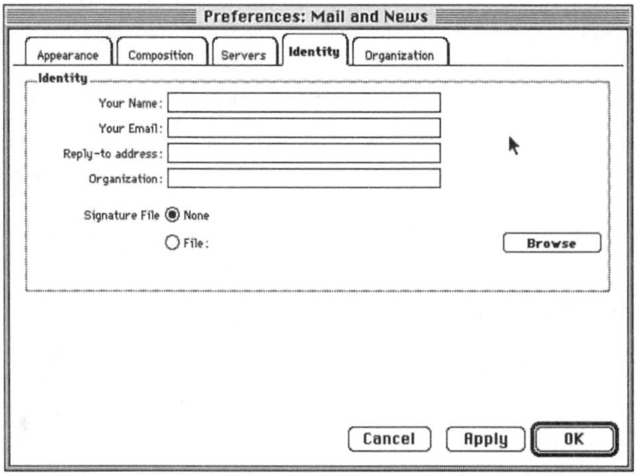

Fig. 12.2

Tell Netscape what identifying information you want to include in your e-mail and newsgroup messages. This is information about you, instead of information about the servers that you'll use.

Now click on the Composition tab to see the information in figure 12.3. This time you're going to tell Netscape what to do when you are composing outgoing e-mail messages:

Send and Post—These two fields allow you to choose how you're going to send mail or post to a newsgroup.

Allow 8-bit—This allows you to send 8-bit characters across e-mail—this may foul up some of your messages unless you know the person you're sending to can receive 8-bit messages.

MIME Compliant (Quoted Printable)—This is the Internet standard for sending e-mail—it allows you to send 8-bit characters by encoding them into a standard format. You will probably want to stick with this option.

Deliver Mail—These options tell Netscape exactly *when* to send messages.

Automatically—Select this to tell Netscape to send a message as soon as you've finished writing it—when you click on the Send button.

Queue for Manual Delivery—Select this to tell Netscape not to send the e-mail when you click on the Send button. Rather, Netscape stores the message (in the message "queue"), and sends all the messages in the queue when you choose File, Deliver Mail Now.

By Default, e-mail a Copy of Outgoing Message to—If you wish, you can tell Netscape to send a copy of every message you send to another e-mail account. Perhaps you plan to use the Netscape e-mail system only for sending e-mail, and want to keep a record of all the messages you send in your main e-mail program.

By Default, Copy Outgoing Message to the File—Netscape will place a copy of every message you send in the file specified in the Mail File text box. There's no need to change this.

Automatically Quote Original Message When Replying—"Quoting" in Netspeak is placing an original message inside a reply. Select this check box to automatically copy all of the original message's text into the reply. Each line of that text will be preceded by >, to indicate that it's quoted.

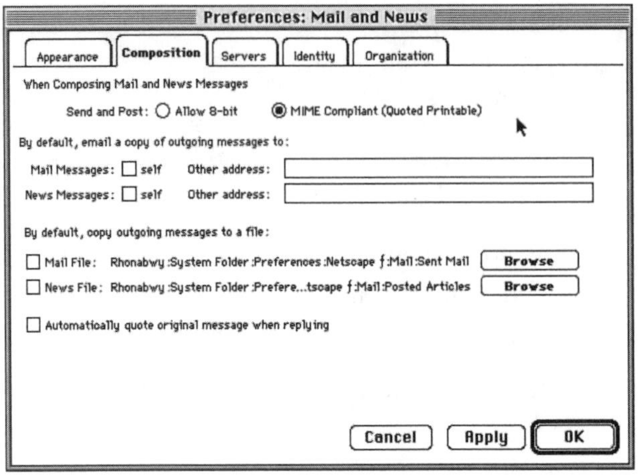

Fig. 12.3

Tell Netscape what to do when you send e-mail messages

There are two other mail option areas. Under the Appearance tab you can define the type of text you want to use for your mail messages—this simply determines what the text will look like when you are reading it, not what text in messages that you send will look like to the recipient. Under the Organization tab, you can tell Netscape to "thread" your messages—that is when replies to your messages are shown next to the original message, making it easier to figure out what's going on. You can tell Netscape how to sort your messages in the message list—by date, subject, or sender. (By default, messages are threaded, and sorted by date.)

Sending e-mail

We'll begin by looking at the basic browser e-mail function—sending e-mail messages. There are four ways to open the Compose window, the window in which you will write an e-mail message:

- Click on a mailto: link in a Web document. You'll often see Internet e-mail addresses in documents that are colored and underlined just like any other link. Hold the mouse pointer over the link and you'll see the URL in the status bar; something like **mailto:william@rotary.com**.

- Type the mailto: URL into the Location bar (type **mailto:robinhood@sherwoodforest.com**, for instance) and press Enter.

- Choose <u>F</u>ile, <u>N</u>ew Mail Message.

- Choose File, <u>M</u>ail Document to send a copy of the current document to someone.

- In the Netscape Mail window (which we'll look at later in this chapter), click on the New Message toolbar button.

- In the Netscape Mail window, choose <u>M</u>essage, <u>N</u>ew Mail Message.

Whichever method you use, the Message Composition window opens; you can see an example in figure 12.4. With the first two examples—using a link that has the mailto: URL, or entering the mailto: URL directly into the Location text box—you'll notice that the e-mail address is already filled in for you.

Fig. 12.4
Write your message and click on the Send button.

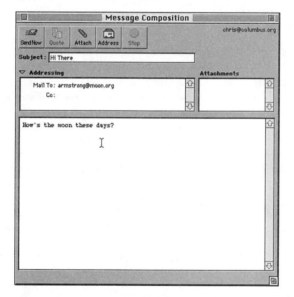

Open the <u>V</u>iew menu. You'll see a list of text fields that you can display at the top of the Message Composition window: Reply To, Mail To, Mail Cc, and so on. You can select from this list, or you can choose <u>V</u>iew, <u>S</u>how All to display all of them at once. By default the window already has four text boxes, as you can see from figure 12.4. Here's a quick description of all the available text boxes:

From	This is your name and e-mail address, from the Mail and News Preferences dialog box.
Mail To/Send To	The Send To text box (identified as Mail To on the View menu), is the address of the person you are sending the message to. If you clicked on a mailto: link or typed a mailto: URL into the Location text box, this is already filled in. Otherwise, type the e-mail address.
Subject	Type a subject if you wish—a quick description of the message contents. If you chose the File, Mail Document from the Netscape window the current Web document's title will appear here.
Attachment	If you are sending a file (you'll see how in "Sending non-text files", later in this chapter), the filename will appear here.
Reply To	This is from the Mail and News Preferences dialog box, though you can enter a different Reply To address if you wish.
Mail Cc/Cc	Choose View, Mail Cc to display the Cc text box (yes, I know this is confusing, having one title on the menu and another on the window, but that's the way they wrote it!). You can then enter the e-mail address of someone to whom you'd like to send a copy of this message.
Mail Bcc/Blind Cc	Choose View, Mail Bcc to display the Blind Cc text field. You can also enter the e-mail address of someone to whom you wish to send a copy of the message. When you use Cc, the address of the person receiving the copy is added to the message header, so the original recipient can see that a copy was sent. But when you send a **blind copy** (Blind Cc), there's no indication in the original recipient's message of a copy being sent.
File Cc	This field only appears if you choose View, Show All. It shows you the file in which a copy of the outgoing message is saved (from the Mail and News Preferences dialog box). You can delete this text, if you don't want to save a copy, or even enter a different filename.
Post To/Newsgroups	Choose View, Post To to display the Newsgroups text box. You can use this to send a copy of the message to a newsgroup. This text box is really intended for use while working with newsgroups—see chapter 13 (UseNet News)—though you can send a message to a newsgroup at the same time you send e-mail to someone. Simply enter the newsgroup name.

Followup To	This field is used when you are responding to newsgroup messages (the same window is used for both e-mail and newsgroup messages). It identifies to which newsgroup you want replies to your message sent.

Once you've entered all the necessary information at the top of the window, place the cursor into the large text area and type your message. Then, when you've finished, click on the Send button, or choose File, Send Message. If you chose Deliver Mail Automatically in the Mail and News Preferences dialog box, Netscape now sends the message out across the Internet. Otherwise it places the message in a queue; it won't send the message until you open the Netscape Mail window (choose Window, Netscape Mail in the main Netscape window) and then choose File, Deliver Mail Now.

Sending the Web document

Do you want to send the Web document you've been viewing to someone? There are several ways to do so. First, try this. Open the Web document you want to mail, and choose File, Mail Document.

Netscape will copy all the text from the current Web document into your Message Composition window, replacing the graphics with [Image] (or its ALT tag if it had one). This is just the text that you can read, not all the HTML tags, by the way. Each line of the text will be preceded by >, to indicate that it's "quoted" text (see fig. 12.5).

You can also send the URL to the document. Okay, this isn't *quite* the same as sending the document itself. But when we're talking about a hypertext system such as the Web, this is almost the same thing…assuming the document is still available and the recipient has access to the Web. Netscape turns the URL into an active link. Try this:

1 In the Netscape window, choose File, Mail Document. Netscape will open the Message Composition window, and place the URL of the current document on the first line of the message (see fig. 12.5).

2 Add a message or comments above or below the URL text.

3 Click on the Send button to send the message to your friend or associate.

4 When the recipient opens the message, he can copy the URL into his browser's URL box to go directly to the document. If he received the e-mail in Netscape 2.0 he'll find that the URL is shown as a link (see "Neat stuff in messages," later in this chapter). All he needs to do is click on the link to display the document in the Netscape window.

Fig. 12.5
I placed the URL into the message by choosing File, Mail Document in the Netscape window, then placed the document text there by choosing Edit, Quote Message.

Here's another way to send the document text:

1 Open the Message Composition window.

2 Click on the Attach button or choose File, Attach File. The Mail/News Attachments dialog box opens (see fig. 12.6).

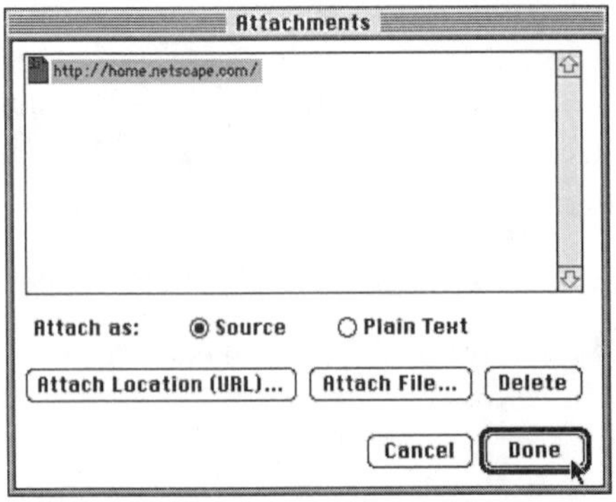

Fig. 12.
You can use this box to attach a URL you're not looking at, or send a file on your machine.

3 In the dialog box that opens, you'll see a button for "Attach Location (URL)..." and "Attach File....". Click on the "Attach Location (URL)..." and type in the URL of the document you want to send (shown in fig. 12.7).

Fig. 12.7
You can type in any URL—even ones you haven't seen yet.

4 Click on the listed URL and choose either the Source or Plain Text option button. If you choose Plain Text, Netscape will send the rendered document—that's the document without any tags in it. If you want to include all the HTML source text, tags and all, choose the Source option button.

5 Click on the Done button and the dialog box closes. You'll see the URL has been placed into the Attachment text box near the top of the window.

6 Write a message, enter the Send To address and any other information you need to include, then click on the Send button to send the message.

7 When Netscape sends the message, it will include the specified text at the end of the message.

What's the difference between the Quote Message and Attach methods?

The difference has to do with MIME. If you quote the document, then the rendered text shows up in the mail message you're sending to someone. When you attach a document, it gets put "outside" of the mail message, but where most mailers can see it. Some older mailers can't read attached documents, so if you're not sure, you might want to use Quote Message to insure the text gets there.

Generally, if a mailer is MIME compliant, it can read and handle attachments.

Sending non-text files

Netscape's e-mail system is intended to be a full replacement for your present e-mail system. No e-mail program would be complete without the ability to send binary files as attachments. What do I mean by "binary files?" (After all, aren't all computer files binary files?) Well, the term generally refers to any computer file that is not ASCII text. You can send ASCII text by simply inserting it into a message—your e-mail message is ASCII text, too. But if you want to send something else (a word-processing file, spreadsheet file, image file, or whatever), you can't just place it in the message, you have to use a program that is able to somehow "attach" the file to the message.

There are generally two ways to do this. One's called BinHex, the other's called MIME. (There's also UUEncode, a system used on UNIX, DOS and Windows, which is very similar to BinHex.) Netscape uses the MIME system. That means that the recipient of the message must be using MIME, too. Here's how to send a file using e-mail:

1 Click on the Attach button, or choose <u>F</u>ile, Attach <u>F</u>ile.

2 In the Mail/News Attachment dialog box (fig. 12.6), click on the File option button.

3 Click on the Browse button.

4 In the Enter File to Attach dialog box, find the file you want to attach and double-click on it.

5 Back in the Mail/News Attachment dialog box, select the file you want to attach and click on the Done button. The dialog box disappears; you'll see the path and filename of the file you selected in the Attachment text box near the top of the Message Composition window.

6 Click on the Send button. When Netscape sends the e-mail message, it converts the binary file and includes it with the message.

TIP **BinHex won't work for Windows users very well. While there is a** version of BinHex for Windows, most people aren't familiar with it and won't be able to use your documents. If you can send them using the MIME format, it's generally better.

How can I send a file to someone whose e-mail program doesn't use MIME?

You have a couple of options. You can tell the recipient to get the Mpack program, which will take the MIME message—it will appear like a jumble of text—and convert it back to the original binary file. (You can find Mpack, at **ftp.andrew.cmu.edu/pub/mpack/**, or by searching for mpack at **http:// vsl.cnet.com/**.) Or you can use the BinHex system. To use that you'll need to get the program BinHex, or some other program which can encode a Macintosh file into BinHex format (StuffIt Lite, for example). Run this program and convert your file into BinHex (it will generally have a suffix of ".hqx" after it) and then you can attach that or even copy and paste it into your e-mail message.

Other things you can do

There are a variety of other minor procedures that can be carried out in the Message Composition window:

Switch to another window—You probably know this, but just in case…you can switch to another window, the Netscape window for instance. Just move the window off to the side and click on the other window you want to view.

Select all the text—Choosing Edit, Select All will select all of the text in the composition area.

Use ROT13—I'll explain ROT13 in the newsgroup chapter (chapter 13, "UseNet News"). This is a method to scramble text by shifting each character 13 characters along in the alphabet (a becomes n, b becomes o, and so on). Try it!

Save the message—Choose File, Save As to save a copy of the message in a text file before you send it.

Print the message—Choose File, Page Setup to define how you want to print your message, then choose File, Print Message(s) to print the message.

Open the address book—Huh, the address book? We'll get to that now.

Using the address book

Netscape has a very simple address book. You can open this from the Netscape, Netscape Mail, or Message Composition window, by choosing Window, Address Book. You'll see a simple box with an icon of a pair of faces at the top (as shown in fig 12.8).

Fig. 12.8
This gives you an overview of all your addresses in your address book.

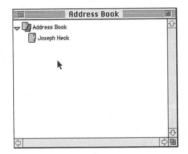

Adding a name to the address book

First, here's how you add a name to your address book:

1 Choose Item, Add User. You'll see a small dialog box with several fields as shown in figure 12.9.

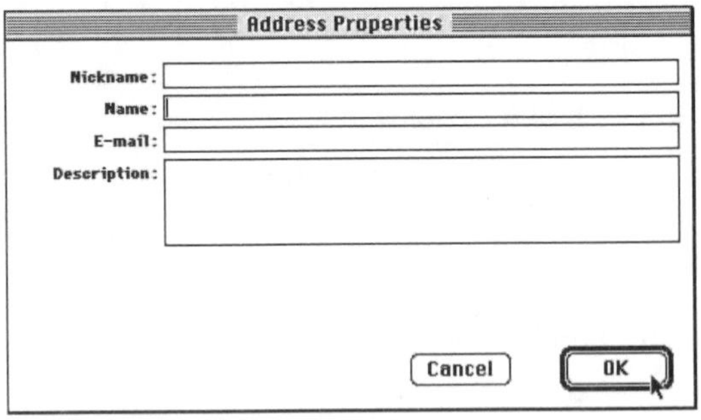

Fig. 12.9
You can type whatever you like in description—it doesn't get sent out to anyone, it's just there for your reference.

2 Type a nickname. This is a name you can use when entering e-mail addresses into the text boxes at the top of the Message Composition window. For instance, if you want to add the **robinhood@sherwoodforest.com** e-mail address to your address book, you might type robinh as the nickname. Then, when you want to send a message to Robin all you need to do is type robinh into the Message Composition window's Send To field.

3 Type the <u>N</u>ame. This is the name by which this entry will be shown in the address book; for instance, type `Robin Hood`.

4 Type the <u>e</u>-mail Address for this person.

5 Type a <u>D</u>escription, if you wish. This can be anything you want, any kind of notes you want to keep.

6 Click on the OK button and the new person is added to the address book (you may need to double-click on the address book folder to see the entry).

You can view (and modify) an entry's information later, by double-clicking on it or by choosing Properties (or click once and choose <u>I</u>tem, <u>P</u>roperties).

Creating a list of people

You can also create a list of people. If you had three people you always wanted to share some information with, you might make a list of them and send the mail to that list.

To create a list:

1 Choose <u>I</u>tem, <u>A</u>dd List. You'll see a small dialog box with several fields as shown in figure 12.10.

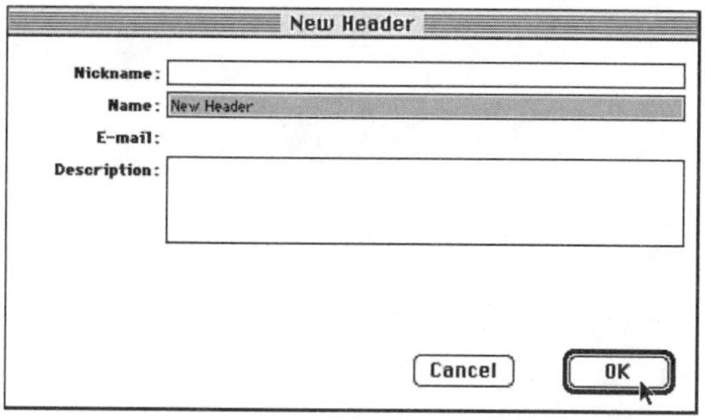

Fig. 12.10

This is very similar to making a normal nickname except you can't specify the e-mail address.

2 Type a nickname. This is a name you can use when you want to send mail to everyone in that list at once.

3 Type the <u>N</u>ame. This is just a name by which you reference everyone— or a name of the list of people, like `my friends`.

4 Type a Description, if you wish. This can be anything you want, any kind of notes about this person that you wish to keep.

5 Click on the OK button and you'll see an icon of a pair of faces show up in your address book.

Once you've created the list, you can drag the icons of one person onto the list icon, and you'll see the names show up below it—italicized—to indicate they've been added to that list.

TIP **You keep your lists pretty compact by clicking on the little tri-angle to the left of the list icons. Clicking on it will toggle the window to show you everything beneath the icon or not in an outline form.**

Other features of the address book

You can delete addresses from your address book as well. Select the address you want to remove and choose Edit, Delete Address. If you select an address that's italicized, it'll only delete that one (it's called an alias). If you choose a normal address, it will ask you if you want to delete all the references to that address as well (its aliases).

Finally, you can mail to someone in your address book by double-clicking on the icon. That will bring up the Message Composition window with all the "To:" addresses filled out.

The Netscape Mail window

Well, we've seen how to send e-mail. How about dealing with the tons of e-mail that you're going to *receive*? You'll do that in the Netscape Mail window, which you can open by choosing Window, Netscape Mail. You can see an example in figure 12.11.

There are three panes in this window:

Folders—The top left pane shows you your e-mail folders. It will contain an Inbox folder. Later, when you delete messages, there will also be a Trash folder. You can add more, too. The columns to the right of the folder icons show you how many messages are within the folders, and how many of the messages are unread.

Messages—The top right pane shows a list of the e-mail messages in the folder selected in the top left pane. The columns show the Sender name, whether you've marked the message (the column with the purple flags), whether you've read the message (the column with the green diamond), and the message Subject. (We'll look at the marked and read columns later in this chapter.)

Message text—The bottom pane shows the text in the message that you've selected in the top right pane. (Double-click on a message to see the text.)

Fig. 12.11
The Netscape Mail window allows you to organize your incoming mail.

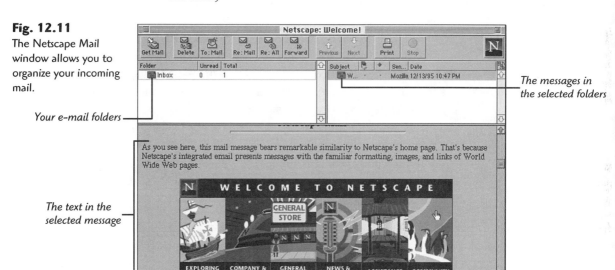

Your e-mail folders

The messages in the selected folders

The text in the selected message

Getting your mail

 The procedure for getting your e-mail is simple; click on the Get New Mail toolbar button or choose <u>F</u>ile, <u>G</u>et New Mail. You'll see a dialog box (as shown in fig. 12.12) asking for your password; this is the password you use to log into your e-mail system and retrieve your e-mail.

Fig. 12.12
The password you enter here is usually the same as your password to your account with your service provider.

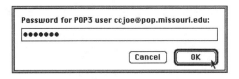

Password for POP3 user ccjoe@pop.missouri.edu:

●●●●●●●

Cancel   OK

Q&A *I don't want to retrieve my mail right away, just read the messages that I already have. What do I do?*

You don't even have to be online when you open the Netscape Mail window. When the dialog box prompts you for your password, simply click on Cancel. You'll be able to read your messages. When you are ready to retrieve new ones, log on to the Internet and then click on the Get New Mail button or choose File, Get New Mail.

Netscape then goes to your service provider's POP server and grabs the e-mail. In a few moments you'll see new mail icons appear in the top right pane, and the contents of the first unread message will appear in the bottom pane. You won't have to enter your password each time you retrieve e-mail; only the first time during a session. Of course, you can change that, too. If you want Netscape to remember your password all the time, you can choose Options, Mail and News Preferences... and click on the tab labeled Organization. In the dialog box that appears (it's shown in fig. 12.13), click on the checkbox next to Remember Mail Password, and Netscape will keep your password in its preferences.

Fig. 12.13
Although Netscape will remember your password, if you ever change it with your service provider, you'll need to turn this option off.

Preferences: Mail and News

| Appearance | Composition | Servers | Identity | **Organization** |

☐ Remember Mail Password

Mail Messages and News Articles can be threaded. Threading means that if you receive a reply, it will be shown next to the original message.

☐ Thread Mail Messages
☒ Thread News Messages

Sorting
Sort Mail by : ⦿ Date ○ Message Number ○ Subject ○ Sender
Sort News by : ⦿ Date ○ Message Number ○ Subject ○ Sender

Cancel   Apply   OK

How do I get people to send me e-mail?

Oh, no e-mail waiting for you? Well, I can't tell you how to make friends and get them to send e-mail to you. But you can test the e-mail system by sending messages to yourself. Follow the instructions for sending e-mail earlier in this chapter, and enter your own e-mail address in the Send To text box. Also, you should already have a message from Mozilla, the Netscape mascot. (This message is placed into the Inbox when you install Netscape.)

So, what will you find in your message? You'll see the message header—the Subject, Date, From, Reply To, and To information at the top of the message. Then you'll see the actual message text. An example of what the screen will look like after you've retrieved your mail is shown in figure 12.14.

Fig. 12.14
Depending on the size of your screen, things may be squished up a bit. You can move those borders with your mouse to make more room.

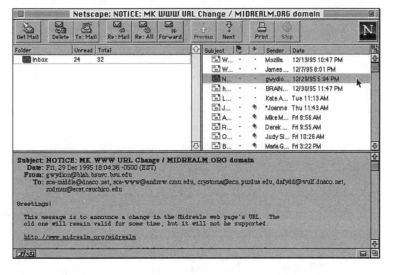

Where's the rest of the message header?

You may know that there's a lot more to a message header than is shown in the message in figure 12.14. There's all sorts of rubbish (Return-Path:, Received:, Message-Id: X-Sender:, and so on) that most people don't want to see, and which just clutters up the message pane. If you *do* want to see this stuff (it's sometimes useful when trying to figure out where a message came from), choose Options, Show All Headers.

Neat stuff in messages

A great reason for using Netscape is when you receive a piece of mail with a URL in it, Netscape will make that reference an active link. If you put your pointer over it, it will change into the hand pointer you're used to seeing when using Netscape to browse the Web. Click on the link and the referenced document will appear in the Netscape window.

Because Netscape treats your e-mail messages like Web pages, rendering the text just as it does with an HTML document, you can see more in the message. If the person who sent the message went through the trouble, you'll also see Web formatting.

TIP **It's unlikely in e-mail—this is more of a newsgroup feature—but** you might receive a jumbled up message, a ROT13 message. ROT13 "rotates" the characters in a message so that a becomes n, b becomes o, and so on. Choose <u>V</u>iew, <u>U</u>nscramble (ROT13). Using ROT13 is kind of a quick encryption – it's something you might do if you don't want it immediately obvious what you're saying. If the message is still unintelligible, you've probably got a UUEncoded message, or someone's sent you some kind of encrypted message. See chapter 13 (UseNet News) for more information about ROT13 and UUEncode.

You may also find pictures inside your messages. If someone sends a message containing a MIME or UUEncoded picture, in the .JPG or .GIF format, that picture will be displayed in your message. I've covered this in more detail in chapter 13 (UseNet News), because pictures are often placed into newsgroup messages.

Moving between messages

So, how do you move from one message to the next? Well, when Netscape first transfers messages, it highlights the first unread message, and displays the contents in the bottom pane. You can click on any other message, to see that message's text. You can also use the menu and toolbar commands:

  Click on the Previous Unread button or choose <u>G</u>o, Pre<u>v</u>ious Unread to read the previous message that you haven't yet read.

  Click on the Next Unread button or choose <u>G</u>o, Ne<u>x</u>t Unread to read the next message that you haven't yet read.

Choose Go, First Unread to read the first unread message in the list.

Choose Go, Next Message to read the next message in the list, whether you've read it or not.

Choose Go, Previous Message to read the previous message in the list, whether you've read it or not.

Replying to messages

If you'd like to reply to or forward a message, you have a few options:

 Reply to the person who sent the message—Click on the Reply button, or choose Message, Reply.

 Reply to the sender and other recipients—Click on the Reply to All button, or choose Message, Reply to All, to send a response to the person who sent the message, *and* to all the people who received copies of the message.

 Send a copy of the message to someone else—To send the message on to another person, click on the Forward button or choose Reply, Forward.

In each case, the Message Composition window will open. Some of the information will be filled in for you; the Send To fields will be filled in if you chose to reply to the message, and the entire text of the message will be in the content area if you are forwarding the message (you can add more of your own text, if you wish). Also, if you chose the Automatically Quote Original Message When Replying check box in the Mail and News Preferences dialog box, the Message Composition window will include the message text (each line preceded by >) in your replies.

About message threads

You saw earlier in this chapter that the Mail and News Preferences dialog box allows you to "thread" your mail messages. That is, when a reply to one of your messages is retrieved, Netscape Mail places the reply indented below the original message in the list. Choose Options, Mail and News, then click on the Organization tab. You'll see the same dialog box as shown in figure 12.13. If you'd like to use this feature, make sure that the Thread Mail Messages check box has been selected.

You can also turn this feature on and off within the Netscape Mail window by choosing View, Sort, Thread Messages.

Working with folders

When you first begin working with Netscape Mail, you'll find that there's only one folder, the Inbox. Others will be added automatically; when you delete a folder, Netscape will create a Trash folder, and place the deleted message there. When you send a message, it will create a Sent folder, and place a copy in that folder. If you want to get rid of those files in the Trash folder, choose File, Empty Trash Folder, and you'll see the items listed in it drop to 0. There's an example of the emptied trash folder after it's been added in figure 12.15.

Fig. 12.15

The trash folder is just another folder to Netscape—except that when you delete things out of it, they're gone for good.

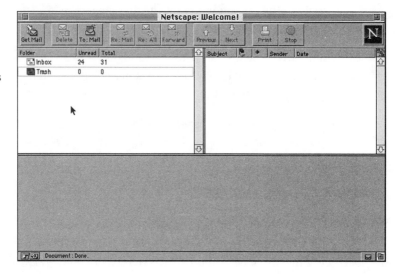

 Q&A *I don't always want to place a copy of an outgoing message in the Sent folder; how do I stop this from happening?*

In the Message Composition window choose <u>V</u>iew, Show <u>A</u>ll, then delete all the text in the Fi<u>l</u>e Cc text box.

You can create your own folders, too. Choose <u>F</u>ile, <u>N</u>ew Folder, type a folder name, and press Enter. You might create a variety of folders for different purposes: Business, Family, Friends, one for each mailing list, and so on.

Right now, there's no way to get Netscape to automatically place messages into the correct folder—when Netscape retrieves e-mail messages from your POP server it places them all in the Inbox. But, as you'll see, you can move messages from one folder to another.

You can sort the messages in your folders. Choose View, <u>S</u>ort and a cascading menu will open. You can then choose to sort the messages by the <u>D</u>ate, <u>S</u>ubject, or Sen<u>d</u>er. You can also turn threading on and off here, and turn the <u>A</u>scending search on and off (for instance, when sorting by date, an <u>A</u>scending search would put the most recent messages at the top; turn off <u>A</u>scending to put the most recent messages at the bottom).

 Netscape Mail always puts incoming messages at the bottom of the Inbox list, regardless of the type of sorting you selected. Choose <u>V</u>iew, <u>S</u>ort, <u>R</u>esort to place the messages in their correct positions.

Moving and copying messages between folders

You can quickly shift messages from one folder to another. Select the message or messages that you want to move, then choose <u>M</u>essage, <u>M</u>ove to open a small cascading menu showing all the folders. Select the folder into which you wish to place the message.

You can use the same method to copy messages between folders, too; this time choose <u>M</u>essage, <u>C</u>opy.

 You can carry out operations on several messages at once. Select multiple messages by holding the Command key while you click on each one; by clicking on the first in a block, pressing Shift, and clicking on the last in a block; by choosing <u>E</u>dit, Select <u>A</u>ll Messages; by choosing <u>E</u>dit, Select <u>M</u>arked messages (to select just those messages that have been marked—the ones with the Purple flags next to them); and by clicking on a message and then choosing <u>E</u>dit, Select <u>T</u>hread to select that message and all the other messages in a thread.

Marking messages—the Marked and Read columns

In the top right pane, the message-list pane, you'll see two columns: one with purple flags and one with a green diamond. The purple flags are for **marked** messages. You can mark a message by simply clicking on the space in the column under the flag—you should see a little flag appear (I've shown an example in fig. 12.16). If it's not marked, all you'll see there is a little dot. You can unmark the message by clicking on the flag again, or by choosing Message, Unflag Message.

Fig. 12.16

You'll notice that the message I've clicked on lost its green diamond (meaning it's been read) and I've chosen to mark with (the purple flag is showing).

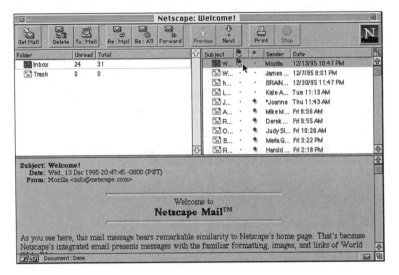

Why bother marking messages? Well, it's a way to group them for an operation. For instance, let's say you receive 20 e-mail messages (easy to do if you subscribe to one of the Internet's thousands of mailing-list discussion groups). As you read each one, you mark the ones you want to shift to another folder. When you've finished reading and marking, you then choose Edit, Select Flagged Messages. Netscape will highlight all the messages you have marked. Now you can choose to forward all those messages, move them into a folder, or perhaps just delete them.

You can also mark messages as read or unread. When Netscape retrieves your messages, each—except the first, which Netscape highlights—is marked with a green diamond (in the Read column). The green diamond means that you haven't yet read this message. Once you've read the message (you click on the message, for instance), the green diamond is removed, showing that you've read the message.

But perhaps you want to mark a message that you have just read as *unread*. Why? Two reasons: you may want to keep the green diamond as a reminder to reread the message, and you may want to make sure that the message remains in the list. You see, there's a Options, Show only unread messages command. By default, this is turned on, so that all the messages in a folder, whether read or unread, will be displayed. But if you choose Options, Show only unread messages, Netscape will only show you the unread messages. So if you commonly use this command you'll want to mark messages as unread if you need to remember to re-read them.

Cleaning up the folders

There are several ways you can save disk space by "cleaning" your folders:

Delete messages—If you no longer need a message, delete it; click on it and then click on the Delete button, or press the delete key, or choose Edit, Delete Message. The message is moved into the Trash folder.

Empty the trash—You can remove messages from the Trash folder the same way. Or remove them all at once by choosing File, Empty Trash Folder.

Delete an empty folder—If you don't need a folder anymore, delete it; click on it and press delete, or choose Edit, Delete Folder.

Compress the folders—Now and again click on a folder and choose File, Compress This Folder to free any disk space used by the folder that is no longer needed (because you've deleted files). Or choose File, Compress All Folders to compress them all at once.

13

UseNet News

● **In this chapter:**

- ● Opening newsgroups from Netscape

- ● What is the newsgroup hierarchy system?

- ● Reading newsgroup messages

- ● Where have the messages gone?

- ● Responding to messages, and starting your own "conversations"

- ● Grabbing sounds and pictures from newsgroups

Netscape provides a link to thousands of discussion groups— through its newsgroups window. . . . . ❯

You may already be familiar with Internet newsgroups. They are discussion groups. Pick a subject, visit the group, read people's messages, respond, start your own "threads" or conversations, and so on. There are tens of thousands of Internet newsgroups spread around the world, on every conceivable subject.

Now, you can't get to all these newsgroups through your service provider. Most Internet newsgroups are of local interest only, and are not distributed throughout the world. But thousands are, through a system known as UseNet. Each online service has to decide which of these UseNet newsgroups it wants to subscribe to. Service providers typically provide from 3,000 to 6,000 groups to around 10,000 or 12,000. Enough to keep a chronic insomniac *very* busy.

 Plain English, please!

News or **Journalism**—which is it?

The Internet uses the word "news" ambiguously. Often, when you see a reference to news somewhere on the Internet, it refers to the messages left in newsgroups (not, as most real peopie would imagine, journalists' reports on current affairs). Newsgroups are, in most cases, discussion groups, though there are some newsgroups that contain real news—real journalism—stories. **99**

Netscape's newsgroup system

Netscape provides a great newsgroup program, integrated into the browser. It's sort of two-way integrated; as you'll see, you can open newsgroups from the Web, and open Web pages from newsgroup messages.

Before you can view newsgroup messages, though, you'll have to spend a few moments setting up the newsgroup system. To save a little space in this chapter, I'm going to refer you back to chapter 12, "E-mail with Netscape," where I explained how to set up the e-mail system. Setting up the newsgroup system is almost exactly the same. In fact once you've set up the e-mail system, you've entered most of the information that Netscape News requires.

So repeating some of what we did in chapter 12 "E-mail with Netscape," Choose Options, Mail and News, then click on the Directories tab. You'll have to fill out that last line with the location of your News Server. You should be able to get this information from your service provider or system administrator.

Fig. 13.1

Assuming you've filled out everything else for mail, all you need to add is the location of your news (NNTP) server.

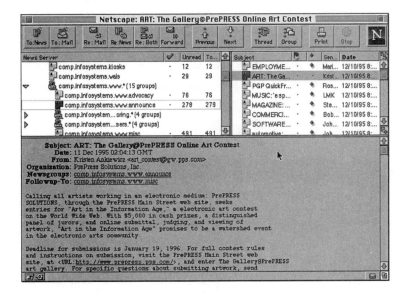

❝ *Plain English, please!*

What is NNTP?

NNTP stands for Network News Transfer Protocol. Just like there is a language for the Web called http, there's a language for news servers. **❞**

The newsgroup hierarchies

Before we look at how to work in a newsgroup, let's quickly learn about the newsgroup hierarchies. Newsgroup names use a hierarchical naming system. The first name is the top level. For instance, in *soc.couples.intercultural* the *soc* bit is the top level. Below that are sub levels. There are many sub levels within the *soc* level, just one of which is *couples*. Then, within the *couples* level are newsgroups, and perhaps more sub levels—one group below the couples level is called *intercultural*. Thus the full name of this newsgroup is *soc.couples.intercultural*. The top-level UseNet groups are shown in the following table.

Top level	Subject matter
comp	Computer-related subjects
news	Information about newsgroups themselves, including software used to read newsgroup messages and information about finding and using newsgroups
rec	Recreational topics—hobbies, sports, the arts, and so on
sci	Science; discussions about research in the "hard" sciences—physics, chemistry, etc.—as well as some social sciences

Top level	Subject matter
soc	A wide range of social issues, such as discussions about different types of societies and subcultures, as well as sociopolitical subjects
talk	Debate about politics, religion, and anything else that's controversial
misc	Stuff. Looking for jobs, selling things, a forum for paramedics. You know, stuff

There are a lot of groups that aren't contained within the "Big 7" list of newsgroups—actually, the official list from UseNet. Many are local groups (groups that contain issues specific to an area), although they may be distributed internationally—through UseNet, just to confuse the issue. Such newsgroups are known as **Alternative Newsgroups Hierarchies**. So there are other top-level groups, as shown in the following table.

Top level	Subject matter
alt	"Alternative" subjects; often subjects that someone has just thought up, and this are includes what many people would consider "inappropriate," pornographic, or just weird. Can also be simply interesting stuff, but the newsgroup has been created in an "unauthorized" manner to save time and hassle
bionet	Biological subjects
bit	A variety of newsgroups from the BITNET network
biz	Business subjects, including advertisements
clari	Clarinet's newsgroups from "official" and commercial sources—mainly UPI news stories and various syndicated columns

continues

Top level	Subject matter
courts	Related to law and lawyers
de	Various German-language newsgroups
fj	Various Japanese-language newsgroups
gnu	The Free Software Foundation's newsgroups
hepnet	Discussions about high-energy and nuclear-physics
ieee	The Institute of Electrical and Electronics Engineers' newsgroups
info	A collection of mailing lists formed into newsgroups at the University of Illinois
k12	Discussions about kindergarten through 12th-grade education
relcom	Russian-language newsgroups, mainly distributed in the former Soviet Union
vmsnet	Subjects of interest to VAX/VMS computer users

Now and again you'll see other groups, too, often local newsgroups from particular countries, towns, universities, and so on.

 Plain English, please!

Anarchists, Lunatics, and Terrorists?

It's sometimes said that **alt** stands for anarchists, lunatics, and terrorists. The alt. groups can be very strange; they're also some of the most popular groups on the Internet. The alt.* groups are constantly changing and you can find some really terrific bits of information there. For that matter, you can find just about anything in the alt.* groups. 🙲

Getting the news

How can you view a newsgroup's list of messages? There are several ways to start:

- Type a news: URL into the location bar (**news:alt.alien.visitors**, for instance) and press Enter. Netscape will open the Netscape News window and connect to your news server. (Note that the news: URL does *not* have the two forward slashes after the colon.)

- Click on a link that contains a news: URL.

- Choose <u>W</u>indow, Netscape <u>N</u>ews, then double-click on a news server in the top left pane.

Now and again you'll find Web documents that contain links to newsgroups. For instance, go to Yahoo (**http://www.yahoo.com**; see chapter 7, "Searching for Information on the Web"), and follow any hierarchy down a few levels and you'll eventually come to a list of newsgroups. For instance, follow the hierarchy to *Entertainment:Music:Usenet*. (You can go directly to this document with this URL: **http://www.yahoo.com/Entertainment/Music/Usenet/**). This document provides links to information about dozens of music-related newsgroups (see fig. 13.2).

Fig. 13.2
Yahoo contains quite a number of links to newsgroups in it's listings.

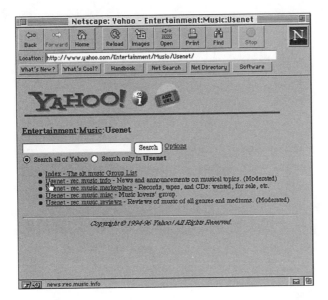

You'll find information about each newsgroup—a short description and the e-mail address of the person running the group—and a link to the group. When you click on the link—a **news:** link—Netscape will open the Netscape News window, and load the newsgroup (see fig. 13.3).

TIP **Another good search site that references newsgroups is Jump City (http://www.jumpcity.com/).** You can select a subject, and you'll find a list of related Web sites and newsgroups. Also, try **http://www.w3.org/ hypertext/DataSources/News/Groups/Overview.html**—you'll find a large list of newsgroups, with links that will open the groups.

Fig. 13.3

If you like a News area you find in Yahoo or another reference area, make sure you bookmark it. The newsgroups are the fastest changing item on the Internet.

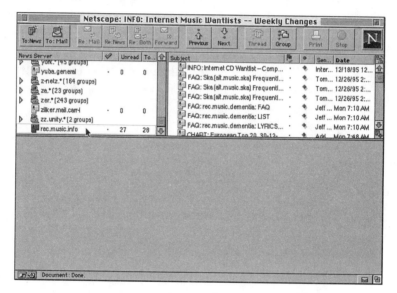

Of course, you might just want to start out looking at news to browse what's out there. If you want to start from the top, you can choose <u>W</u>indow, <u>N</u>etscape News, and you should see a window appear much like the one in figure 13.4.

Fig. 13.4
Netscape's News
window has three
default groups—all
worth reading if you're
new to UseNet news.

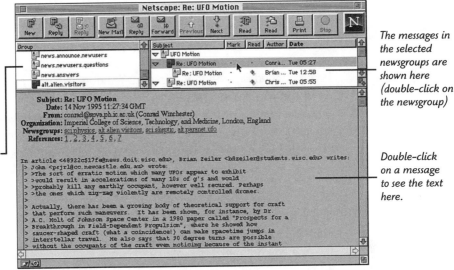

The messages in
the selected
newsgroups are
shown here
(double-click on
the newsgroup)

*The news servers are
shown here; click on a
server to see a list of
newsgroups*

Double-click
on a message
to see the text
here.

Netscape opened the News window, but why didn't it display the newsgroup?

If the news server you've specified in the Mail and News Preferences dialog
box doesn't have the newsgroup, Netscape can't display it. Each news server
subscribes to a different list of newsgroups, so now and again you'll run
into a server that doesn't have the newsgroup referenced by the link you
clicked on.

If you still want to read the newsgroup's messages, you can choose another
news server. See "Give me another news server," later in this chapter.

Working in the newsgroups

What will you see when you open the newsgroup window? Perhaps
something like figure 13.5. To display the window like this I typed
news:alt.alien.visitors, the URL to a popular newsgroup, in the Location
text box and pressed Enter. The window opened, then after a few seconds (it
can take a little while), the list of messages appeared in the top-right pane. I
then double-clicked on a message, and the message text appeared in the
bottom pane.

TIP **Some newsgroups are huge, and it can take a while to download** the message listing. If it's taking too long, click on the Stop toolbar button or press ⌘+".".

If you opened the window using the <u>W</u>indow, Netscape <u>N</u>ews command, what you will see will be different; you'll see no list of messages, and now message text in the bottom pane, because you haven't yet told Netscape which newsgroup you want to read. I'll explain how to do that in a moment (see "Displaying the newsgroups—and subscribing", below).

If you've read chapter 12, "E-mail with Netscape," you'll already be familiar with the News window, because it's very similar to the Mail window. The major difference is that the top-left pane shows a list of news servers (in the Mail window it shows folders, of course). You'll see one news server at least, the one you defined in the Mail and News Preferences dialog box. You can add more, though, as you'll see in "Give me another news server", later in this chapter.

The top-right pane shows a list of messages in the newsgroup. And if you double-click on a message, you'll see the message text in the bottom pane.

Displaying the newsgroups—and subscribing

If you used the <u>W</u>indows, Netscape <u>N</u>ews command to open the News window, you haven't yet selected a news server or newsgroup. Here's what you need to do.

In the top left pane of the news window, there should be a news server listed. Click on the little triangle to the left of it. Netscape News will display a list of newsgroups below the server icon. These are the newsgroups that you have subscribed to.

Now, notice the Sub column, which has a check box next to each newsgroup name. If there's a check mark in the box, you have subscribed to the group. (If you clicked on a link to a newsgroup, or typed the news: URL, one of the listed newsgroups may show a check box *without* a check mark; that means that the URL took you to a newsgroup to which you haven't yet subscribed.)

TIP **Because newsgroup names and message subjects are often very** long, you may need to drag the bars between the panes to the left or right, to make more room for the text. Also, you can drag the column dividers to the left or right to make more room. (Drag the line immediately before Sub in the left pane, or the line immediately before M in the right pane.)

Why doesn't Netscape simply show you all the newsgroups that the server has available? That might be thousands, and could take a long time (you'll see how long in a moment). So, instead, it allows you to **subscribe** to newsgroups. Then, each time you double-click on that news server, Netscape gets information about those few newsgroups, which it can do relatively quickly.

Here's how to pick a few newsgroups and subscribe to them. First, choose Options, Show All Newsgroups. You'll see a message-box warning that it might take a while; click on OK and Netscape will begin retrieving the information. (How long will this take? Well, as an example, it took Netscape about a minute to retrieve information about my service provider's 6,000 newsgroups; I'm using a 28,800 bps modem.)

Take a look at figure 13.5. I've expanded the top-left pane a little to the right (drag the bar between the two top panes to the right) and removed the bottom pane (drag the bar down), to show you what you'll see once Netscape News has retrieved a list of newsgroups:

- **Computer icons with + signs**—Remember the newsgroup hierarchy I told you about? Well, these little computers represent groups of newsgroups. Netscape shows how many newsgroups the folder contains in parentheses. Click on the triangle next to one to see a list of the groups (and perhaps more groups of groups) below.

- **Newsgroup names in bold text**—If the newsgroup name is shown in bold, it contains messages.

- **Newsgroup names in regular text**—If a newsgroup name is *not* bold, it's empty; there are no messages in the group.

- **The Sub column**—The check box in the Sub column shows you if you've subscribed to the newsgroup; an empty box means you haven't, a pair of glasses means you have.

- **The Unread column**—This shows how many messages in the newsgroup you haven't yet read (or which you have marked as unread, more of which later).

- **The Total column**—The total number of messages held in the group, both read and unread.

- **???**—In some cases you may see ??? shown in the Unread column. This means either that Netscape is grabbing information about the group (the ??? will be replaced with a number in a moment), or that Netscape was unable to get the numbers (perhaps because you're off-line).

Fig. 13.5

Adjust the panes and the columns to make more room for the listings; here's a list of newsgroups.

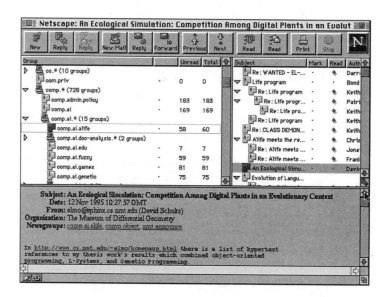

Now you've got a full list of all the newsgroups, you can move down the list, clicking on the check boxes of the ones you want to subscribe to. You don't have to subscribe to a group to see its messages, though. You can always view a group to which you have not subscribed. You can do that by typing **news:*newsgroup.name*** into Netscape's Location bar and pressing Enter. Or you can choose Options, Show All Newsgroups again. (Subscribing to a newsgroup is simply a convenience that allows you to quickly see a list of your favorite newsgroups.) Once you've finished with the full list of newsgroups, you can choose Options, Show All Newsgroups to return to your subscribed list.

TIP **If you select another news server, or close and reopen the** Netscape News window, Netscape News will display only the list of subscribed newsgroups—it will turn off the Show All Newsgroups option.

Displaying messages

Now you've got a list of newsgroups, you can display messages from any one. It doesn't matter whether you've subscribed or not; if the newsgroup name is listed, you can double-click on it to display its message list in the top-right pane—assuming that the newsgroup has messages, of course. Netscape will transfer the list of messages, which may take a moment or two.

Once you've got a list of messages in the top-right pane, you can double-click on one to view the text in the bottom pane.

What's in the text?

What will you find in the message text? Well, this is very similar to what we looked at in chapter 12 when we looked at an e-mail message. You'll find the header—the Subject, Date, From, and Organization (newsgroup messages typically have an organization identifier; you can enter yours in the Mail and News Preferences dialog box). You'll often find Newsgroups: and References entries too, and you'll see that they are active links (colored and underlined).

The Newsgroups entry shows you to which newsgroups the message has been posted; many are posted to multiple newsgroups. Click on a newsgroup name to open that newsgroup. And the References entries show you related messages, other messages in the thread. Click on a reference to see another message displayed in the main Netscape window. We'll talk more about threading in a moment.

Below the header you'll find the message text. (If you want to see the *full* header, all the strange routing stuff, choose View, Show All Headers.)

You may see other stuff, too. If there's a URL in the message you'll notice that Netscape News has converted the URL into an active link; click on it and the referenced document will appear in the Netscape window. Newsgroup messages often contain lists of newsgroup names at the top of the message, in the header; these are newsgroups to which the message has been posted (people often submit a single message to multiple newsgroups). Click on one to open that particular newsgroup.

As with e-mail, Netscape treats your newsgroup messages like Web pages, rendering the text just as it does with an HTML document. So the person sending the message could add some HTML tags to format the text. The message might have bold and italic text, for instance, or lines across the text, and so on. You won't yet find many newsgroup messages using this sort of thing, but who knows, with the popularity of Netscape it may become common soon.

Keeping the News up to date

As I mentioned earlier (and probably will again), News is the fastest changing item on the Internet. Changing as it is, it's important to keep up to date on what you're reading. If you're reading a particularly active group, your server could easily have received more messages while you were working your way past the last 200 or so.

If you want to update the list, you can click on the newsgroup name (in the upper left pane of the News window) and it will re-list all the messages. You can also choose <u>F</u>ile, <u>G</u>et More Messages to do update the list a little quicker.

 TIP **Netscape News uses the same Find system as Netscape Mail, so** you can search your list of messages for a particular person or subject. See chapter 12, "E-mail with Netscape," for more information.

Pictures from words

Newsgroup messages are simple ASCII text messages. You can't place any character into a message that is not in the standard ASCII character set. So if you want to send a computer file in a newsgroup message—maybe you want to send a picture, sound, or word processing document—you must convert it to ASCII.

There are three ways to do this; you can **binhex** a binary file, **uuencode** a binary file, or you can use **MIME**. You saw in chapter 12, "E-mail with Netscape," how to attach files to messages, and the process is the same when posting to newsgroups.

But how about converting back from UUENCODE or MIME? The newsgroup message is simply garbage text, a huge jumble. But Netscape may be able to convert this text for you, automatically. When it begins transferring a newsgroup message, it looks for evidence of a MIME or UUENCODE attachment. If it finds it, it tries to convert it; it can do so if the binary file that has been encoded is a .JPG or .GIF image file, as you can see in figure 13.6.

Fig. 13.6
I found this picture of a bat in the newsgroup **alt.binaries.pictures. animals**. Netscape converted the UUENCODED message to a picture automatically.

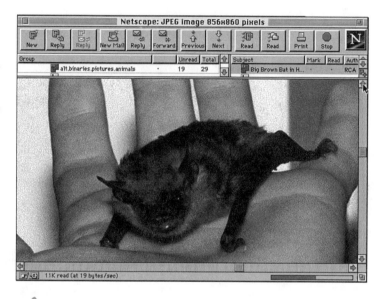

 TIP **You can save a picture, once it's converted, by clicking on the** image and holding down the button until the pop-up menu appears. Then choose *Save This Image As*.

Netscape won't always be able to convert the file, though, for a number of reasons:

- The picture's not one of the image types that Netscape can work with.

- It's the correct image type, but it's split into multiple newsgroup messages (many binary files are UUENCODED, then divided into several parts because the entire block of text is too big for a single message).

- It's not even a picture; perhaps it's a sound, for instance.

- It wasn't encoded properly in the first place. Somewhere between 10% and 20% of all the uploaded binary files are "damaged" in some way and can't be decoded.

If Netscape can't convert the information in the file, you'll see something like figure 13.7. You'll often see BEGIN — Cut Here — cut here near the top of the file, too, meaning that the following text is the encoded binary file.

Fig. 13.7

This sound, from alt.binaries.sounds. cartoons, couldn't be converted by Netscape, so all you get is the UUENCODED text.

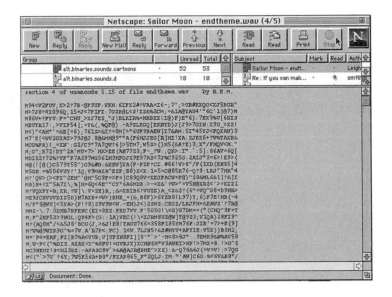

If Netscape can't handle it

What are you going to do if Netscape can't handle the attached binary; if it's not a picture, for instance, or if it's split between several files? Well, you can decode the file using a special UUDECODE program (the vast majority of files in the newsgroups are attached using UUENCODE, not MIME; however, if you have to convert a file attached using MIME, use Mpack; see chapter 12, "E-mail with Netscape," for more information.)

When you find a file that you want to decode, save it as a text file by choosing File, Save As. Then you can use a shareware decoder (such as UULITE) to decode the file.

TIP **If the encoded file is split into several messages you may see**
Subject lines that say something like Picture.zip 1/3, Picture.zip 2/3, Picture.zip 3/3, for instance. In such a case, save each message in a separate text file. Most decoders can pick up each message in sequence while it decodes—see the instructions of your decoder for more information.

What's this gibberish message? ROT13

Now and again, especially in the more contentious newsgroups, you'll run into messages that seem to be gibberish. Everything's messed up, each word seems to be a jumbled mix of characters, almost as if the message has been encrypted. It has.

What you are seeing is **ROT13**, a very simple substitution cipher (one in which a character is substituted for another). It's actually very easy to read. ROT13 means rotated 13. In other words, each character in the alphabet has been replaced by the character 13 places further along. Instead of A you see N, instead of B you see O, instead of C you see P, and so on. Got it? So to read the message, all you need to do is substitute the correct characters. Easy. (Or *Rnfl*, I should say.)

For those of you in a hurry, there is an easier way. Choose <u>V</u>iew, <u>U</u>nscramble (ROT13), and like magic the message changes into real words (see fig. 13.8).

Fig. 13.8
I ROT13ed this news.announce.newusers message to show you what a ROT13 message looks like. If you have time to kill, try decrypting it!

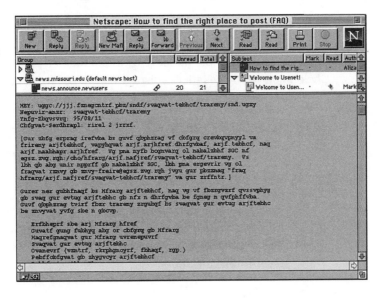

So what's the point? Why encode a message with a system that is so ridiculously easy to break? People don't ROT13 messages as a security measure, in order to make them unreadable to all but those with the "secret key." After all, anyone with a decent newsgroup reader has the key. No, ROT13ing (if you'll excuse my use of the term as a verb) is a way of saying "if you read this message, you may be offended, so if you are easily offended, *don't read it!*" ROT13 messages are often crude, lewd, or just plain rude. Offensive. Nasty. Converting a message into ROT13 forces readers to decide whether or not they want to risk being offended. And if they do, then that's their problem.

Threading and references

Most of the messages you will see in the newsgroups are replies to earlier messages. Someone sends a message with a question or comment, then someone replies, then someone else replies to the reply, and so on.

If all you saw was a chronological list of messages in the newsgroup, you'd find it very difficult to figure out what's going on. For this reason you'll want to choose Thread <u>N</u>ews Messages in the Mail and News Preferences dialog box (under the Organization tab). You can also choose <u>V</u>iew, <u>S</u>ort, <u>T</u>hread Messages to turn threading on and off. Figure 13.4 shows the messages are threaded; you can see that messages are indented one below the other, replies below the messages to which they are replying.

You'll also notice that many messages have a References line in the header. This shows a series of numbers, each of which is a link to a particular message—generally the message to which the one you are reading is a reply. Click on one of these links to display that message in the main Netscape window.

Q&A ***Why can't I find the original message in the list of messages, even though I'm using threaded view?***

Just because you are viewing the messages in a thread doesn't mean you'll see the entire thread. Messages are not held in a newsgroup forever; the newsgroup files your service provider maintains have to be cleaned of old messages all the time, to make room for new ones. So if the thread is more than a few days old, you may not be able to find the message that began the thread in the first place.

Moving between messages

You can move between messages by simply double-clicking on each one. Or use one of these methods:

- Choose <u>G</u>o, <u>N</u>ext Message or click on the Next button to read the next message.

- Choose <u>G</u>o, <u>P</u>revious Message or click on the Previous button to read the previous message.

- Choose <u>G</u>o, <u>F</u>irst Unread to move to the first Unread message in the list. (Unread messages are marked with a green circle in the R column.)

- Choose <u>G</u>o, Ne<u>x</u>t Unread to move to the next Unread message in the list.

- Choose <u>G</u>o, Pre<u>v</u>ious Unread to move to the previous Unread message in the list.

Putting in your own two cents—posting and responding

You can just **lurk** in the newsgroups if you wish; just read, without taking any part in the discussions. Or you can put in your own two cents worth, by responding to messages or even starting your own discussion. There are several ways to do this:

- **Reply to a message**—To send a reply to the selected message to the newsgroup, choose <u>M</u>essage, P<u>o</u>st Reply, or click on the Post Reply button.

- **Reply to the author**—To e-mail a response to the person who originally sent the selected message (not to the newsgroup itself), choose <u>M</u>essage, Mail <u>R</u>eply, or click on the Reply button.

- **Reply to the newsgroup *and* the author**—To reply to the newsgroup and e-mail a copy of your reply to the author of the selected message, choose <u>M</u>essage, Post and Mail Reply, or click on the Post and Reply button.

- **Forward the message to someone**—To e-mail a copy of the selected message, choose <u>M</u>essage, <u>F</u>orward, or click on the Forward button.

• **Send an e-mail message**—You can send an e-mail message to some-one (anyone, not just a newsgroup correspondent) by choosing Mes-sage, New Mail Message, or by clicking on the New Message button.

 • **Send a new message**—To begin a new "conversation" in the newsgroup, choose Message, Post News, or click on the Post New button.

In each case the Message Composition window will open, and you'll be able to type your reply. Some of the fields will be filled in for you, of course. If you are replying to the newsgroup or the author of the message, the correct Send To address is filled in. If you are forwarding the message, the message will be in the Message Composition windows content area (as it also will when you reply to a message if you selected the Automatically Quote Original Message When Replying check box in the Mail and News Preferences).

Read versus Unread messages

When you double-click on a newsgroup and Netscape retrieves the list of newsgroup messages, does it retrieve the entire list? No. It retrieves a list of all the messages that have been marked as read.

How, then, does a message get marked as read? Well, when Netscape dis-plays the message contents in the bottom pane, it marks the message as read, removing the green circle from the R column in the top-right pane. But there are other ways to mark messages as read, too. You can mark a message as read even if you've never actually read it. You can do this so that you don't see the message the next time you view the contents of this newsgroup. For instance, you might read a message's Subject line and know you're not interested in the message contents. Or maybe you've read the first message in a thread, and know you don't care about the rest of the messages in the thread. Mark them as Read, so they don't appear in the list next time. Here's how:

• Click once on the green circle in the R column, removing the circle.

• Select a message and then choose Message, Mark as Read.

- Select a message and click on the Mark Thread Read button; all the messages in the same thread as the selected message are marked as Read.

- Click on the Mark All Read button; every message in the newsgroup is marked as Read. The next time you view the newsgroup you'll only see new messages listed.

Of course you can go the other way, marking messages that you *have* read as unread. Why bother? So that the next time you view the contents of the newsgroup, that message will still be there. (Maybe you're pondering something in the message, and want to reply to it later.)

- Click once on a message and then choose Message, Mark as Unread.

- Click on the little dot in the R column; Netscape will replace the green diamond, marking it as Unread.

TIP **When Netscape marks a message as read, that message remains** displayed during the current session—until you close the window or choose another newsgroup. (When you return, the Read messages will not be there.) However, you can tell Netscape to remove a Read message as soon as you move on to another message by choosing <u>O</u>ptions, Show Only <u>U</u>nread Messages.

I want the messages back!

So, you read some messages, or manually marked them as Read, and now you want them back. What can you do? No problem; choose <u>O</u>ptions, <u>S</u>how All Messages. Netscape will retrieve a complete list from your service provider's system, marking all the messages as Unread.

Of course this doesn't mean that the message you want is there; it may be too old to remain on the newsgroup. Still, you'll see everything that your service provider has for that newsgroup.

Saving and Printing messages

You can save newsgroup messages if you wish. In fact, if you find a useful message, don't simply rely on marking it as Unread so you can come back to it later. If the message is removed from your service provider's computer—as it will be eventually—you won't be able to retrieve it.

To save a message, choose File, Save As, and you should see a standard Save dialog box as I've shown in figure 13.9. Pick where you want to save it, name the message, and click on Save.

Fig. 13.9
If you're collecting FAQ's or other useful messages, you might want to make a folder just for them.

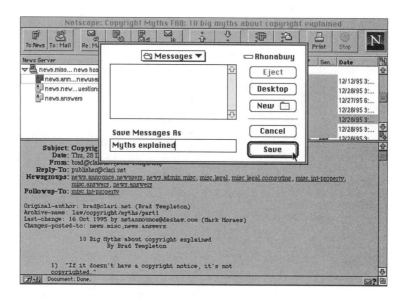

Of course another way of saving messages is by printing them out. You can print the news message just as easily as you print Mail. Click on the Print toolbar button, or choose File, Print... (You get can more details on printing from chapter 8, "Saving Stuff from the Web").

TIP   **After you've saved a couple dozen news messages you found**
where interesting, you might note that you can't keep track of them. Well, there's not a good solution for that yet, but something I might suggest is creating your own organization of folders and files based on subject (or whatever). Just make sure you save the news message into the correct folder, and it will be much easier to track down when you need it.

Tracking down newsgroups

Netscape News provides a few methods to help you manage your newsgroup lists, so you can find the ones you need:

List the default newsgroups—Choose Options, Show Active Newsgroups.

List only subscribed newsgroups—Choose Options, Show Subscribed Newsgroups.

List all available newsgroups—Choose Options, Show All Newsgroups.

List new newsgroups—Choose Options, Show New Newsgroups to see a list of newsgroups that your service provider has added since the last time that you use the Show All Newsgroups command.

Give me another news server

Each news server is different. Some only subscribe to 2,000 or 3,000 newsgroups. My university subscribes to about 11,000. Another local provider subscribes to about 17,000—about as many as is possible.

If you find that your service provider doesn't subscribe to a newsgroup that you want to use, ask them to do so. Most will oblige. It may take a few days, though. If you are in a hurry, or they refuse to get the group you want, you may have another option. You *may* be able to connect to another news server.

Choose File, Open News Host, type the host address of the host you want to use, and press Enter. Netscape will connect to the host and display another host icon in the top-left pane. You can now use this in the same way that you use your default host. Click on it and choose Options, Show All Newsgroups to get started.

Which news server are you going to connect to, though? Ah, well that's the problem. Most service providers won't let you connect unless you have an account with them.

You can remove a news server that you've added this way by clicking on it and choosing File, Remove News Host.

Secure News

There is one news server that you can always connect to—Netscape's. In fact, they've even gone to the length of making it a secure transaction—they encrypt the information from their news server and Netscape automatically decrypts it for you.

If you take a look at the Netscape User's Group page (**http://home.netscape.com/commun/netscape_user_groups.html**), you'll see quite a number of links. Each of these links is to one of Netscape's secure news groups. For example, you might be interested in the Netscape Navigator User's group (see fig. 13.10). If you click on that link, it will bring up Netscape's secure news server for you and display it's set of mail messages (see fig. 13.11).

Fig. 13.10

The Netscape Navigator User Group area is a good place to catch up on the latest tidbits with Netscape and how to do things.

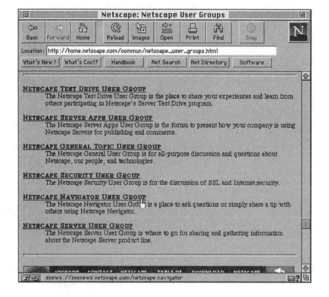

Fig. 13.11

Netscape actually maintains quite a collection of secure newsgroups, most of them technical in nature.

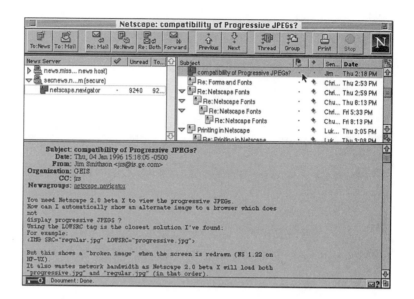

14

Not by Web Alone— Gopher, Finger, Telnet, and More

● In this chapter:

- **Gophering around in Gopherspace**

- **Searching WAIS through the Web**

- **What's Finger, and how do I use it?**

- **Chatting through the Web?**

- **Starting Telnet sessions**

We haven't finished yet—there are a lot more Internet services available through Netscape. . . . . ➤

We've looked at three major "non-Web" services that Netscape can help you with—FTP, E-mail, and newsgroups. But there are a host of other non-Web services out there, many of which Netscape can handle: Gopher, Finger, and WAIS. We'll start with the simplest, Gopher.

Traveling in Gopherspace

Before the World Wide Web become popular—Mosaic wasn't in wide use until the middle of 1994, and Netscape wasn't released until late in 1994—the really easy way to travel around the Internet was through Gopher. Compared to other Internet tools—which were about as easy to use as threading a needle in the dark—Gopher was a revolution. The Gopher system provided a nice menu system from which users could select options. Instead of remembering a variety of rather obscure and arcane commands to find what they needed, users could use the arrow keys to select options from the menu. Those options could take the user to other menus, or to documents of some kind. In fact the Gopher system is, in some ways, similar to the World Wide Web. It's a world-wide network of menu systems. Options in the menus linked to menus or other documents all over the world. These Gopher menus made the Internet much easier to use, and much more accessible to people other than long-term cybergeeks.

The Gopher system is still alive and well, for a couple of good reasons. First, there were already many Gopher systems set up before the Web became popular. And secondly, there are still millions of Internet users who don't have access to graphical Web browsers, for whom Gophers are the easiest tools available. There's a lot of interesting information on Gopher servers around the world. And, fortunately, you can get to it with Netscape. That's right; Netscape may be primarily a Web browser, but you can use the Web to access Gopher.

Digging around with Gopher

You can get to a Gopher server—a computer that maintains a Gopher menu system—in two ways; by clicking a link that some Web author has provided, or by typing the **gopher://** URL into the Address text box and pressing Enter. For instance, typing **gopher://wiretap.spies.com/** will take you to Internet Wiretap Gopher server, which you can see in figure 14.1.

Fig. 14.1
The Wiretap gopher contains lots of interesting and strange documents.

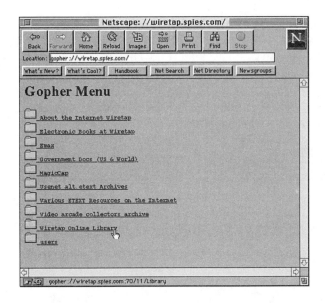

In some cases you can ignore the **gopher://** bit. You've already learned that you can type a URL into the Address text box without including the **http://** bit. Well, if the gopher address starts with the word **gopher** you can type the address and forget the gopher:// part. For instance, you could type **gopher.usa.net** instead of **gopher://gopher.usa.net**. (Of course, the Wiretap address I've just given you won't work this way.)

TIP **For a list of links to Gopher servers, go to gopher://gopher.micro.umn.edu/11/Other%20Gopher%20and%20Information%20Servers**. Or, if you don't want to type all that, go to **http://www.w3.org/hypertext/DataSources/ByAccess.html** and click on the Gopher link.

How, then, do you use a Gopher server with Netscape? The Gopher menu options are represented by links—click the link to select that option. If the option leads to another menu, that's what you'll see in the window. If it leads to a file of some kind, the file is transferred in the normal way, and if Netscape can display or play it, it does so. If it can't…well, you'd better go back and see chapters **x** Audio and Video and **x** More on Viewers.

You'll find that most of the documents at Gopher sites are text documents; Netscape can display these text documents within its own window. Of course you won't find any links to other documents within these text documents—they're not true Web documents, after all—so once you've finished you'll have to use the Back toolbar button (or Alt+Right Arrow) to return to the Gopher menu you were just viewing. In figure 14.2 you can see a text document that I ran across at the Wiretap site. I selected the *Electronic Books at Wiretap* menu option, followed by the *Beowulf* menu option.

Fig. 14.2

If you select a menu option that leads to a text document, you'll see it in the Netscape window.

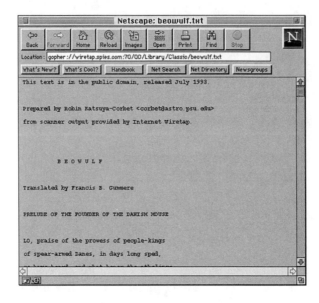

You'll notice that the icons to the left of each menu option indicate what the option leads to:

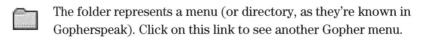 The folder represents a menu (or directory, as they're known in Gopherspeak). Click on this link to see another Gopher menu.

The page represents a document or computer file of some kind. Click on this link to read, view, or transfer the file.

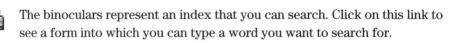 The binoculars represent an index that you can search. Click on this link to see a form into which you can type a word you want to search for.

Veronica and Jughead

Gopher servers have two types of search tools: **Veronica** (Very Easy Rodent-Oriented Net-wide Index to Computerized Archives) and **Jughead** (Jonzy's Universal Gopher Hierarchy Excavation and Display). Do these acronyms mean much? No, but you try to create an acronym from a cartoon character's name!

 Plain English, please!

Veronica and Archie?

Why **Veronica** and **Jughead**? They are characters in the famous Archie cartoon strip. **Archie** arrived on the Internet first. Archie is a system that enables you to search the Internet for particular computer files—you can type a filename, and Archie will tell you where the file is (you learned about Archie in chapter 11, "Software Libraries—Using FTP"). Why Archie? The legend is that Archie is derived from the word *archive*. Remove the V, and what have you got? *Archie*. Some say this is *not* how the name was derived, so who knows. Personally it makes sense to me. Anyway, the people who created the Gopher search systems figured Archie needed company, and named their systems Veronica and Jughead. **"**

Veronica lets you search Gopher servers all over the world. Jughead lets you search the Gopher server you are currently working with (though many Gopher servers don't yet have Jugheads).

If you want to search **Gopherspace**—this giant system of Gopher menus that spread across the Internet—find an appropriate menu option somewhere. For instance, at the **gopher://gopher.cc.utah.edu/** Gopher site, you'll find menu options that say *Search titles in Gopherspace using veronica* and *Search menu titles using jughead*. At other sites you may have to dig around a little to find the menu options you need. Most sites have at least links to Veronica—Wiretap is an exception rather than the rule.

Both systems are quite easy to use. However, you must understand that Veronica provides two ways to search, and also allows you to choose a particular Veronica server. Veronica searches *all* of Gopherspace—Gopher servers all over the world. Something called a **Veronica server** stores an index of menu options at all of these Gopher servers, so you are actually searching one of these indexes; you get to pick which one.

But at the same time, you have to decide whether you want to limit your search. You can search all menu options, or only menu options that lead to other menus. Let's assume, for instance, that you went to **gopher:// gopher.cc.utah.edu**, then chose the *Search titles in Gopherspace using veronica* option. You'll see something similar to figure 14.3.

Fig. 14.3

Veronica allows you to choose a server, and pick the search type.

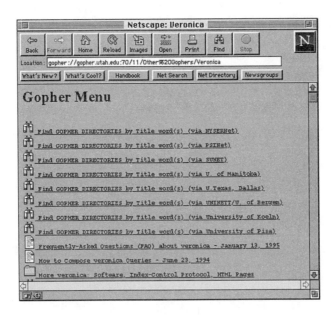

If you now select *Find GOPHER DIRECTORIES by Title Word(s) (via U of Manitoba)*, you will be looking for menu options that lead to other menus (often called **directories** in Gopherspeak) using the University of Manitoba Veronica server. If you select the *Search GopherSpace by Title Word(s) (via University of Pisa)*, you will be searching all menu options, both "directories" and options leading to files and documents, at the University of Pisa Veronica server.

When you make your selection, you'll see a box into which you can type the keywords you are searching for. You might type **electronic books**, **publishers**, **sports**, or whatever your interest. Then press Enter and the search begins.

What happens next? Well, there's a good chance you'll get a message saying **** Too many connections—Try again soon. ****, or something similar. Try another server. Or perhaps Netscape just seems to wait and wait, and nothing seems to happen. These servers are very busy, so it often takes a long time to get a result. Eventually, with luck, you'll get a list of links you can click on to continue moving through Gopherspace, to sites and documents related to your interests.

Using Jughead is similar to using Veronica, but easier; you don't get to pick a server or search type, you simply enter the keywords you want to search for.

Q&A   *Can I use "and" and "or" in my searches?*

Yes, you certainly can. The "and" and "or" are known as **boolean** operators—the result is always yes or no. Boolean operators allow you to mix
keywords and define how they relate to each other; you could search for
book or publisher, or book and publisher, book not publisher, and so on.
For more information about exactly how to search, read the information
that most Gopher sites place close to the Veronica and Jughead menu
options. Most have menu options titled something like *How to Compose
Veronica Queries*, or *About Jughead*. When using Jughead you can search for
?help to see a link to the documentation.

WAIS Database Searches

WAIS means Wide Area Information Server, and is a system that's been used
for some time to allow Internet users to access information on hundreds of
databases around the world.

The WAIS servers are one of the most infrequently used tools on the Internet,
partly because the WAIS interface is rather confusing. You can get to the
WAIS servers in several ways. There's a wais:// URL, but it won't work unless
you have a special WAIS proxy installed. (If you installed Netscape on a dial-
in line to a service provider, you are out of luck. If you use a copy on your
network at work though, ask your system administrator if there's a WAIS
proxy installed; there almost certainly isn't.)

There are other ways to use WAIS, though. Many gopher servers have links to
WAIS servers—use Jughead or Veronica to find them. But perhaps the best
way to use WAIS is through the WAIS gateway at WAIS, Inc., the company
that owns the WAIS software. Use Netscape to go to **http://wais.wais.com/
newhomepages/wais-dbs.html** where you'll find the WAIS, Inc. Directory of
Servers page. (You can also go to **http://wais.wais.com/** to enter the WAIS,
Inc. site "at the top," where you can find plenty of information about the
WAIS software.)

As you can see in the following illustration (fig. 14.4), this page has two
elements; a Search area, and a list of databases.

Fig. 14.4

WAIS, Inc., probably
the best way to use
WAIS through
Netscape

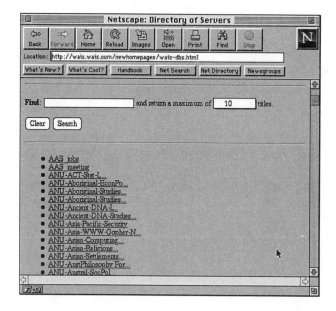

You now have two options. You can search for a useful database by entering
a word related to the subject in which you are interested into the Find text
box and clicking on Search. The system finds matching databases and then
displays a list; you can then search the database that you think will be most
useful.

The other option is to scroll down the list of databases and click on one that
sounds like it might help you. You'll see information describing the list, along
with a text box that allows you to search the list.

Using WAIS can be tricky, but it's worth taking a look, just to see what's
available. You'll find hundreds of databases, from AAS Jobs (from the
American Astronomical Society Job Register) to Zipcodes (the U.S. Zip Code
directory), from The Book of Mormon to ANU-Buddhist-Electrn-Rsrces (the
Buddhist Electronic Resources Directory). It's a fantastic resource that is
well worth learning.

TIP   **Try using the Edit, Find command to search this—and other—long**
lists of links.

Finger

The UNIX *Finger* command lets you find information about someone's Internet account. If you typed **Finger username@hostname** at a UNIX prompt and press Enter, you would see information about that person's real name, whether they are logged on, and so on. And, more importantly, you'll see the contents of their *.plan* file. This is often used to distribute information, about anything that takes the account owner's fancy—sports scores, weather information, earthquakes, and so on.

You can't use Finger directly from Netscape; there's no **Finger://** URL! But there are Finger "gateways." You can find a gateway at **http://www-bprc.mps.ohio-state.edu/cgi-bin/Finger.pl**, for instance.

Finger gateways provide a text box into which you can type the address you want to Finger. For instance, Finger smith@csn.org; this will produce a list of all the Smiths with accounts at that particular host computer. Or Finger an account that is being used to distribute information. Try **quake@andreas.wr.usgs.gov**, for instance. You'll see something like figure 14.5.

Fig. 14.5
An earthquake report, via Finger

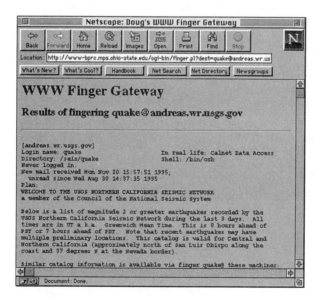

The sort of information you can get back depends on how the machine you are "Fingering" has been set up. Some provide a lot of information, some just a little. Some sites won't give out any Finger information at all.

TIP **For more Finger "gateways," search Yahoo (see chapter 7,** "Searching for Information on the Web") for the word Finger, or go to **http://www.yahoo.com/Computers_and_Internet/Internet/ World_Wide_Web/Gateways/Finger_Gateways/**.

By the way, some Web pages have links that automatically use a Finger gateway to grab Finger information. For instance, search Yahoo for the word Finger, and you'll find a few of these Finger links. Or go to **http:// www.jou.ufl.edu/commres/jlist/JL_05.htm**, the Finger list in the Journalism List Web document. This contains links that will get Finger information from a variety of sources, on a variety of subjects: auroral activity, NASA's daily news, a hurricane forecast, earthquake information, and all sorts of other, wonderful information. Some of these Finger documents even contain small pictures; while .plan files are text files, they can contain links to images, just like HTML Web documents. If the document is retrieved through the right sort of Finger gateway, those images appear in the document when it's displayed in your Web browser.

Chatting Online

Chat is a service that isn't well developed on the Web, but now and again you may run into some kind of chat system. For instance, at **http:// www.rock.net/webchat/rwchat.html** you'll find the RockWeb chat system. You type a message into a form and press Enter. Your "view" of the chat is then updated, so you can see your message. If you know a bit of HTML (see chapter 19, "Creating Your Own Web Page"), you can even include HTML tags in your message, so you can use bold, italics, underlines, and so on—even include a link to somewhere. In other words, someone reading your message could click on the link in your message to go somewhere else. (If you are going to do this fancy stuff you'll probably want to prepare it beforehand in a word processor, copy it to the Clipboard, and paste it into the chat as shown in fig. 14.6.)

Fig. 14.6
The WebChat page is also a good example of some more advanced Netscape features—Frames.

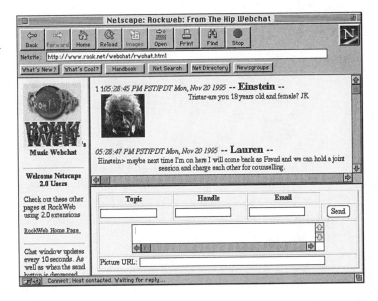

66 *Plain English, please!*

What is a chat system?

A **chat** system is one that allows people to hold "conversations" in "real time." You type a message, and others can read it almost immediately, and respond to you. 99

If you want to be really geeky, you can tell the system to display a picture next to your name each time you "say" something in the conversation. You'll have to provide the picture, though, and enter a URL pointing to the picture on a system somewhere. (From what I've seen, very few people are using the fancy features that are available in this chat—mostly it's just plain old text.)

TIP **Netscape Communications has a product called Netscape Chat** which can be integrated into the Netscape Navigator browser. Unfortunately, it only works on the Windows version of Netscape at this time. It provides a chat interface, through which you can use Internet Relay Chat (an Internet-wide chatting system), or set up your own private chat links (similar to what is known as talk to UNIX users on the Internet). Those private chats can be between two people, or an entire group, either with everyone in the group allowed to take part, or with one person "presenting" to the group.

Telnet sessions

Telnet is a system that lets you log on to other computers that are connected to the Internet. You can play games, search library catalogs, dig through databases, and so on. Netscape can't do this for you directly, it doesn't support Telnet sessions. Instead it can run a Telnet program that you specify.

Choose Options, General Preferences, and then click on the Applications tab. You'll see several text boxes. It's the first two that we are interested in, Telnet Application and TN3270 Application. TN3270 is very similar to Telnet; TN3270 sessions run on certain IBM computers. Most Telnet programs don't handle TN3270 sessions very well, so you may need to use an actual TN3270 program to run such sessions.

Use the Browse buttons to select the programs that you want Netscape to launch when you run Telnet or TN3270 sessions. Like many of the viewers, if you have the ones Netscape expects, it'll automatically link them into place.

If you don't already have Telnet, you can find a copy of it at **ftp://sumex-aim.stanford.edu/info-mac/comm/tcp/ncsa-telnet-26.hqx**. Likewise, you can find a copy of TN3270 at **ftp://sumex-aim.stanford.edu/info-mac/comm/tcp/tn3270-23d26.hqx**.

Starting a Telnet session

There are several ways to start Telnet sessions from Netscape. You'll occasionally find links from Web documents to Telnet sites (using the **telnet://** URL). Clicking on one of these links will launch the Telnet program you have specified. You can also start a Telnet session by typing **telnet://** followed by a Telnet host address into Netscape's Location text box and pressing Enter. For instance, if you type **telnet://pac.carl.org** and press Enter, your Telnet program launches and connects to the Denver Public Library's site. (Type PAC and press Enter to log on.)

TN3270 sessions are started in the same way, except that you (or the Web author) will use the **tn3270://** URL.

Using HyTelnet

To get a taste for what's available in the world of Telnet, take a look at HyTelnet, the Telnet directory. This used to be available only through Telnet itself, but now you can view the directory at a World Wide Web site, a rather more convenient method. Open your Web browser and go to **http:// library.usask.ca/hytelnet/**, and you should see a page like the one shown in figure 14.7. You can also find a HyTelnet site at **http://www.cc.ukans.edu/ hytelnet_html/START.TXT.html**, but it's rather out of date; and at a gopher site, **gopher://liberty.uc.wlu.edu/11/internet/hytelnet**.

Fig. 14.7
The HyTelnet site is nicely organized to make it a little easier to find what's there.

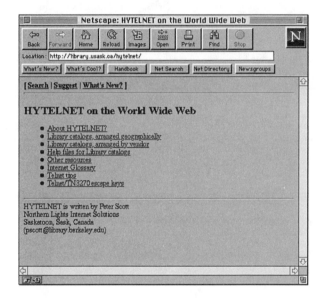

Each Telnet site is different. You can find Telnet sites on which you can play chess, or search databases of satellite photographs, or try experimental "chat" systems, and so on. But once you are connected to a Telnet site, that site's rules take over. Each system is a little different; each has a different set of commands, or menu options perhaps.

So if you want to use Telnet your first step is to get to know your Telnet program, and the second step is to carefully read the instructions that are often shown when you enter a Telnet site. For example, if you wanted to look at Arizona State University's Research Library, you could dig up the page under HyTelnet at **http://library.usask.ca/hytelnet/us1/us138.html**, where it would show you some simple instructions as displayed in figure 14.8.

Fig. 14.8

Pay attention to the instructions if you're going to use HyTelnet, the systems aren't very easy to work with.

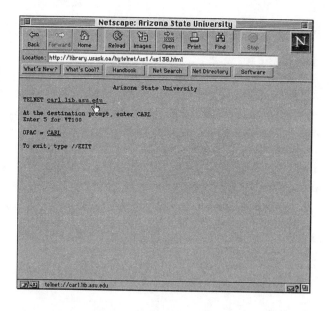

Then you can click on the link to the server (**telnet://carl.lib.asu.edu**), and you'll see a telnet session open (as shown in fig. 14.9). At this point, you're working in someone else's computer with their system.

Fig. 14.9

I've already followed the instructions given on the Web page to get into the Library system this far.

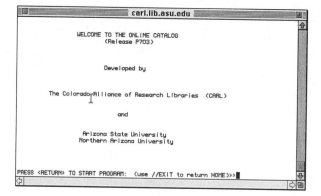

Part IV: Netscape's Advanced Features

15

Security on the Internet

● **In this chapter:**

The Web is an open system; someone who understands networking can look in on all your transactions. Here's how to make transactions private. . . . . ❯

The big question on the Web these days seems to be, "Is it safe?" People are concerned that information they send out across the Internet can somehow be intercepted by someone in-between the browser and the Web server.

For instance, let's say that you want to buy something from an online mall; you fill out a form, entering your name and address, the product you want, and your credit card number. You click on the Submit button, and off that information goes, across the Internet, to the Web server that is managing this particular Web store. What happens to that data between here and there? Where is there, even? It might be the other side of the country, the other side of the continent, or even the other side of the world. Could someone in-between take a look at that message as it shoots by, and grab your credit card number?

Well, yes, it can be done. Not too many people can really do it—but it's getting easier all the time.

It's not that dangerous!

I know people who wouldn't dare to send their credit card numbers across the Internet. They seem to have this strange idea that every host computer has some evil soul lurking around, checking every e-mail message for credit card numbers.

While it's probably not that dangerous, you should also know that most of the fraud that has happened with credit card numbers is from when the transaction reached the other end. Make absolutely sure you know who you're sending that information to; a little time checking up could save you a lot of money!

Public-key encryption

Regardless of the risks (or lack of), it does make sense that the companies building software for the Web should do everything they can to reduce the risks. The more transactions made over the Web, the more potential for trouble. And once the Web has been made secure, it could be used for transmitting data far more valuable than credit-card numbers—corporate financial and management data, research data, even government communications.

Netscape Communications has incorporated something called **public-key encryption** into its browsers and servers to ensure that online transactions are safe.

Public-key encryption is a concept that few people have heard of, and fewer still understand. First, let me describe **private-key encryption**, which most people do understand. Private-key encryption takes a private key (kind of a secret code word—also known as a secret key) and encrypts a file so that it appears to be garbled characters. Tell the program the name of the file you want to encrypt, and tell the program the private key—the code—and the program uses a mathematical algorithm to encrypt the file. How can you decrypt the file? You do the same thing; give the program the name of the encrypted file, give it the private key, and it uses the algorithm to reverse the process, to decrypt the file. The key is what controls how to get into the information. Needless to say, you don't want to share that key too widely, or everyone could read your file. That's why it's called **private** key encryption.

Public-key encryption uses two keys, though, a private key and a public key. Through the magic of mathematics, these keys work together; they are in some way mathematically related. If you encrypt a file with one key, that key cannot decrypt it—the message can only be decrypted with the *other* key! Encrypt a file with the public key, for instance, and it can only be decrypted with the private key. Sounds a little odd, but that's how it works (don't ask me how; as far as I'm concerned, it's magic. The best I can say is that it's complicated mathematics).

How, then, does this apply to Netscape? Netscape can use public-key encryption to encrypt information from a form before it sends it to the server. Here's how. When you load a secure Web document—a form, for instance— the Web server sends its public key along with the form. (That's why it's called a public key. Because it's available publicly, no attempt is made—nor needed—to protect the key.) You fill in the form, then click on the Submit button, and your browser takes the public key and encrypts the data in the form, then sends it back to the server. The server then uses its *private* key to decrypt the message—remember, anything encrypted with the public key can only be decrypted with the private key. Because the people running the server keep that private key secret, your information is safe. If anyone intercepts it, they can't decrypt it.

TIP **Remember, there are two required components in this procedure.** Your browser has built-in security software, but not all servers do. Only special **https** servers (also known as **Secure Sockets Layer** servers) have the security software required for secure transactions. You'll find out how to identify this when you are connected to an https server under "How do I actually use this?," later in this chapter.

Different size keys

There are actually two different versions of the Netscape security software—there's a 40-bit version and there's a 128-bit version. These numbers refer to the length of the key—the code—that is used to encrypt data. The longer the key, the more secure the transmission. The 128-bit software is built into the Netscape servers and browsers sold to customers within the United States. The 40-bit software is built into Netscape servers and browsers sold to customers outside the United States, *and* in the browsers that can be downloaded from the Netscape Web and FTP sites, and the various mirror sites.

In other words, if you want the very highest security, you need to be living within the United States of America, you must (according to law) be a citizen or a resident alien, and you must buy a copy of Netscape—the software will be shipped to you.

Does it really matter? In most cases, no. The 40-bit software is strong enough for all but the most critical of applications; for instance, a government department could use the Web to transfer information throughout the world (if they wanted to; I don't know if any do). Using 128-bit encryption they could be sure that the message was unbreakable.

Why, then, are there two different versions? For one reason only: ITAR, the United States Government's International Traffic in Arms Regulations. Encryption software using keys over 40-bits long is considered an armament—SAM missiles and the like—and cannot be exported. Kind of crazy, but true. The Federal government has decided that hiding information is as much a weapon as a missile.

So there are two parts to the security equation: the browser and the server. What happens if you have a 40-bit browser, and you connect to a 128-bit server? The data encryption will be carried out using a 40-bit key. What if you have a 128-bit browser, and you connect to a 40-bit server? The encryption is still carried out using a 40-bit key. You'll only get full security when both browser and server use the 128-bit security software.

Q&A *How safe is Netscape's encryption?*

Very. Data encrypted using the U.S. version, the 128-bit key, is essentially unbreakable. (That's why various U.S. lawmakers have suggested banning this form of encryption; in some countries it's already illegal.) Messages encrypted with the 40-bit key can be broken, but at a very high price. It takes about 64 MIPS-years to break (a million instructions per second for 64 years). A French graduate student recently broke a 40-bit-encrypted message by using spare time on multiple computers. Netscape estimates that it costs $10,000 of computing time to do so. That's a high price to grab one credit card number! (Note that the 128-bit system is not simply three times as strong as the 40-bit system, it's thousands of times stronger; there's no known way to break it.)

How do I actually use this?

Let's see how all this works. Go to the Netscape store; you can get to it from the Netscape home page, or go directly to **http://merchant.netscape.com/netstore/**. We're going to look at how to buy something (don't worry, you can cancel the operation at the last moment).

TIP **If your system administrator has set up your connection to the** Web behind a "firewall"—a security system that limits the type of communications between your network and the outside world—you may find that Netscape is unable to communicate properly with a secure server. If so, talk with your system administer about modifying the firewall.

When you get to the store, click on a link to select the type of product you might want to buy; Software or Bazaar (T-shirts and so on), for example. Continue following links until you come to a product that is for sale. I went into the Surfer Mozilla Boxer page, for instance; just what I've always wanted, boxer shorts with a surfing lizard on them. Make the appropriate selection—color, size, quantity, and so on—then click on the Add to Basket button. In a few moments you'll see the dialog box in figure 15.1. This informs you that you are entering a secure form, and that the data you enter into the form will be transmitted back to the server in an encrypted format.

Click on the Continue button (if you don't want to see these message boxes each time you enter a secure form, clear the Show This Alert Next Time check box). Now you'll see the secure form, something like the one in figure 15.2.

Fig. 15.1
You'll see this message box when you enter a secure document.

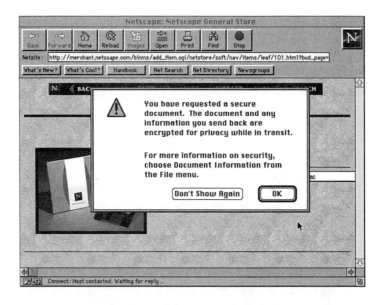

Fig. 15.2
Secure forms are identified by the key in the bottom left corner, and the blue bar at the top.

The URL shows https:// rather than http://

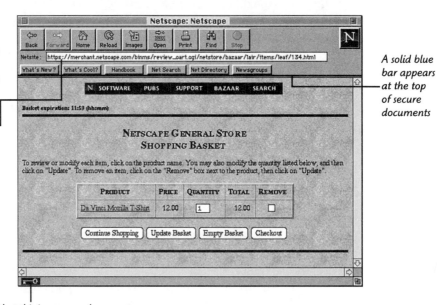

A solid blue bar appears at the top of secure documents

The key indicates that this is a secure document

Notice the blue bar at the top of the content area, and the key icon in the left side of the status bar; these both indicate that you are currently working in a secure document—a document at an **https** server (a secure server).

There are three possible key icons that represent a secure document. The first has just one tooth; it indicates that you will be using the medium security method, the 40-bit method. You'll see this if your browser has the 40-bit software, or if the server has the 40-bit software even though your browser has the 128-bit software.

 Another key icon has two teeth. This indicates that both your browser and the server are using 128-bit software, so the transaction will use high security.

 TIP **You can further confirm the type of security by choosing _V_iew,** Document _I_nfo. In the lower frame you'll see something like: *This is a secure document that uses a medium-grade encryption key suited for U.S. export.* This refers to the 40-bit key.

 Now and again you'll come across mixed-security documents, documents containing some information that will be transferred securely, and some that will go *without* encryption. There's no simple way to figure out which bits will be secure, and which not; but Netscape will indicate that it's a mixed document by ??.

What do you have to do to send information from the form using the encryption? Nothing. Just leave it up to Netscape. Use the form as normal—type the information, click on the Submit or Send button, and so on—and Netscape does the rest. It's all invisible to you; the browser quickly encrypts the data and sends it to the server.

 TIP **Just because Netscape provides security features, doesn't mean** you are totally safe. There are other things that can go wrong. You have no control over what happens to information you send across the Internet once it's received and decrypted by the server. And if other people have access to your computer, they can subvert your attempts at security.

By the way, Netscape is also selling a secure news server. This would allow you to send messages to a newsgroup, and read messages from the group, entirely securely. The messages would be encrypted between the browser and server. Why bother? After all, newsgroup messages are public anyway, aren't they? Well, a secure news server would let an organization set up private newsgroups. A company might have newsgroups in which employees all over the world could discuss private business completely securely, for

instance. To see a secure news server in action, type **snews://
secnews.netscape.com/netscape.server** into the Location text box and
press Enter. You should come up with a window much like figure 15.3.

Fig. 15.3
Very much like normal
news, except you can
see the solid blue bar
and the key indicating
it's a secure document.

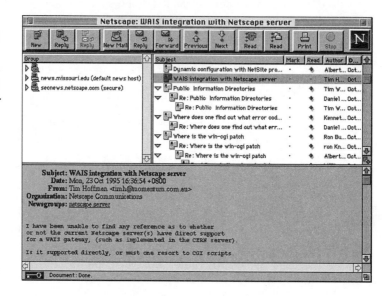

The security messages

By default Netscape will display message boxes informing you of certain
operations: when you enter or leave a secure document, when you enter a
document with a secure and insecure mix, and when you submit information
insecurely. For instance, you click on a Send or Submit button in a form that
is not on a secure server.

You can turn these message boxes off if you wish; choose Options, Security
Preferences, then click on the General tab. Or simply clear the Show This
Alert Next Time check box when one of the messages appears.

The most irritating of these messages is the Submitting a Form Insecurely
message. Most forms on the Internet are insecure, and in any case, in most
cases you won't be submitting anything of importance. For example, each
time you use one of the search sites (as in chapter 7, "Searching for Information on the Web"), you'll be submitting data from a form, but there's no
security risk. So you may want to turn this message box off. Fortunately, this
is pretty easy to do. Choose Options, Security Preferences... and click on the

tab labeled General. You should see a window as in figure 15.4. Then simply click on the check boxes to toggle the options on or off. I tend to prefer off.

Fig. 15.4

If you turn off these

Preferences: Security

General Site Certificates

ace (Server)
ce (Server)
re/Insecure Mix

Cancel   Apply   OK

secure documents or view their source, but
t save them in the cache, so they'll always be reloaded from
you ask for them.

other messages that you have no control over.
ou of the following situations:

mes from a secure server, but submits your data to an

mes from a secure server, but the script that is used to
(the **CGI**—Common Gateway Interface—script) is
aps the CGI referenced by the document is on a

Using certificates

A security **certificate** is a special document that is used to **authenticate** a site or person. It's all part of the public-encryption system. Here's how it works.

A company that's setting up a secure site on the Internet has to get a certificate—otherwise the server can only operate in an insecure manner. The company applies to a **certificate authority**; Netscape has arranged for RSA Certificate Services (which is owned by the company that created the encryption system used by Netscape) to issue certificates, though other companies will issue certificates eventually.

The company uses special software to electronically create the certificate (this is an electronic, not paper, certificate), and sends it to the certificate authority, which then checks that the company applying for the certificate is really what it says it is. The authority then digitally signs the certificate.

 TIP **This public-key encryption thing can get very involved. Suffice it** to say that you can sign a document by using a private key to encrypt it. If someone wants to check the authenticity, they can use the associated public key to decrypt it. Because the private key is secret, and because only the associated public key can decrypt documents encrypted with the private key, that person can be sure that the document is authentic.

The company now has a valid https security certificate, and can install that in its server. When you enter a secure document, the certificate is sent to your browser; choose Options, Document Info and you'll see, in the lower frame, that information (see fig. 15.5).

Fig. 15.5
Choose View,
Document Info to see
the site certificate
information.

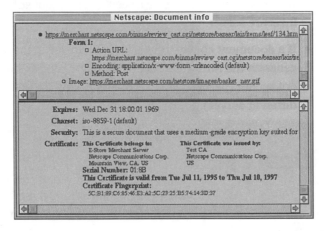

What's it for?

How does a certificate help you? First, without a certificate a server cannot turn on its security features; it cannot accept encrypted transmissions of data from your browser. The name of the issuing authority will also be listed in there—and they're banking their name against these secure transactions.

Editing certificates

You can view lists of the certificates that you have accepted, and the certifying authorities, by choosing Options, Security Preferences, and clicking on the Site Certificates tab. You'll see the dialog box in figure 15.6.

Fig. 15.6
The Site Certificates are of the Security Preferences dialog box, where you can view and edit certificates.

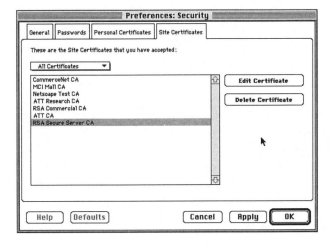

The drop-down list box at the top of this area allows you to modify the contents of the list box; you can view All Certificates, Site Certificates, or Certificate Authorities (the Certificate Authorities list shows the site certificates belonging to the organizations that issue site certificates). Click on an entry and then click on the Edit Certificate button, and you'll see something like figure 15.7.

In this case we clicked on a certification authority in the list. At the top you can see information about the site certificate; it tells you who owns the certificate and who issued it (in this case both the same organization, because this is RSA Data Security, Inc., the company that licensed the encryption software to Netscape Communications, and which also issues certificates).

Fig. 15.7
The Edit A Certifica-
tion Authority dialog
box allows you to tell
Netscape whether to
accept sites authorized
by this authority.

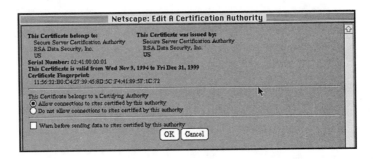

You'll see the certificate's serial number, the dates between which it is valid, and the **fingerprint**. The fingerprint provides a physical way to check the authenticity of a certificate. A company could publish its fingerprint; anyone wanting to confirm that they really have connected to the correct site—and not one masquerading as a site—could compare the fingerprint in the dialog box with the fingerprint in the company's publications. There's no practical way to forge the fingerprint, forcing a forged certificate to use the forged fingerprint.

You have two option buttons in this dialog box; the default selection is Allow Connections to Sites Certified By This Authority. In other words, if your browser connects to a secure site, and that site sends a certificate that has been signed by this certifying authority, the browser should assume that it's safe. (How does Netscape know? You won't see any of this, and don't need to worry about it; the site sends the certificate to Netscape, and Netscape can read the digital signature on that certificate.)

The other option is Do Not Allow Connections to Sites Certified By This Authority. Why would you ever use this? If for some reason you suspect that the certifying authority has certified sites incorrectly. Perhaps the site accidentally issued certificates to a company that is carrying out fraudulent transactions, or somehow the certification procedure was subverted and certificates were issued incorrectly. Either way, you can block this certifying authority. (How will you hear about certification problems? I don't know; this is all in its infancy. Perhaps Netscape Communications would issue warning via e-mail, or post such news at their home page.)

Finally, there's a check box at the bottom: Warn Before Sending Data to Sites Certified by This Authority tells Netscape to display a warning message if the server you are about to send data to was certified by this authority. Again, there may be a problem with some of the certificates issued by this company.

TIP **There's another way to get to all the security information; type about:security** into the Location text box and press Enter. You'll see the Certificate Management Web document with links that let you View Certificates, Delete Certificates, Edit Certificate Trust, and List Certificates.

Other security measures

Netscape has introduced some very important advances in Internet security. Right now, though, Netscape's security features are really not terribly useful to the average user. Yes, they may come in handy now and again, and maybe soon they'll be essential. But there simply aren't many servers using them yet. I took a look at the list of Netscape secure servers (you can find it at the Netscape home page, in the Galleria—**http://home.netscape.com/escapes/ galleria.html**), and there were only about eighty.

But there are other ways to stay safe on the Internet. There are a variety of cybermoney systems around, in use by a few Web sites here and there:

- **First Virtual**—You can open a First Virtual account, then use your account number to buy things online. The store sends your account number to the First Virtual people, who send e-mail to you asking you to confirm. When you confirm, they charge your credit card. For more information, go to **http://firstvirtual.com/**

- **NetCash**—This is like online cash. You apply for an account via e-mail. Then, each time you want money, you ask for a coupon (which is really a serial number representing a sum of money). To buy, you give the merchant the number. **http://www.teleport.com/~netcash/ ncquick.html**

- **Ecash**—Another form of online money (this one's often known as DigiCash—after the company that developed it—or CyberCash). This one uses a special program. You use this program to get money from the "bank" (which takes it from your checking account), and to transfer this ecash to the store. **http://www.digicash.com/ecash/**

16

Netscape and Java— Programs Built Into the Web

● **In this chapter:**

● **What is Java?**

● **Where can I find Java?**

● **Playing an applet**

● **Developing Java on the Macintosh**

Web documents have gone a long way, and Java takes them farther. With Java, you can now download and run programs from anyone who cares to serve them to you. Sound, animation, and most importantly, interaction are now at the door. ➤

One of the most exciting new technologies on the Web is Java. Java is a programming language originally created by Sun Microsystems, Inc. and based on the language C++. It allows a programmer to create a small program (called an **applet**) that can be pulled down through the Web and run on your machine. Netscape has developed a plug-in that allows it to run the Java applets directly. This language might first appear limited, but its capabilities are really quite amazing. There's even a simple Web browser called HotJava written with Java.

So what are Java programs going to do? Right now, they're being used to bring sound and animation into Web documents. Some examples that are available now in Java include:

Frequent document updates—The Web document may contain information that is updated regularly and frequently. As you view the document the information changes before your eyes: stock quotes, weather reports, news reports, and so on.

Expert graphics rendering—A Java applet may be used to display high-resolution graphics, or video—much like RealAudio, except with video and inside the Netscape!

- **User interaction**—A Java applet may contain a game; a crossword puzzle, chess, tic-tac-toe, word-match games, and so on. Games just happen to be the most common example of interaction—you could also search a database in real time, or change the entries for a simulation.

Animation—Web authors can animate their documents: along with the blinking text and images we can place in cartoons that move and react, or perhaps scrolling text and images.

Sounds—Web authors can also use Java to add sounds to their documents; background music, a voice over, a welcome-to-the-page statement, and so on.

After Java is well integrated into the Web (as I mention in my tip—it's not available while I'm writing this book), the Web will have a completely different look and feel. It will be more like using a multimedia CD; very interactive, in motion, and more responsive.

TIP **Java applets are designed to be secure. If the applet provides** interaction between you and the server—you might be able to enter information, and receive information back from the server—the information is transferred securely. Java also has protection against viruses and tampering, but you have to make sure to enable those features.

To protect you against malicious programming, Java is set so that it can't access your hard disk. It's up to you to choose the programs you trust in Java and give them permission to access your hard disk.

If you want to be extra secure, you can also disable Java. Choose Options, Security Preferences, and click on the Disable Java check box. You'll still be able to view Web pages with embedded Java applets, but a blank space will be left where the applet should go.

Where can I find Java?

As I'm writing, Java isn't available for the Macintosh. But Java is out there! Shortly after this book is published, perhaps while you're reading this, you'll be able to go out and find Java for the Mac and start running with it.

If you want to browse the Web and check out Java, the site to start with is Sun's Java page: **http://java.sun.com/**, shown in figure 16.1.

Fig. 16.1
Sun's Java page is the central server for the latest breaking news regarding Java on the Internet.

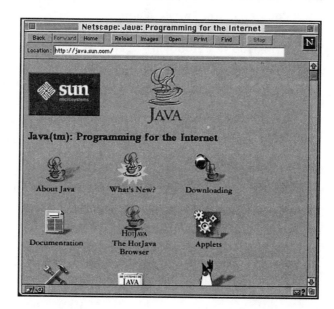

From Sun's Java page, you can get the details on various applets that are available by clicking on the applets icon. This will take you to **http://java.sun.com/applets/** as shown in figure 16.2.

Fig. 16.2

The Java applet page isn't the place to find the applets themselves, but it's guaranteed to point to somewhere that does list them!

One of the sites that probably will maintain lots of links to Java applets is Gamelan. Working closely with Sun, they're providing a constant registry of new and old Java applets. You can find their central index of applets at **http://www.gamelan.com**, shown in figure 16.3.

TIP   **While you're out looking at applets, you'll notice there are both alpha and beta applets.** Sun made some significant changes to the Java language when it was developing it, hence the indication. Netscape will be set to run **beta** applets, not alpha. Many links, especially at the Gamelan Registry, will indicate whether you are about to view an alpha or beta applet.

In the age old feature of the Internet, several folks have created a Java Frequently Asked Questions index. You'll find a great number of FAQs about topics on the Internet, and the more complex the topic—probably the more FAQs will exist. In the case of Java, there's an index of some of the FAQs pages. You can find it at **http://java.sun.com/faqIndex**, shown in figure 16.4.

Fig. 16.3
Gamelan provides an index to not only the applets, but also the code so that if you wish to develop your own Java applets, you can see what others have done.

Fig. 16.4
The FAQ index will provide a list of pages that should answer a large number of your questions. They're updated frequently and are excellent resources!

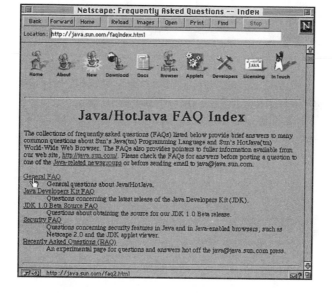

Playing an applet

What do you have to do to play one of these applets? Nothing. At least, nothing beyond what you normally do when entering a Web page; click on the link, or type the URL and press Enter, or whatever. When the Web page opens, Netscape will load the Java applet at the same time.

TIP **The progress bar doesn't work well with Java applets. It works for** a short while, during the time that the Java applet is being transferred to your computer. But then the progress bar stops working, even though nothing may be happening. You might see a blank gray box, for instance, while nothing else is happening. However, listen for your hard drive; your drive is probably churning away, preparing the applet.

Netscape has some information about Java, which you can find at **http:// home.mcom.com/comprod/products/navigator/version_2.0/ java_applets/index.html**, shown in figure 16.5. As I'm writing this, they're saying Java is going to be available very soon, but don't give much more information other than it will be forthcoming.

Fig. 16.5

The Netscape Java page will let you know about the latest developments in Netscape and how it works with Java.

Of course, after the applet is loaded, it might want you to interact with it. If the applet is a game, for instance, you'll have to know how to play the game; a good applet will provide instructions, of course.

TIP **If a Java applet is a play-once applet—a welcoming message in the** Web author's voice, for instance—you don't have to leave the page to replay it. Simply click on the Reload button.

Developing Java on the Macintosh

The first folks out there with a development kit for Java on the Macintosh appears to be Natural Intelligence, Inc. If you're interested in developing Java, or just can't wait for Netscape to incorporate Java into its browser, you can check out their development kit at **http://www.natural.com/pages/ products/roaster/flyer.html**, shown in figure 16.6.

Fig. 16.6

Roaster is the first Java development kit out for the Macintosh.

If you're lacking a compiler on the Macintosh, there's even a public domain Java byte code compiler. Located at **http://mars.blackstar.com/** and shown in figure 16.7, it uses the latest Netscape features to allow you to choose a file to upload to it and returns a compiled Java applet.

In addition to any development kits you find or use, Netscape should be able to help you troubleshoot your applets. Click on a link to a Web page containing a Java applet, then quickly choose Options, Show Java Console. A large window opens, and displays the program as it runs.

Fig. 16.7
The Black Star public compiler is making it easy for anyone who wants to get involved to develop Java applets.

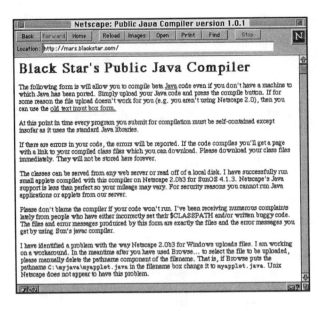

17

Netscape Scripting with JavaScript

● **In this chapter:**

● **What is JavaScript?**

● **What can JavaScript do?**

● **JavaScript versus Java**

● **Where to learn about JavaScript**

● **What events can JavaScript watch for?**

● **JavaScript examples**

JavaScript—another way for Web authors to add interactivity
to their documents . . . . **➤**

There's another way that a Web developer may create active Web documents, documents that do things and allow you to do things to them. Developers can use **JavaScript**, Netscape and Sun's new scripting tool.

What is JavaScript

Well first off, it's not Java. JavaScript was designed by both Netscape and Sun to accompany Java. Think of JavaScript as a macro language for Netscape. Like Java, (see chapter 16, "Netscape and Java—Programs Built Into the Web") it adds function to a Web document, but unlike Java, it doesn't require the heavy-duty programming skills. If a Web author can understand how to create HTML documents, he can probably understand how to work with JavaScript. JavaScript is actually based on Java, but it's a much easier to use version.

TIP **If you're familiar with Hypercard's language, HyperScript, you may** notice a lot of similarities between the two. Instead of dealing with cards, you have pages and documents, and instead of buttons, you get URLs and Form input tags.

This core similarity is an aspect of the language (JavaScript really is a programming language—so is HyperScript) known as Object Oriented Programming. Basically, it's just passing messages back and forth between objects—those objects being things like pages, frames, and Form input tags in Netscape.

What can JavaScript do?

So what can JavaScript actually do? It allows a Web author to script events, objects, and actions. The author can tell the document to watch for certain actions: when the document is opened by a browser, when the browser moves from the document to another one, when the reader clicks the mouse button, and so on. It then allows Netscape to act upon those actions. It could link the Web document to a Java applets, or load another URL in a new window. It brings a lot of other (external) features into the Web document without requiring a whole lot of programming skills.

The developer might use JavaScript to add sounds to a document—a sound may play when the document is opened by the browser, or when a reader clicks the mouse button on an icon. Another possibility is an inline picture may change according to the time of day. One of the neatest features is that Web forms can now quickly check that the correct information has been entered, *before* that information is transmitted back to the server (that is, making sure a field that wants a telephone number didn't get an e-mail address).

Another possible use to link it to a Java applet. For instance, the reader may choose a particular model, type, or color from an order form. The Java applet—on receiving JavaScript instructions generated when the reader made his selection—could then display the appropriate object.

JavaScript versus Java

I said JavaScript was different from Java, but what are the differences?

Well, the differences are plenty. For one thing, only Netscape can do JavaScript right now—although plenty of other folks are starting to want to be able to add this feature as well. But that only really tips off the differences.

JavaScript is a flexible language, much like HyperScript. Like HyperScript, it's easy to understand—the basic concept is that all the parts of a Web page can talk to each other. In essence, they're sending messages. While this itself isn't different from the function of Java, the programming of it is. In JavaScript, you simply specify the event that a piece of the Web page is looking for, and what it does if that happens. An easy example would be to say when someone looking at your page clicks on this link, load up a sound file and play it.

JavaScript is also easier to program because you dont have to be as finicky with the variables. Java is based on C++, and like C++ it has what's known as strong type-checking. This means you can't fudge and assume the program knows if you want to treat a number like a letter or vice-versa. JavaScript is a lot more forgiving, in fact—it's made so that you don't have to worry about all those details—you can just write up what you want it to do in general terms. It's those general terms that make it easy to work with.

One of the downsides to JavaScript is that it's slower. Since Java is already compiled, it can run much faster. JavaScript needs to be interpreted by Netscape each time Netscape loads the page. With Java, it just downloads the program and runs it.

Java is also more flexible for the really complex tasks. Java itself is a more complex programming language, and where that makes JavaScript easier to learn, it also makes Java much more powerful, and generally capable of more things.

Finally, the last benefit of JavaScript is that it's already embedded into the Web page. Java applets are separate documents that you have to download. Once you've gotten a page with a JavaScript, it's there and ready to go.

Where to learn about JavaScript

If you're interested in learning about how to create JavaScripts to use in your Web pages, Netscape keeps the definitive home for the language. You go to **http://home.netscape.com/comprod/products/navigator/version_2.0/ script/script_info/index.html** for an overview and index. As I'm writing this book, JavaScript is still under development, but a good amount of it has been documented, as you can see in figure 17.1.

Fig. 17.1
Youll notice that this page is making use of frames as well—which we looked at in chapter 18, "Web Hypertext Grows Up— Frames."

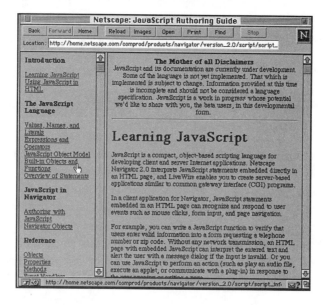

From this page, you can get references on the language—what items Netscape recognizes as objects, what commands you can perform, and how they talk to each other. Netscape has the beginning of a tutorial there, located at **http://home.netscape.com/comprod/products/navigator/ version_2.0/script/script_info/authoring.html**.

What events can JavaScript watch for?

When can JavaScripts run? Web authors can set up their documents to run JavaScripts when events such as these occur:

- When Netscape opens a Web page or other document.

- When you move from one Web page to another—by using the history list or bookmarks, for instance.

- When input focus changes; for instance, when you press Tab to move the cursor from one field in a form to another.

- When you select text in a field.

- When you modify text in a field.

- When you click on a button.

- When you click on a command button.

- When your browser sends the contents of the form back to the server.

- When you click on a link.

- When you simply point at a link.

Although I can't really go into the details of how to create JavaScripts, this should help give you an idea of whats possible with JavaScript.

JavaScript examples

Right now there are only a few examples of JavaScript in action. While I was writing this book, they fully announced JavaScript and a lot of sites have yet to make heavy use of it. In fact, I've been able to find only one, a reverse polish notation calculator (also known as Postfix Notation Calculator), at **http://home.netscape.com/comprod/products/navigator/ version_2.0/script/calc.html** (which you can see it in fig. 17.2).

This doesn't look much different from something you might do in a Java applet. That, of course, is the point of JavaScript—authors can create objects and events in their documents that might be created using Java, but with much less effort. In effect, this is a form, but with much more interactivity than most forms you'll find on the Web. Most allow you to enter information and click on a button to send the information. But this JavaScript example does more; it responds by returning the results of your actions directly to the form. It works just like a calculator (of course you have to understand reverse notation to use it; read the instructions above the calculator.)

Fig. 17.2

This reverse notation calculator is run using JavaScript.

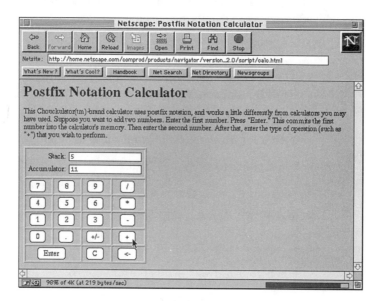

Another example using the calculator idea is located at **http://home.netscape.com/comprod/products/navigator/version_2.0/script/interest.html**. In figure 17.3, the JavaScript uses the fields in the form to calculate the monthly payments depending on what you type in for interest rate, number of payments, and principal loaned.

Much like Java has a central repository for Java applets, there is also a central storehouse, if you will, of JavaScript programs. Like Java, it's maintained at Gamelan (**http://www.gamelan.com/**) at **http://www.gamelan.com/Gamelan.javascript.html**, also shown in figure 17.4.

TIP **If you want to view the JavaScripts themselves in these documents,** choose View, Document Source to display the files. Some of them will be long, but you should be able to figure them out if you're interested.

Fig. 17.3
Although the form has a compute button, it's set to work out the details once you've filled in three fields.

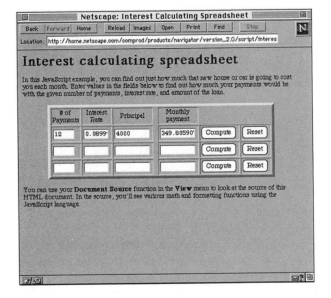

Fig. 17.4
Since Gamelan is working closely with Sun, this archive will probably have good information and examples of JavaScript when you're reading this book.

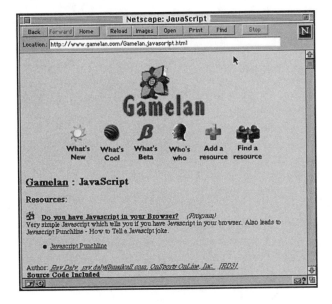

18

Web Hypertext Grows Up—Frames

● In this chapter:

● **What are frames?**

● **Uses and examples of frames**

● **The problem with frames**

● **Targeted windows**

Finally, multiple frame (or pane) Web documents . . . . . . ➤

For all the excitement about the World Wide Web, it's actually a fairly primitive form of hypertext. I'm not talking about all the multimedia stuff—the sound, video, pictures, and so on. I'm talking about the basic way in which documents are handled. Until recently Web browsers could only display one document at a time. Click on a link and the current document would disappear and another would appear. The best that you could do was to open another window in which to display a new document. For instance, in Netscape you can right-click on a link and choose New Window With This Link. A new Netscape window opens and displays the referenced document. But what you are really doing in such a case is starting a new Web session. You'll end up running multiple Web sessions, but the documents within are still single-view documents.

 TIP **There was one browser, created early on, that tried to work with** Frames and make the Web easier to browse, but it didn't address the need for the Web documents themselves to be built that way. With the Frames supported by Netscape, it's the document telling the browser how to format instead of the other way around.

Some other forms of hypertext handle documents in a different way. They may allow the hypertext author to open secondary windows, for instance; the reader would click on a link, and another window would open showing the referenced document. The first window would remain open. This, at first glance, appear to be the same as Netscape's New Window With This Link command. It's not, though, because in this case the author is determining that a new window should open, so it's the author who can determine the flow of the session. You are not opening another hypertext session, you are following the flow of the document according to the wishes of the author.

What are frames?

Another way that other hypertext systems can handle text is by using multiple panes. In other words, while you may be viewing only one window, there may be two or three individual areas within the window, maybe more. One pane may contain special controls needed, another may contain a picture, another may contain a list of cross reference links.

Well, Netscape has now introduced both these concepts; Web authors can now create documents that open multiple panes within a Netscape window (in Netscape-speak they are known as **frames**), and can also tell Netscape when to open a new window. The basic concept of the feature is to give the HTML author a little more control over the page layout, and when done properly, frames can really enhance the usability of a Web site.

Uses and examples of frames

Lets consider how frames can be used, and take a look at a few examples. Here are a few ways youll see frames employed:

- Authors can add banners to their documents. The banner at the top (a corporate logo, for instance) remains static, while you can scroll through the contents of the document in the lower frame. Static areas such as this are known as **ledges**.

- A form in one frame may be used to accept data from you, while the other frame displays the results after you've submitted the form. For instance, you might enter information for which you want to search in the form, submit the form, then view the results in the second frame.

- An author may add a control bar in one frame, the document in the other; clicking on the control bar would take you out of the current document, to another part, to a different framed document, and so on. This is another form of ledge.

- A table of contents might be displayed in the left frame, with the document in the right frame. Clicking on an entry in the table of contents would display the selected document in the right frame.

- A company may choose to keep its copyright information in a frame, so it's a constant reminder to the reader.

Different framed documents will work in different ways. Here are few things to look for:

- Frames may be fixed in place.

- Frames may be movable. Point at a border between a frame; if the pointer changes to two parallel lines with two arrows (see fig. 18.1) you can drag the border to reposition it.

- Links within documents can be set up to take you to away from the framed document to a completely different document, to replace the contents of the frame, or to replace the contents of one of the *other* frames in the document.

- Frames are independently scrollable; that is, you can scroll through the contents of one frame while the contents of the other frames remain static.

- Frames can even contain different documents. For instance, clicking on a link in one frame may change the contents of one of the other frames, bringing in a document from a different location entirely. Now you have two different documents displayed in the same window.

A table of contents

Figure 18.1 shows a good example of frames used to create a table of contents. This is JavaScript reference information (see chapter 17, "Netscape Scripting with JavaScript", for information about JavaScript). The left frame is the table of contents. When you click on an entry in the left frame, the referenced document appears in the right frame. Notice the mouse pointer on the border has changed; this means you can move this border.

Fig. 18.1

The left frame provides a permanent table of contents; click on a link to change the document in the right frame. (Notice the mouse pointer, indicating that the border is movable.)

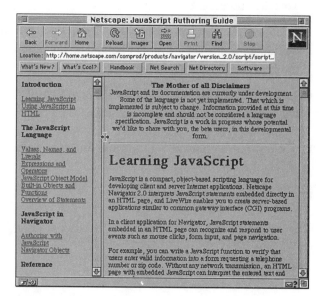

Q&A *Where can I find more framed documents?*

You can find lots of samples of framed documents from the Netscape home page. In particular try the Companies Using Frames document (**http://home.m.com.com/comprod/products/navigator/version_2.0/frames/frame_users.html**).

A table of contents and a ledge

The Web page in figure 18.2 contains three frames; the one on the right is a table of contents (using pictures instead of words), the one at the top is a ledge containing links to other areas of Fashionmall's Web site (**http://fashionmall.com/**), and the large area is the content area. Both the content area and the table of contents are scrollable. (Notice the mouse pointer on the horizontal border, by the way; it hasn't changed form, so these are non-adjustable borders.)

Fig. 18.2
This document has a table of contents on the right and a ledge containing other links at the top.

Input/output frames

The example in figure 18.3 shows how an author can set up one frame in which you input data, and another in which you view the results. This is the Ecola Tech Directory site, where you can search for Web sites maintained by high-tech companies (**http://www.ecola.com/techcorp/frames.htm**).

Fig. 18.3
Enter your data in the top frame; see the results in the lower frame.

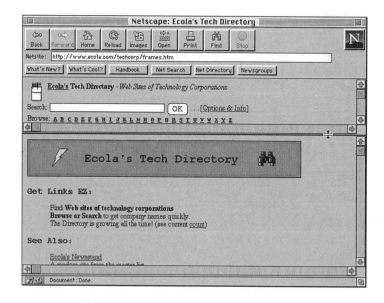

A banner (and more)

Here's an example of a banner. The document in figure 18.4 (**http://www.piper-studios.com/**) has a banner at the top containing the company name; scroll through the content area (the large frame), or choose something from the table of contents in the left frame, and the banner remains in place. There's also a ledge at the bottom of the window. (Of course the banner is a form of ledge, too; they are both non-scrolling areas.)

Fig. 18.4
Here's an example of a frame used to place a banner at the top.

My favorite example

One of the nicest framed documents I've seen so far is actually a demo document. It's the How We See document, which you can get to from the Netscape home page (**http://home.mcom.com/comprod/products/ navigator/version_2.0/frames/eye/index.html**). The largest frame contains a picture of the eye, with callouts pointing to the eyes various components. Each callout is a link; click on a callout to change the contents of the frame on the right side. The top frame is a static banner. You can see this document in figure 18.5.

Fig. 18.5
The How We See demo document.

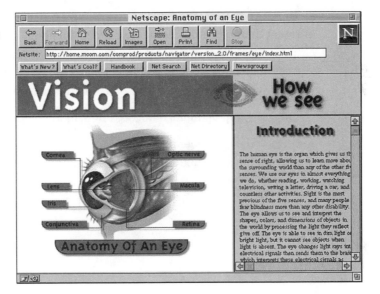

The problem with frames

Frames can be irritating if they are not used properly. There's a tendency for many Web authors to use every neat toy that's available, without considering whether they are really appropriate. We're going to see a lot of frames on the Web pretty soon, placed there not because authors feel they *should*, but because they know they *can*!

Frames can sometimes clutter up the Netscape window, particularly for people using small screens. I've already heard complaints from Web users about frames, and there are very few out there yet. And I've run into one extremely annoying situation. I found a document with a ledge at the bottom.

When I clicked on links in the main area, though, the frame remained in the window; the author had set up the document to change the content of the main frame, but retain the frame at the bottom. The problem with this is that Netscape assumes you are in the same document, and doesn't record your travels at the other site in the history list. So when you try to go back through those travels, using the history list or Back button, you can't! (Back will take you out of the framed document, back to the document you viewed immediately before viewing the framed document.)

There are a few ways around this problem:

- To return to the previous document displayed in that particular frame—rather than returning all the way to the document that was displayed immediately before you entered the framed document—move the pointer inside the frame and hold down the mouse button until the pop-up menu appears. Then choose Back in this Frame.

- Using the pop-up menu, choose New Window With This Link.

- Using the pop-up menu, choose Copy This Link Location, paste the link into the Location text box, and press Enter.

Targeted windows

The other feature I mentioned earlier—allowing Web authors to automatically open another window and place the referenced document in that window—is known as **targeted windows**. The extensions that are built into Netscape to make Frames work allows the Web author to create names for any framed document—including a document with no frames at all. The Web author can assign a document to a new blank window, a frame that's already open, or a previous frame (or window). When you click on the link, Netscape will look around for the named frame or window and either place in the document or open a new window and put the document inside.

For example, if you look at the WebSpace home page (**http://webspace.sgi.com/Mission/index.html**) shown in figure 18.6, you'll see a document with a graphical table of contents on the left and an information frame on the right.

Fig. 18.6

As an aside, WebSpace is a powerful program that should be ported to the Macintosh very soon. Definitely a wave of the future.

If you select one of the items on the left, the Web author has made these pages so that they show up in the frame to the right. Clicking on WebSpace Navigator, for example, bring up a Web document in the right hand frame about the program itself.

Other examples may include clicking on one of those subject items and having a new window open with the appropriate information, or may replace the document in the second window with the new document. The end result is this capability gives the author a little more control over how you're viewing the Web page.

19

Creating Your Own Web Page

● In this chapter:

- Why create your own home page?

- Opening the Editor

- How do I place text in my new home page?

- Creating links to other Web documents

- Creating a multiple documents

- The Sections of a Web Page

- A little about HTML codes

At the time of this writing, you couldn't use Netscape Navigator to help you create Web pages, but there are other programs out there to help you. Web Weaver is one of them . . ▶

When the Web was originally conceived, the whole thing was supposed to be a bunch of documents that anyone could edit. Obviously that's not how it's developed today, but it's still very easy to publish your own stuff. In addition to just being fun, it's a great way to get a feel for how HTML works, and you'll produce something you can use, too. How do you go about producing a home page? Well, there are plenty of freeware, shareware, and commercial HTML authoring tools you can use. But we're going to look at one in particular—Web Weaver.

Web Weaver was written to use Netscape as a helper to show the pages you develop, and internally has some great authoring and editing tools that help you create a Web page from scratch. In this and the following chapters, I'm going to assume you are working with Web Weaver, which you can find at **ftp://ftp.cdrom.com/pub/mac/umich/util/comm/www/ htmlwebweaver2.53.sit.hqx**, and at other Macintosh software archives.

 TIP Windows users have the advantage of using Netscape's Navigator Gold software. This version of Netscape allows people to create their own pages WITH Netscape, instead of some other program.

Your First Home (Page)

What is a home page? Here's a quick refresher:

- It's the page that appears when you open Netscape. (Assuming you have the Preferences set up to display a home page—choose Options, General Preferences, then look under the Appearance tab.)

- It's the page that appears when you click on the Home toolbar button or choose Go, Home.

As I've mentioned earlier in this book, there's currently some ambiguity about the term home page. The term *home page* has come to mean two things. The original meaning is the page that appears when you open your browser or use the Home command. The new meaning is a page that you have published on the Web, a page that others on the Web can view (as in the Rolling Stones' home page). Most people referring to home pages today will be talking about pages that someone published on the Web.

Why would you want to create your own home page? For these reasons:

- Everyone uses the Internet in a different way. The page provided by Netscape may be okay to start with, but it won't have all the links you want, and it may contain plenty that you don't. You can certainly create a home page with all the links you like, and use it instead of the one Netscape provides.

- You can provide some general information about yourself to others out in the World Wide Web, or even just put up a page with topics you find interesting.

How do you open the Editor?

Web Weaver is the editor itself. Getting it started is as simple as running the program. If you just wanted to start from scratch, you could just run the program by double-clicking on the icon. Figure 19.1 shows a new window opened in Web Weaver.

You could also start with editing a text file you have already created by dragging that file onto the Icon of Web Weaver. Now why would you want to do this? Well, eventually you'll want to edit some of the documents you've created, or you might want to take something from a word processor and mark it up by hand to make sure it looks like what you want in the Web.

Fig. 19.1
The Editor window provides the tools you need to create or modify a Web page.

The editing screen (notice your pointer turns into an I-beam, indicating it's ready to edit)

The toolbar

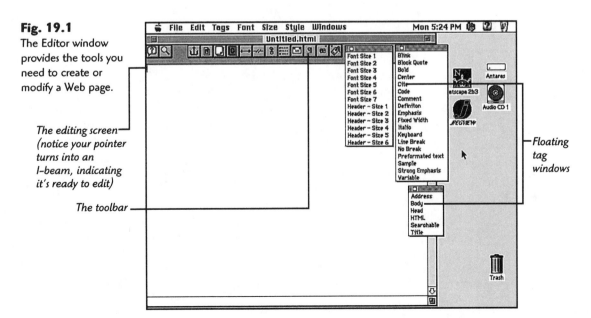

Floating tag windows

Here's a quick summary of what each button does.

 Balloon Help—Click here to turn on and off Balloon help. Balloon help will give you an overview of what items on the screen do, including these other buttons.

 Preview—Click here to preview your HTML document.

 Anchor—This button brings up a dialog box to help you create an anchor tag within a document.

 Images & Files—Pressing this button will bring up a dialog box helping you place graphics within your Web page.

 Forms—Another button that brings up a dialog box— this one to help you create forms.

 Glossary—This button allows you to define words in a Glossary, which Web Weaver can later expand upon.

 Horizontal Rule—This button drops a horizontal line into your web page.

 Line Break—Another button to drop a single tag into your document— a line break tag.

 Link—Clicking on this button will bring up the dialog box to help you create a link to another document or web page.

 List—This button brings up a dialog box to make creating lists on the Web easier.

 E-mail To—A simple dialog box appears when you click this button to help you create mailto links in your document.

 Paragraph Break—Clicking this button drops a paragraph break into your document.

 Special Characters—To use this button, you need to click and hold down the mouse button. It then shows you a list of possible special characters— characters which don't otherwise work easily in Web pages.

 Format tags—Another button you need to click and hold down the function. This brings up a list of formatting tags for your web page.

Entering your text

Let's start creating a home page. Type this text into the Editor window (you can see an example in fig. 19.2):

Fig. 19.2
Oh, and change the last line to be your name and today's date.

Right now all we have is basic text. If we previewed this in Netscape, it would look horrible—all run together. To keep it from doing that, we need to insert the special codes—the HTML tags—that will make it appear the way we want.

Making these changes is very easy. For instance, try this:

1 Highlight the text *My Home Page*, then select **Header—Size 1** from the floating boxes on the side. You'll see the text get significantly larger, and the HTML tags will appear to either side: <H1> and </H1>.

2 Highlight that whole line of text again, click the Format Tags button and hold it down until the menu appears. Select center from the list, and you'll see more tags appear around the text.

TIP   **What we've really just done is show you two ways to get the same** thing accomplished. You can select those tags either from the floating palettes that side along-side the editor window or from the Format Tags button.

3 Now click just above the last line you typed in— the stuff with your name and date. Press the Horizontal Rule button and you'll see the <HR> tag appear above your final line of text.

Q&A ***Why are there so many header sizes?***

HTML is a derivative of a language called SGML, which is used in professional typesetting to lay out books and similar documents. In SGML, there were a number of headers based on what part of the document you were in. For example, the title of the document would have the largest header, while chapters would have a slightly smaller header, and sections in each of those chapters would be smaller still. These have carried over into HTML, and so we have six different header sizes, with one being the largest and six the smallest.

Now what have we got? Let's go ahead and preview this document by clicking on the Preview Button. You should then see your page (an example is shown in fig. 19.3). When you're done checking it out, go back to Web Weaver and the document source that we're creating.

Fig. 19.3
It's not perfect—but it's definitely a start!

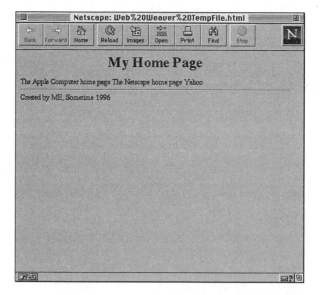

TIP **If you haven't ever used Web Weaver before, it's going to want to** know what program to use to preview these pages you're creating. All you have to do is locate your copy of Netscape in the dialog box provided, and it will remember the rest.

Before we go on, let's save what we've done; saving in Web Weaver is like any other Macintosh application, just choose <u>F</u>ile, <u>S</u>ave and type in the name for the file in the dialog box provided. As a side note, you generally want to end all Web pages with the suffix .html, because that's how most machines identify what kind of file it is—by that suffix.

Where'd my line breaks go?

In the preview you probably noticed that even though we typed Apple Computer and Netscape on separate lines they were run together. This is because Netscape (and all the other Web browsers) ignore linebreaks unless you specifically tell them to exist.

But why did the last line show up correctly? Well, it's really pretty simple: the horizontal rule code implies that you're going to have a new line beneath it. So do any of the header items.

So you want to enter those breaks? Okay, pretty easy. Go back to your Web Weaver program (if you're not already there) and click at the end of the line with Apple Computer. You should see a vertical bar blinking there—now click **line break** from the tag list on the floating palette. You'll see a <BR> tag appear.

Now you might want a larger break—like the break between paragraphs. Again, just click at the end of the line—this time the line with Netscape in it, and click on the paragraph button in the tool bar.

Q&A *I've made changes to my document, but want to go back to the way it was the last time I saved it—how can I do that?*

Press ⌘+R or choose <u>V</u>iew, <u>R</u>eload.

How about links?

Now we're going to get fancy. Let's add a **link** to another document. For instance, you may want to add a link to the Netscape home page (on the other hand, you may not; you can always choose <u>D</u>irectory, <u>N</u>etscape's Home to get there, even if you are using your own home page), or perhaps a link to a favorite site. Since I asked you to type in the line *The Netscape home page* we might as well create a link to it.

Plain English, please!

The HTML tags used to create links are also known as anchors; but there's a number of different kinds of anchors. Some can be used to link into this document, and some are for making links to other pages. The one we're creating now is for linking to another web page. **"**

Highlight the line *The Netscape home page* and click on the link button, or choose <u>T</u>ags, <u>L</u>ink. You should see the dialog box as in figure 19.4

Fig. 19.4
Enter the address of the page you want to link to, in this case home.netscape.com.

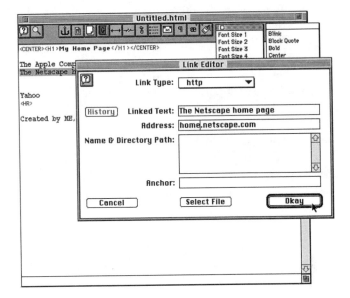

When you've typed in the location you want to link to, click Okay and you'll see a lot of tags appear around the text. Try the same for the Apple Computer home page and Yahoo. The locations for these places are **www.apple.com** and **www.yahoo.com**.

Where do I get these URLs?

A number of places; you might use Netscape to go to the page you want and copy the URL from the Location bar. Remember also that you can use the pop-up menu to copy a link location, which would be perfect for this.

What about pictures?

No self-respecting Web page would be complete without a picture or two, would it? Luckily the Editor provides a way for you to insert pictures.

Where are you going to get pictures for your documents? You can create them yourself, using an graphics program that can save in a .JPG or .GIF format (many can these days). You can also grab them from the Web, remember! Find a picture you want, right-click on it, and choose Save This Image As. (Note, however, that you don't *own* the image, as it may not be in the public domain. You can use it on your own system, but don't put it on a Web site open to the public unless you have permission to use it or know for sure it's in the public domain.)

 TIP   **Want to find some icons you can use in your documents? Go to an** *icon server:* a Web site from which you can download icons or even link your documents across the Web to a particular icon. Try these:

http://www.bsdi.com/icons
http://www-ns.rutgers.edu/doc-images
http://www.di.unipi.it/iconbrowser/icons.html
http://www.cit.gu.edu.au/~anthony/icons/

Clicking on the File and Images button will bring up a dialog box as shown in figure 19.5.

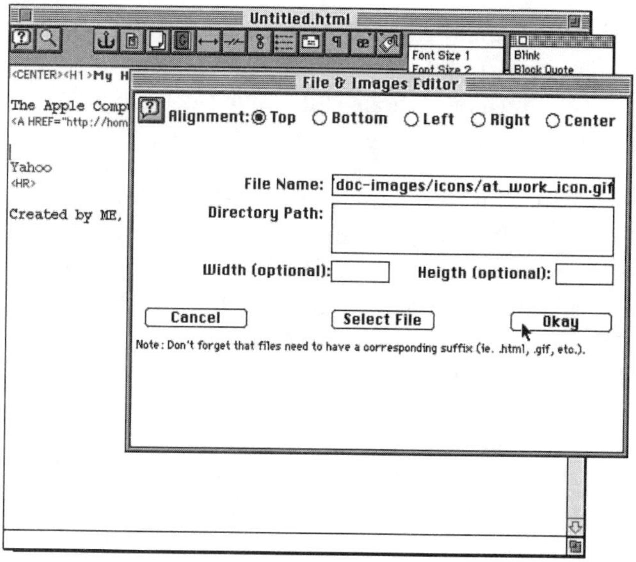

Fig. 19.5
You're going to need to know the location of the image you want to link to—this could be the most difficult part, if Netscape didn't make it so easy to find them out.

Once you have the dialog box open, you can choose what image you want to link in. An extremely common image is the under construction icon that appears all over the place. If you want to join the fad, the location is **http://www-ns.rutgers.edu/doc-images/icons/at_work_icon.gif**.

TIP **There's a special line break command that makes sure that text** placed after an image is not "wrapped" around the image. This tag forces the text to appear *below* the image.

Unfortunately, Web Weaver doesn't include it normally. The easiest way to create it is to change the tag yourself. Change the tag **
** to say **<BR CLEAR=LEFT>**, and that'll do the trick.

Creating Multiple Documents

You may want to create a group of documents. You could, for example, create a page that appears when you open Netscape, with a table of contents linked to several other documents. In each of those documents, you could then have links related to a particular subject—one for business, one for music, one for your kids, and so on.

This is very simple to do. Create and save several documents in Web Weaver (I suggest you put them all in the same folder, for simplicity's sake). Each time you finish one, choose File, New Document to clear the screen so you can create the next one.

When you want to link to a document in the same folder, that's called making a relative link. Instead of going to the trouble of specifying out every little detail about where the page is, we just tell it the file's name and it assumes the file is in the same folder as the original page. For example, if you wanted to link to a file called fred.html, you would fill out the link dialog box as shown in figure 19.6.

Choose **local html file** from the link type pop-up menu, and type **fred.html** in for the location. Remember, this file has to be in the same folder as the one you're linking it from to work properly.

Fig. 19.6
Relative links make pages much easier to move because you can move whole clusters of them at a time.

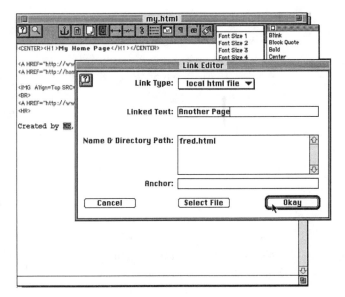

How can I use my home page?

You've created a home page; now how do you use it? Follow this procedure:

1 Click on the Preview icon to bring up Netscape and show your document (if it's not already there).

2 Click in the Location text box, highlighting the URL.

3 Press ⌘+C to copy the URL.

4 Choose Options, General Preferences, and click on the Appearance tab.

5 Click on the Home Page Location option button (in the Startup area) is selected.

6 Click inside the text box below this option button.

7 Press ⌘+V to paste the URL into the text box.

8 Click on OK.

Now, the next time you start your browser, you'll see your very own home page. Pretty neat, huh?

Here's a good one...let's change it

Web Weaver allows you to open up other HTML documents and modify them for your own use. If you see a page you like, one that has many links that you'll need in your home page for instance, or one that uses a particularly attractive format, you can open that page and make changes to it, then save it on your hard disk.

 CAUTION **Be aware that you don't own something you "borrow" from the** Web. If you borrow something from the Web and simply keep it for your own use, there's no problem. But if you publish it—creating a Web site using pictures and text you grabbed from another Web site, for instance, you may be guilty of a copyright violation. If you use the borrowed stuff as a template, replacing everything in the page with your own stuff, in most cases there's no problem (though it's possible for a particular design to be copyrighted, too).

First, we need to have that page to edit it.

1 Display the page you want to modify in the Netscape window. Now you have save this document to your hard drive so we can edit it with Web Weaver.

2 Choose <u>F</u>ile, <u>S</u>ave As..., and select source from the pop-up menu that appears. Type in a name for the file and save it to your hard drive..

3 Go to Web Weaver and choose <u>F</u>ile, <u>O</u>pen to open the file we just saved.

Now you have the best of both worlds; you've got the document you need open in Web Weaver, and the browser's still open so you can move around on the Web to find things you want to add to your document.

 TIP **Just because you can edit HTML documents doesn't mean it's** going to be easy. Web Weaver doesn't make it easy to read other HTML documents, and you're going to have to learn a little about HTML tags to really edit it. Still, one of the best ways to learn is to play with it yourself.

The Sections of a Web page

More than just the text of a web page is actually in a web page. There's really two sections to a page, the header and the body. The header is where you put the title of the page, and the body is where you put the rest.

In Web Weaver, there's a floating palette with Body, Head, HTML and TITLE listed. Here's the order they fit in:

<HTML>

   <HEAD>

         <TITLE>Some Title</TITLE>

   </HEAD>

   <BODY>

         your HTML document here

   </BODY>

</HTML>

Generally, you technically want to put the HTML tags around your whole document. Now in reality, almost nothing checks for this, so if you miss it, it's not going to hurt anything. But the HEAD and BODY tags are a lot more important.

The HEAD tag marks off where the TITLE of the document will go (it's own tag) and it's mostly important because the majority of the search engines out on the Internet will list pages by their TITLE. The Title of the document is what will show up in the Window title of Netscape's browser window.

The BODY just marks off where everything else goes—your Web page.

A little about HTML codes

There's a lot written about how to create good HTML documents, what all the codes mean, and how to put it all together. We'll get into the details in the next chapter, but I wanted to list a couple of URLs for you in case you wanted to browse around the web and see what's there already:

- **http://www.ncsa.uiuc.edu/demoweb/html-primer.html**

- **http://home.netscape.com/assist/net_sites/index.html**

Netscape has added a lot of goodies to the pile to make their pages more interesting. You can find lists of what they've added at this site.

20

Advanced Web Authoring

● In this chapter:

- Links, links and more links

- All the different kinds of lists

- Paragraph Styles

- The whole document—backgrounds and text colors

- Text sizes, superscript, and subscript

- Special Characters

The previous chapter only covered the very basics of creating Web pages. There's a lot more to making a good Web page, and not just more codes. . . . . **>**

In the last chapter you learned how to use Web Weaver to create your own home page. But there's more. In this we'll go over some of the advanced things you can do with a Web page. You may want to make your home page really cool, or even use your new skills to publish your own stuff on the Web.

Q&A *I want to publish on the Web. Once I've created my Web pages, where do I put them?*

Ask your service provider if you can place Web pages up on their server. Many allow people to set up Web pages for little or no cost. You can transfer them from your computer to your service provider's site using an FTP program such as Fetch (see chapter 11, "Software Libraries—Using FTP," for more information).

Lots more formatting

There are a number of formatting tools we didn't get around to looking at in chapter 19. There are a number of ways that you can format a paragraph, by setting up indents and alignment, as well as by choosing a paragraph style. And you can modify particular words or individual characters, too, by changing colors and type styles.

While there are possibly hundreds (if not thousands) of variations to making Web pages, let me caution you right from the outset. Not all of these nifty items are going to work for your aesthetics, and not all of them should be used. There's a lot of pages out there in the Web that are just a bunch of neat things and cool links that are utterly and horribly unusable. Design is of utmost importance if anyone other than you is going to see these pages.

You have to be able to convey your information to make the effort worthwhile.

Links, links and more links

As we mentioned in chapter 19, "Creating Your Own Web Page," there are a couple kind of links. They all involve how much of a URL is listed and what the browser is going to have to assume. You might list only the file name, in which case the browser (Netscape) will know to look in the same folder or directory where the file is located. You might list the path from the front of some server—you'll probably only do this if you're creating Web pages for someone else. Or you might just want to list out the whole thing—down to exactly where it's located. The first two types of links are called **relative URLs**, and the last is called an **absolute URL**.

In relation to Web Weaver, when you're putting in an absolute URL, you'll want to fill in the location field of the link (that's the host name of the machine the page resides on) and the location/path field (that's the stuff after it—the directions into that machine to find the URL).

Finally, pay attention to what text you have linking to other pages. It might seem simple at first to make click here link to some neat page, but really that's not a very effective way of making the Web work for you. Instead, try listing what the site is. For example, instead of:

> <A HREF=www.apple.com>Click Here</A> for Apple's Home Page

you could put

> More information about <A HREF=www.apple.com>Apple's Home Page</A>

All the different kinds of lists

 Web Weaver makes is pretty easy to create lists in an HTML document. You just click on the lists button, and you'll see a dialog box as shown in figure 20.1.

Fig. 20.1

You can create Unnumbered, Numbered, or Descriptive lists by choosing from the radio buttons at the top of the dialog box.

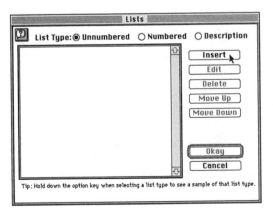

There's essentially three kinds of lists: Unnumbered, Numbered, and Descriptive. You would use them for three different things really, but the Unnumbered lists are probably the most useful. Unnumbered list are also known as bulleted lists.

Unnumbered lists are simple lists with each item preceded by a bullet (a small figure to mark the entry—usually a dot or box). Numbered lists are, not surprisingly, numbered in the order in which you create them. A neat feature is that HTML takes care of the numbering for you—you don't need to worry about renumbering items 6-9 if you remove number item 5.

The final kind of list is a descriptive list. This list is kind of a dual list with two parts—a description title and a description. The Description titles aren't indented, and the descriptions are. These can make for some really great annotated lists.

If you wanted to add some items to the list you're creating, click on the Insert button and you'll see another dialog box as in figure 20.2.

Fig. 20.2

Just type in what you want listed, and click Okay.

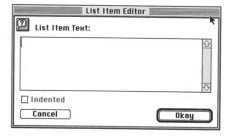

After creating a number of items, you can reorder them, delete items, or edit them. One thing you'll notice is the indent checkbox—that's for the descriptions in the descriptive lists. If you don't have Descriptive list chosen, it won't allow you to choose it.

Finally, there's nothing to keep you from creating a list inside a list. I've seen numerous cases of using an unnumbered list inside a descriptive list to make an outline sort of format on a Web page. To do this in Web Weaver, just make your Descriptive list first, and then set the cursor inside the list and create a new unnumbered list. Violà!

Paragraph Styles

Netscape provides a number of paragraph styles to make your document more effective. You can have normal paragraphs (the default), you can have citations, you can make blocked off quotes, you can mark off text as lines of code, and you can have address paragraphs. Finally, you can also keep text exactly the way you type it in using the preformatted text tags.

You make a paragraph any one of these styles by highlighting the text you want to effect and choosing any of these styles from the floating palettes. Their effects generally appear as:

- Cite

When you set a bunch of text to cite, it generally appears in italics in Netscape. You would use this (strangely enough) for common citations, such as books or magazines. If you're really lucky, you can link your citation to it's source—if it's on the Web.

- Block Quote

Setting block quote indents the section of text and makes it stand out as obvious not part of the surrounding document. Great for listing an extended quote from another source—make sure you cite your sources.

- Code

Used for marking off examples, or lines of programming code, this generally is displayed in a monospaced font.

- Address

Used for marking off addresses, they appear almost the same as citations, just using italicized text.

- Preformatted Text

When you set preformatted text, it appears in a monospaced font (every character is the same width) exactly as you typed it. This can be really handy for lining up quick and dirty tables, or making some fun art with text characters.

Paragraph Alignment

Netscape includes some tags to allow you to justify your text as you like. As you might have noticed, you can also do this with images—it's just a matter of writing the tags correctly. When last I checked, Web Weaver didn't make this easy, but it's not hard to understand so you can do it yourself.

In the paragraph tag (<P>), you can add an **element** to further specify how you want that tag to act. An element is an internal piece of the whole HTML tag. For example, the standard paragraph tag <P> is the same as <P ALIGN=LEFT>. The element that's assumed is the ALIGN=LEFT. Needless to say, you can specify the alignments for paragraphs or images to right, left, or center.

If you wanted to make a paragraph wrap around the left side of an image, you might make the image ALIGN=LEFT and then add the text normally below it.

What if you don't want it to wrap? Well, we actually mentioned this in passing in the last chapter, although we didn't explain it. You add a clear element to a line break tag: <BR CLEAR=ALL>. Clear left makes sure there's a clear left margin before it continues displaying text or images. Clear right does the same for the right margin, and clear all makes sure both sides are clear of images or text.

While we're talking about alignment, let me also point out a tag that I've found handy and which a lot of people seem to use—<CENTER>. You can put the <CENTER> tag around about anything and it will center that on the Web page. Although it's still in common use, the more proper form is to specify justification with an option in the paragraph tag (<P>), so instead of <CENTER> you would use <P ALIGN=CENTER>. As you might expect, you can put in left or right to have the text justify to either side.

The whole document—backgrounds and text colors

Just like there's additions to the paragraph, image, and line break tags, there's additional elements for the <BODY> tag to change the whole document.

Now before I go on to tell you how to use these great effects, I'm going to remind you one more time to make sure your pages are readable first, and cool second. Using some cool features that make your page illegible just makes it worthless.

The additional elements to the BODY tag are BACKGROUND, BGCOLOR, TEXT, and the three LINK elements: LINK, VLINK, and ALINK.

BACKGROUND and BGCOLOR serve essentially the same function—and are not generally used together—they change the background color of the Web page—or put an image there. For example, if you wanted a completely black background, you could add in BGCOLOR=#000000 to the BODY Tag. The codes that go along with these colors are rather obscure, but you can find a list of them at: **http://www.missouri.edu/mu/colors.html**.

TIP **Remember: the backgrounds are supposed to enhance the** document!

Now if you change your background color (or set a background image), you're probably going to want to change you TEXT so it's readable. If you wanted your text to be white on the black background, you would add the element TEXT=#FFFFFF to the BODY tag.

LINK, ALINK, and VLINK are similar to text - they describe links yet to be chosen, links currently being chosen, and links that have already been chosen respectively.

Now, your final BODY tag might read: **<BODY BGCOLOR=#000000 TEXT=#FFFFFF LINK=#00FF00 ALINK=#FF00FF VLINK=#777777>**

Text sizes, superscript, and subscript

A couple of other Netscape tags that can make your document really something are the Text Size, superscript, and subscript tags.

In Netscape, if you want to just increase the size of one character, you can wrap it in a FONT tag. This isn't supported in Web Weaver (to my knowledge anyway), but it's easy to do. If you wanted the size to get one step bigger, you could write **<FONT SIZE=+1>My text</FONT>**. You can specify either bigger or smaller using + or -, and it doesn't force a line break like headers normally do.

It's very much the same with subscript or superscript. The tags for subscript are **_{Some Notation}** and superscript **is <SUPER>Some Notation</SUPER>**.

Special Characters

The last bit about special tags I'll list is that there are some special characters out there in the Web. Originally, it was just kept to an ISO standard (that's an international standard which includes a number of common symbols from other languages) and a few additional special characters. In HTML, they look rather odd—for example the copyright symbol is listed as **©**. Some other relatively common symbols are also listed in this way—the ampersand **&**, the less than **<**, and the greater than **>** sign. They're listed with special symbols because they make up the codes in HTML documents.

In Web Weaver, you can choose to place any of these symbols by simply selecting them from the Special Character button on the toolbar.

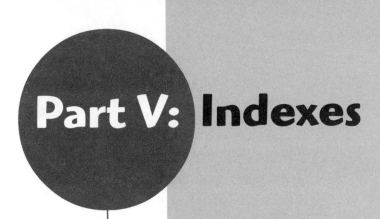

Part V: Indexes

Help Index

Action Index

Help Index

If you have this problem...	You'll find help here...
Where do I find a viewer?	p. 125
What is "RealAudio"?	p. 126
Where is the Virtual Reality on the Web?	p. 132
What is Adobe Acrobat?	p. 128

If you have this problem...	You'll find help here...
What is Gopher?	p. 142
What is FTP?	p. 143
How do I find software for my Mac?	p. 148

If you have this problem...	You'll find help here...
Send a file with e-mail	p. 160
Add someone to my address book	p. 168
How do I set up e-mail?	p. 156

If you have this problem...	You'll find help here...
What is "BinHex"?	p. 194
How do I set up a news server?	p. 182
The message is all scrambled	p. 197

If you have this problem...	You'll find help here...
What is a Key?	p. 224
What is a certificate?	p. 231

If you have this problem...	You'll find help here...
Want to learn to program with Java	p. 243
What is "Java"?	p. 238

If you have this problem...	You'll find help here...
What is JavaScript?	p. 246
What's the difference between Java and JavaScript?	p. 247

If you have this problem...	You'll find help here...
What are Frames?	p. 254

If you have this problem...	You'll find help here...
Where do I find Icons and Pictures?	p. 270
What should I put on my home page?	p. 264
How do I create a link to another page?	p. 269
What HTML editor can I use?	p. 265

If you have this problem...	You'll find help here...
What is a relative URL?	p. 279

Action Index

When you need to...	You'll find help here...
Create a bookmark	p. 70
Change a bookmark	p. 71
Save a bookmark for a friend	p. 74
Use a bookmark	p. 74

When you need to...	You'll find help here...
Use a search engine	p. 79
Find a place	p. 86
Get information on a product or company	p. 91

When you need to...	You'll find help here...
Save this Web page on your machine	p. 99
Copy the graphic that's on the screen	p. 100
Print a document you found	p. 102
Send a Web page to a friend	p. 106

When you need to...	You'll find help here...
Install a sound player for Netscape	p. 115
Install a plug-in Netscape	p. 120

When you need to...	You'll find help here...
Find a new viewer for a video format	p. 125
Find RealAudio	p. 126
Install RealAudio	p. 127
Install another viewer for Netscape	p. 130
Find out about Virtual Reality on the Web	p. 132

When you need to...	You'll find help here...
Find something on the Internet that is not on the Web	p. 143
Use FTP	p. 144
Find a specific program	p. 148
Search through the Macintosh software archives	p. 149

When you need to...	You'll find help here...
Set up your mail program to work	p. 156
Send e-mail to someone	p. 160
Keep an address book of e-mail addresses	p. 168
Read your e-mail	p. 172
Save your e-mail	p. 176

When you need to...	You'll find help here...
Read the UseNet News	p. 193
Get pictures and programs from Newsgroups	p. 194
Post your own news message	p. 199

When you need to...	You'll find help here...
Dig around in Gopherspace	p. 208
Find something via Gopher	p. 211
Search through full-text archives	p. 213
Connect to another machine	p. 218

When you need to...	You'll find help here...
Make sure your transaction is secure	p. 227
Add or remove a certificate	p. 231

When you need to...	You'll find help here...
Find a site with Java	p. 239
Play a Java Applet	p. 241

When you need to...	You'll find help here...
Find a site with JavaScript	p. 246
Learn how to create JavaScript	p. 248
Find more examples of JavaScript	p. 249
Watch JavaScript in action	p. 249

When you need to...	You'll find help here...
View a site with Frames	p. 255
Get a document into its own window	p. 261

When you need to...	You'll find help here...
Learn basic HTML	p. 264
Create your own home page	p. 265
See someone else's HTML codes	p. 275

When you need to...	You'll find help here...
Format a paragraph differently	p. 278
Center a paragraph or image	p. 282
Change the colors in a Web page	p. 282
Change the text size	p. 283
Create a list in HTML	p. 284

Index

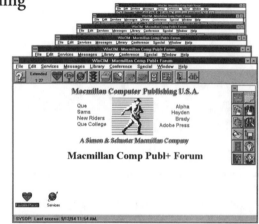

Complete and Return this Card
for a *FREE* Computer Book Catalog

Thank you for purchasing this book! You have purchased a superior computer book written expressly for your needs. To continue to provide the kind of up-to-date, pertinent coverage you've come to expect from us, we need to hear from you. Please take a minute to complete and return this self-addressed, postage-paid form. In return, we'll send you a free catalog of all our computer books on topics ranging from word processing to programming and the internet.

☐ Mrs. ☐ Ms. ☐ Dr. ☐

ne (first) [ ] (M.I.) [ ] (last) [ ]

dress [ ]

[ ]

y [ ] State [ ] Zip [ ]

ne [ ] Fax [ ]

npany Name [ ]

nail address [ ]

Please check at least (3) influencing factors for purchasing this book.

nt or back cover information on book .... ☐
cial approach to the content .... ☐
mpleteness of content .... ☐
thor's reputation .... ☐
blisher's reputation .... ☐
ok cover design or layout .... ☐
ex or table of contents of book .... ☐
ce of book .... ☐
cial effects, graphics, illustrations .... ☐
er (Please specify): _____ ☐

How did you first learn about this book?

v in Macmillan Computer Publishing catalog .... ☐
commended by store personnel .... ☐
v the book on bookshelf at store .... ☐
commended by a friend .... ☐
ceived advertisement in the mail .... ☐
v an advertisement in: _____ ☐
ad book review in: _____ ☐
er (Please specify): _____ ☐

How many computer books have you purchased in the last six months?

s book only .... ☐   3 to 5 books .... ☐
ooks .... ☐   More than 5 .... ☐

4. Where did you purchase this book?

Bookstore .... ☐
Computer Store .... ☐
Consumer Electronics Store .... ☐
Department Store .... ☐
Office Club .... ☐
Warehouse Club .... ☐
Mail Order .... ☐
Direct from Publisher .... ☐
Internet site .... ☐
Other (Please specify): _____ ☐

5. How long have you been using a computer?

☐ Less than 6 months   ☐ 6 months to a year
☐ 1 to 3 years   ☐ More than 3 years

6. What is your level of experience with personal computers and with the subject of this book?

	With PCs	With subject of book
New	☐	☐
Casual	☐	☐
Accomplished	☐	☐
Expert	☐	☐

Source Code ISBN: 0-7897-0729-2

7. Which of the following best describes your job title?

Administrative Assistant ☐
Coordinator ☐
Manager/Supervisor ☐
Director ☐
Vice President ☐
President/CEO/COO ☐
Lawyer/Doctor/Medical Professional ☐
Teacher/Educator/Trainer ☐
Engineer/Technician ☐
Consultant ☐
Not employed/Student/Retired ☐
Other (Please specify): _____ ☐

8. Which of the following best describes the area of the company your job title falls under?

Accounting ☐
Engineering ☐
Manufacturing ☐
Operations ☐
Marketing ☐
Sales ☐
Other (Please specify): _____ ☐

9. What is your age?

Under 20 ....
21-29 ....
30-39 ....
40-49 ....
50-59 ....
60-over ....

10. Are you:

Male ....
Female ....

11. Which computer publications do you read regularly? (Please list)

_____
_____
_____
_____
_____
_____
_____
_____
_____
_____

Comments: _____

Fold here and scotch-tape to